T R O M P E T A

Chappottín, Chocolate, and the Afro-Cuban Trumpet Style

Rick Davies

The Scarecrow Press, Inc.
Lanham, Maryland, and Oxford
2003

SCARECROW PRESS, INC.

Published in the United States of America
by Scarecrow Press, Inc.
A Member of the Rowman & Littlefield Publishing Group
4501 Forbes Boulevard, Suite 200
Lanham, Maryland 20706
www.scarecrowpress.com

PO Box 317
Oxford
OX2 9RU, UK

British Library Cataloguing in Publication Information Available

Library of Congress Cataloging-in-Publication Data
Davies, Rick, 1951–
  Trompeta: Chappottáin, Chocolate, and the Afro-Cuban trumpet style /
Rick Davies.
     p. cm.
  Includes bibliographical references (p.).
  ISBN 0-8108-4679-9 (alk. paper) — ISBN 0-8108-4680-2 (pbk. : alk.
paper)
  1. Popular music—Cuba—History and criticism. 2. Latin
jazz—Cuba—History and criticism. 3. Trumpet—Performance—Cuba. 4.
Chappottáin, Fâelix, 1907–1983. 5. Armenteros, Chocolate. I. Title.
ML3486.C8 D38 2003
788.9'2165'09227291—dc21

                                                    2002153311

⊗™ The paper used in this publication meets the minimum
requirements of American National Standard for Information
Sciences—Permanence of Paper for Printed Library Materials,
ANSI/NISO Z39.48-1992.
Manufactured in the United States of America.

CONTENTS

ACKNOWLEDGMENTS

A number of extraordinary people were instrumental in the creation of this book. First, I wish to thank Alfredo "Chocolate" Armenteros. Not only did he contribute enthusiastically to this book, Chocolate also has inspired me over the years with his music. It was very fortunate that I was able to include input from one of the giants of Afro-Cuban music.

Two talented musicians, Andy González and Wayne Gorbea, generously assisted me in the interviews with Armenteros, and translator Ricardo Luiggi spent many hours transcribing the interview tapes. Andy, a widely acknowledged expert on Afro-Cuban and *salsa* music, also helped me get a handle on the subject matter through late night discussions and listening examples from his extensive collection of classic recordings. Wayne is a good friend and one of my closest musical colleagues. I have been associated with his ensemble, Salsa Picante, for almost two decades. In addition to Wayne, I would like to acknowledge band members Frank Reyes, Ruben Borgas, Juan Rodríguez, Frank Otero, Richie San Quintin, Rafi Malkiel, Raul Navarette, and Tomer Levy.

I would like to mention several other musicians from whom I have learned a great deal: Johnny Colon, Ray Santos, Santiago Cerón, Manny Oquendo, Jimmy Bosch, Reynaldo Jorge, Papo Vásquez, Harvie S., Arturo O'Farrill, Willie Martínez, Sam Furnace, Curtis Fowlkes, Jaki Byard, and many others.

Because this book contains a significant amount of material that was originally presented in my doctoral dissertation, I would like to thank the members of my doctoral committee at New York University: Dr. Tom Boras, my dissertation advisor and committee chair, gave advice on music analysis issues that was particularly important to this study; Dr. John Gilbert guided me in terms of topic and proposal development as well as research techniques; and Dr. George Yúdice, with his background in American Studies and Spanish, gave this project greater cultural insight than it would have had otherwise.

Additionally, I want to acknowledge my colleagues at Plattsburgh State University who were encouraging and tolerant during the final stages of putting this book together. Jo Ellen Miano is the perfect music department chair—always cheerful and ready to help in any way. Likewise, Professor Dan Gordon and Dean Kathy Lavoie have been supportive and enthusiastic about my pursuits.

A number of other individuals contributed directly or indirectly to my writing. John Child and David Barton, two Brits, have long espoused Latin music and have collaborated together on articles and interviews. (John's numerous biographical sketches for *The Penguin Encyclopedia of Popular Music* were especially helpful.) Max Salazar, another writer, provided early interviews with Chocolate that helped tremendously when I began this project. Al Angelora, a New York City radio DJ, has encouraged me since the late 1980s when I appeared occasionally on his legendary live broadcasts on WBAI.

The people at Scarecrow Press generously guided me through the often-daunting process of publishing a book. Many thanks to Shirley Lambert, who initiated this project and was very encouraging in the past few years. Melissa Ray was an indispensable guide and troubleshooter in pushing the project forward. Likewise, Debra Schepp and her team were extremely helpful in the copyediting and typesetting process.

I want to thank my parents, Emlyn and Ruth Davies, who have given me support constantly throughout my sometimes uncertain and hectic career as a musician, writer, and educator. Most importantly, I lovingly dedicate this project to my wife Karen Hildebrand, not only for her incredible love and forbearance but also for her indispensable professional editorial assistance. I could not have done this without her.

INTRODUCTION

Afro-Cuban music, like its North American cousin jazz, has had a long and colorful history that roughly corresponds to the twentieth century. Like jazz the Cuban tradition has been the product of a countless number of musicians both obscure and celebrated. However, also as in jazz certain individuals stand out at various points in the historical continuum of Afro-Cuban music. In the same way that a Louis Armstrong, Charlie Parker, or Miles Davis exemplifies the jazz of his time, certain individual singers, percussionists, wind players, and other musicians are pivotal figures in the different eras in the development of the Cuban style.

In the history of Cuban brass playing two individuals stand out: Félix Chappottín and Alfredo "Chocolate" Armenteros. Coming from two separate generations, either Chappottín or his younger colleague Armenteros have been present at many of the significant turning points in the history of the music.

Chappottín (b. 1907) almost single-handedly established the renowned *septeto* trumpet style when he recorded with the seminal Septeto Habanero starting in 1928. He became the most famous

Cuban trumpet player when he was featured with the most celebrated group of the 1940s, the *conjunto* led by Arsenio Rodríguez.
When the group was taken over by Chappottín in the early 1950s
(after Rodríguez emigrated to New York City), this ensemble remained one of the most important in Cuba. Renamed Chappottín
y Sus Estrellas, the band featured singer Miguelito Cuní and Pianist
Luis "Lilli" Martínez Grinan and remained a fixture on the Cuban
music scene for over thirty years.

The torch was passed when twenty-one-year-old Alfred "Chocolate" Armenteros joined the veteran Chappottín in the trumpet
section of the Arsenio Rodríguez *conjunto* in 1949. Armenteros became, arguably, the most important Cuban trumpet player of the
second half of the twentieth century. After firmly establishing his
reputation in 1950s Cuba by performing and recording with the
likes of Sonora Mantancera and his first cousin, the legendary
singer Beny Moré, Armenteros went on to become the most celebrated trumpet player on the New York–centered *salsa* scene of
the 1960s and 1970s, where he recorded with almost every major
group at that time. His reputation continues to flourish to this day
and he has recorded several albums as a leader over the past two
and a half decades.

By analyzing the music of Félix Chappottín and Alfredo "Chocolate" Armenteros, the entire history of mainstream Afro-Cuban
music and *salsa* can be examined. As the early innovations in
Cuban trumpet playing by Chappottín and his contemporaries
eventually evolved into the mature Chappottín style of the 1940s
conjunto and the even later developments in the *salsa* world of
Armenteros, the major developments and historical movements
of Afro-Cuban music are demonstrated. In the same way that looking at the playing of both Louis Armstrong and Miles Davis would
expose the entire history of jazz from ragtime to jazz/rock, Chappottín and the younger Armenteros between them were involved
in almost every phase of Afro-Cuban music.

AFRO-CUBAN MUSIC

Cuban music is one of the most important musical genres to have emerged from the cultural ontology that was generated over the last five hundred years as part of the European colonization of the Western Hemisphere. An original style was formed: "The synthesis of Spanish, African, French, and North American musical traditions to create uniquely Cuban music represents a definite contribution to world culture" (MacGaffey and Barnett 1962). Like its counterparts in both North America and South America, modern Cuban music resulted from a syncretism of the various cultures involved in the imperialist-inspired reorganization of the New World. Although Europeans initiated this example of civilization building, the cultural input of Africans who were brought (forcibly) to the Americas has had the greatest impact on the development of the Cuban musical style (Manuel 1995).

As the Cuban style developed, a number of musical elements evolved that both defined and identified the music. The most fundamental formal element of Cuban music is the *clave*[1] (see chapter 1, figure 1.1), which is a two-measure rhythmic pattern that repeats for the entire length of a composition. The way in which the various members of the Cuban ensemble have expressed the *clave* has determined how the performance style of their instruments has evolved, as exemplified by the emergence of the traditional *son*[2] in the early twentieth century.

In the same way that unique percussive, vocal, and other instrumental styles and techniques emerged, a distinctive Cuban brass tradition was created. The first complete integration of the Cuban brass style arose in the 1920s in the form of the *septeto*[3] trumpet tradition—so called because the trumpet was often the seventh instrument added to the *son* ensemble. From the basic elements of the *son* and *septeto* traditions evolved the modern Cuban trumpet style, which reached its maturity in the *conjuntos*[4] of the 1940s. It is the soloing of trumpet players like Félix Chappottín and Alfredo "Chocolate" Armenteros from this era that establishes the common practice of the Cuban brass performance style.

NOTES

1. *Clave*—the fundamental rhythmic unit of Cuban music. The two-measure pattern, once established, is repeated throughout the performance. The clave pattern consists of a "two-side" and a "three-side." In its simplest representation, the two-side contains two downbeat quarter-note rhythms on the second and third beats, and the three-side consists of three notes on the downbeats of one and four and the upbeat of two. The *clave* of a particular piece can be either three-two or two-three.

2. *Son*—the single most popular dance music genre of twentieth-century Cuba, usually (but not always) performed by a group comprised of six pieces. Considered a perfect balance of African and Spanish musical elements, the *son* is the most common influence on modern Cuban music and *salsa*.

3. *Septeto*—Spanish for *seven*; refers to the Cuban trumpet style that evolved when the *son* ensemble of the 1920s and 1930s added a seventh performer: a trumpet player.

4. *Conjunto*—a term most often associated with the type of ensemble led by *tres* player Arsenio Rodríguez in the 1940s. The *conjunto* evolved from the *son* ensemble of the 1920s and 1930s. The addition of the *conga* drum and the creation of a brass ensemble are two of the main changes between the early *septeto* and the modern *conjunto*.

①

HISTORICAL OVERVIEW

The importance of Cuban music is widely acknowledged both as an independent entity and as an influence on other musical styles, but researchers have subjected it to little systematic examination. This study will provide one such analysis using performance style to develop a historical and technical description of Cuban brass playing, specifically, and the Cuban music style in general. Because of the important place of brass playing in Cuban music and the extensive influence of this music on American and other musical traditions, the development of Cuban brass playing (which originated with the *septeto* school in the 1920s) must be accorded a complete and timely academic examination. To understand this music better, an analysis of the music of Chappottín, Armenteros, and the other brass players who most closely represent the Cuban style needs to be undertaken.

In the last half-century, the Afro-Cuban genre of American music has had a major impact both in its own right and as an influence on other types of Latin music; on jazz and rhythm and blues; and on a large variety of international popular music forms. Since the 1920s, a great tradition of trombone and trumpet performance has evolved around this Caribbean-rooted style. A golden age arrived in the 1940s when pioneering players like Félix Chappottín and Alfredo "Chocolate" Armenteros brought this style of brass playing to maturity and enormously influenced later Cuban or Cuban-derived (or *salsa*) brass performers. Even as Armenteros continues to perform regularly (most notably at this point in time with bassist Israel "Cachao" Lopez and with the so-called Conga Kings), he and his generation have spawned newer generations of extraordinary brass players.

As the twenty-first century progresses, a resurgence in Cuban and *salsa* brass performance has produced some of the finest trumpet and trombone players in the world. While almost every country in Latin American has produced excellent brass performers, the best of the modern artists playing in the Cuban tradition come from Cuba, Puerto Rico, and the multicultural stomping ground of New York. Among these modern virtuoso brass players are Cuban trumpeters Arturo Sandoval and Jesús Alemañy, Cuban trombonist Juan Pablo Torres, and New York trombonists Jimmy Bosch and Papo Vásquez (who continue the *salsa* tradition of Barry Rogers) (O'Neill 1997).

In addition to those musicians involved primarily or exclusively with *salsa* music, most of the jazz brass players spawned during the modern jazz era have also been exposed to Cuban music at some level. Well-known jazz trumpet players who have been notably involved in Latin jazz projects include Dizzy Gillespie, Kenny Dorham, Lee Morgan, and Freddie Hubbard.

The importance of researching the music of Chappottín and Armenteros is increased by the fact that some of the best straight-ahead jazz brass players to have recently emerged (e.g., Arturo Sandoval, Ray Vega) come from a Cuban or *salsa* background. The relationship between Cuban music and American jazz is an area that needs to be explored, as well as the direct impact of the Cuban style on jazz technique (and vice versa) in recent years.

Although modern Cuban music has flourished for over fifty years and historically corresponds roughly to the era of modern jazz, there has been relatively little research into this vital and significant musical style. The existing academic studies on music in Cuba are, in many cases, concerned with composers using Cuban elements in the composition of music in the European mold; journal articles exist, but in limited number; and dissertations in the United States that focus on major performers and composers working in indigenous Cuban styles are virtually nonexistent.

This book is concerned with the playing of Afro-Cuban and *salsa* brass players; however, it might also serve either as a prototype or as inspiration for research into other significant musicians working in the Cuban tradition. Timeliness is an urgent issue; many of the original musicians and "scholars without portfolio" who are familiar with this music, while still alive, are aging. It is vital that the music of seminal musicians like Beny Moré, Machito, Cachao, Arsenio Rodríguez, Tito Puente, and Eddie Palmieri (to name a few) is one day accorded full academic examination.

The focus of this study historically is the modern era of Cuban music from when the trumpet was introduced to the *son* ensemble to the present. In order to establish a contextual setting for this era of common practice, it is useful to review in brief the history of Cuban music with an emphasis on the styles immediately preceding the modern era. In addition to examining general historical issues, it is important to explicate the specific moves that led to the modern brass style as exemplified by the playing of Chappottín, Armenteros, and others.

EARLY CUBAN MUSIC

Cuban music, like most of the musical systems that were formulated as a result of the European colonization of the Western Hemisphere, is a product of the syncretism of European and African styles. The music genres that developed in the Americas (North and South) as a result of this melding of cultures expressed a wide range of stylistic formulations, containing both similar and disparate elements. A multitude of variables must be taken into account when tracking how and why a particular music ontology was formed.

On the surface, the various music genres that evolved in the United States and Cuba share a common ancestry of European and African elements. However, there exist as many differences as similarities. In order to set a context for examining the way in which the elements of the Cuban style evolved, a brief analysis of how European and African music influences were combined and expressed in Cuban music is necessary. For purposes of clarification through comparison and contrast, examples of North American music such as blues and jazz will be cited occasionally.

At least one scholar advocates that African music is even more pervasive in the Cuban music system than it is in North American musical styles like jazz and blues. Peter Manuel, in *Caribbean Currents: Caribbean Music from Rumba to Reggae,* asserts that it was "much easier for Cuban slaves to buy their freedom than it was in the United States or British West Indies" (Manuel 1995), and, therefore, free blacks in Cuba were able to retain African elements in their music in a purer form than the more encumbered North American blacks. The African elements of Cuban music were also reinforced by the continuation of slavery in Cuba throughout most of the nineteenth century, as opposed to the abolition of slavery that came about in the United States as a result of the American Civil War: "[although] the import of slaves to the United States and the British colonies had dwindled by 1800, most Cuban slaves (especially the Yoruba) were brought in the subsequent sixty years, so that neo-African musical traditions continued to be invigorated by fresh infusions of hapless captives" (Manuel 1995). For Manuel and other pundits, Cuban-created music is rhythmically closer to the music of Africa than the music of North America is.

Though music from the jazz and blues traditions is considered, in many cases, to be more sophisticated in its melodic and harmonic usage than the Cuban style, this sophistication is usually accompanied by a less exacting rhythmic basis than that of the Cuban musical tradition. As Miles Davis, John Coltrane, and others discovered in the modal and free jazz movements of the late 1950s and early 1960s, greater complexity is possible in the rhythmic realm when harmonic and melodic elements are static.

Another factor that created a tight bond between Cuban and African cultures were the social clubs, or *cabildos*, in which the slaves gathered starting in the early eighteenth century. Sponsored by the Spanish Catholic Church, these "mutual aid societies" allowed the slaves to socialize with other members of their African culture (e.g., Yoruba, Abakwa, etc.) in the interest of promoting an autonomous support system (Manuel 1995). As a result of this socialization action, former Africans reestablished many of their cultural and artistic traditions, including music. The music that evolved from the *cabildos* took both secular and religious forms, and the Afro-Cuban music that emerged from the practices of the *santería* religion is rich and multifarious; however, it is the secular music that is the most relevant to the brass tradition.

Two early indigenous secular Cuban musical genres that were closely associated with *cabildos* and exemplified a strong African heritage were the *rumba* and the *comparsa*. Both the original *rumba* and the *comparsa* fall into a premodern category of urban folk music traditions that Argeliers Léon (Manuel 1991) considered the "primary sources" for many of the main twentieth-century Cuban styles. Although the *rumba* evolved and was incorporated in a modified form into the main current of Cuban popular dance music, the traditional version of the *rumba*, along with the *comparsa*, was strongly African-influenced ensemble music consisting solely of percussionists and singers, with dancers providing the visual element. While mature Cuban musical styles like the *son* and the *danzón* contain a more democratic mixture of European and African elements, these styles also strongly reflect the influence of earlier urban Afro-Cuban folk music, especially the *rumba*. The vitality of early Afro-Cuban genres like the *rumba* is borne out by the existence of modern Cuban groups, such as Los Muñequitos de Matanzas, who continue to perform traditional *rumba* to international acclaim in the twenty-first century.

Even though the African influence on Cuban music is of paramount importance, the influence of European culture cannot be discounted. The main European influences on Cuban music came from the folk music and literature of Spain. In the same way that English hymns came to influence the formal structures of spirituals and gospel music in the United States, various Spanish dance and poetic forms played a major role in the formation of Cuban music (Manuel 1991). In fact, the argument that Cuban music is "more African" than North American music can be bolstered by the close association that existed at various times in history between Spain and certain African cultures, especially the North African Moorish culture. This African influence is noticeable in the frequent use of minor and pentatonic modes in many traditional Spanish melodies and a rhythmic sophistication in forms from Spain such as the *flamenco* (Manuel 1991).

The most important direct European influence on Cuban music is comprised of various dance forms that led to the *contradanza* (also called *habanera*), "thought to derive from the English country dance" (Roberts 1979). The specific precursor to this form was the French *contredance*, which was brought to Cuba in the early nineteenth century by refugees of the Haitian revolution. Over the course of the century, the *contradanza* gradually absorbed Afro-Cuban elements into its European-derived form until it evolved into the *danzón* during the latter half of the nineteenth century (Moore 1997). The *danzón* is viewed as "the first form of national music" in Cuba; it became very popular in the ballrooms of the black middle class around the 1870s, performed for dances by the *orquesta típica,* which contained primarily standard European orchestral instruments.

The *orquesta típica* was the first Cuban ensemble to use brass instruments, but these instruments were dropped in the first decade of the twentieth century as the *orquesta típica* evolved into the *charanga francesa* (Roberts 1979). Consequently, the modern Cuban trumpet tradition actually traces its stylistic origins to the 1920s, when the trumpet was added to the popular *son* ensemble.

The *charanga francesa* is the precursor to the (still popular) *charanga* group, with its instrumentation of piano, bass, violins, flute, and the African-derived *timbale* and *guiro*. One reason for this "taming" of the instrumentation was that the original *orquesta típica* was considered too crude for the sensibilities of the white and black middle-class members of the various social clubs in which the *danzón* was performed. While the *danzón* was harmonically and formally the same as its *contradanza* predecessor, many of the Cuban social elite took issue with its newly added African elements. This is ironic in that the *danzón* is relatively devoid of Africanisms when compared to the *rumba* or the *comparsa*. However, as in the United States, racism played a pivotal role in how Cuban music developed. One effect of race and class discrimination in Cuba was the recurring ban on the public performance of the *rumba, comparsa,* and other Afro-Cuban music genres in the first decades of the twentieth century. Robin D. Moore, in his book *Nationalizing Blackness: Afrocubanismo and Artistic Revolution in Havana, 1920–1940,* describes the social processes at work in the development of various mainstream Cuban music styles such as the *danzón* and *son* and in the transformation of the traditional *rumba* into the "commercial *rumba*" (Moore 1997).

The development of mainstream Cuban music often involved a give and take between the pure Afro-Cuban styles and a white or mulatto interpretation of these styles, often by the same people who despised and denigrated the musicians whose music they were co-opting. At various times during the first decades of this century, the discrimination against the pure black "street" styles in Cuba reached the point where laws were enacted banning the public performance of the *comparsa* and traditional *rumba* (Moore 1995). One of the reasons for the great success of the *danzón* was that, although it was based on Afro-Cuban music, it sufficiently watered down the African elements to avoid offending the sensibilities of the mostly white upper class.

Beginning in the 1920s, the *son* musical genre supplanted the *danzón* as the primary form of Cuban music. In many ways the most

perfect syncretism of European and African elements, the *son* provides the underpinning for almost all modern Cuban and Cuban-
derived music. Most of the elements contained in what is now called
salsa originated in the Cuban *son* ensembles of the 1920s (Robbins
1990).

The *son* originated in the province of Oriente, initially a rural
genre that came out of the mountains of this eastern-most
province. However, by the end of the first decade of the twentieth
century, the *son* had been "brought to the capital by the soldiers of
the permanent army" (Robbins 1990). In particular, a musical
group made up of soldiers, the Trio Oriente, moved to Havana in
1909 and became very popular after adding a *bongó* player.

Because the *son* is seminal to the development of the modern
trumpet style, the next chapter will focus on the *son* style and some
early practitioners, including the Sexteto Habanero and Septeto
Nacional.

Many of these early *son* groups recorded prolifically in the 1920s;
these recordings, along with the early development of radio broadcasting in Cuba, helped to disseminate the *son* throughout the island.
The colorblind medium of radio also allowed the Afro-Cuban *son* to
become popular among the middle- and upper-class white popula-
tion, which normally would have had little to do with a black art form.

An event that is often cited as starting the "rhumba craze" in the
United States was the appearance of Justo "Don" Azpiazu and his
Havana Casino orchestra at the Palace Theater in New York City
starting in 1930. In addition to being popular in its own right, the
Azpiazu group spawned a number of other ensembles including that
of Spaniard Xavier Cugat, who had a wildly successful long-term
stint at the Waldorf Astoria Hotel. Cugat became the house bandleader at the Waldorf starting in 1932 and achieved stardom through
his coast-to-coast radio broadcasts from the hotel later in that
decade (Moore 1997). Although Cugat was often criticized for lacking authenticity as a *rumbero*, his orchestra did introduce several
Cuban singers and other performers who later became internation-

ally famous, including Machito, Miguelito Valdés, and Tito Rodríguez. The Azpiazu orchestra also performed its jazz-influenced *rumba* with much success in Europe (Moore 1997), and Azpiazu (like white musician Benny Goodman in black-dominated jazz) was one of the first white Cuban bandleaders to include black musicians in his ensemble (Roberts 1979).

An unfortunate side effect of the global popularity of ensembles like the Azpiazu and Cugat orchestras was the appropriation of the term *rumba* (rhumba) to refer to almost any type of Cuban (or even non-Cuban) music. Most of the music performed by these groups was in fact *son* and had little direct relationship to the traditional *rumba*. The Cugat orchestra performed a large variety of musical styles from American jazz and commercial music to songs from virtually every Latin American country. Despite this, the North American music industry used the term *rumba* to refer to all of this music (Moore 1997). By the end of the 1930s, almost any piece of music with a Latin American reference was called a *rumba*—even works composed or performed by American musicians like Paul Whiteman, Cab Calloway, and Cole Porter.

The white co-option of the black *son* form also fed the so-called rhumba craze of the early 1930s: the first time that Cuban music made a major impact on the international music scene. (This development was similar to the exploitation of black jazz in the 1930s by white big band leaders like Benny Goodman and Glen Miller.) Several white Cuban bands and composers traveled (and sometimes immigrated) to the United States and Europe, primarily to New York and Paris.

Another source of the spread of Cuban music internationally during the early 1930s was the work of Cuban theater and movie composers such as Ernesto Lecuona and Eliseo Grenet. Lecuona was most noted as a composer of salon music and *zarzuelas*. Although his early work was primarily in the European tradition, he eventually incorporated Afro-Cuban elements in most of his work and became one of Cuba's most beloved and famous composers.

Eliseo Grenet was one of the most important purveyors of the Cuban style in Europe. Primarily a theater composer, Grenet was forced to flee Cuba in 1932 when one of his songs was deemed subversive by the Cuban government (Moore 1997). Grenet first settled in Madrid and garnered considerable success as a composer and producer of *"zarzuela*-like theater productions" (Moore 1997). In 1934, he achieved even greater success in Paris with *comparsa*-influenced compositions that created a so-called *conga* craze in the Parisienne ballrooms. This development eventually spread throughout Europe and to the United States.

MODERN CUBAN MUSIC

Starting in the late 1930s, the two primary genres of Cuban music, the *danzón* and the *son*, went through a maturation process that for the most part established their finalized form. Two musical organizations are often cited as the primary modern consolidators of the *danzón* and *son* styles: the *charanga* of Antonio Arcaño, the most important *danzón* organization of its day; and the Arsenio Rodríguez *conjunto*, considered the personification of the modern *son* ensemble. These groups represented separate historical perspectives, but they also shared many elements that became the central elements of all modern Cuban and Cuban-derived styles. Because of their importance to the history of brass playing, the *son* and *conjunto* will be examined in detail in later chapters. However, certain innovations of the Rodríguez *conjunto* will be referred to in this chapter when they become pertinent to this historical overview. For example, because of the importance of the Arsenio Rodríguez *conjunto* in the development of New York *salsa* in the 1960s and 1970s, it will be impossible to completely postpone discussion of the *son* genre entirely. By changing the instrumentation of the *son* ensemble and extending the form, *tres* player and bandleader Rodríguez established a standard that has been a primary influence on almost all modern-day *salsa* groups (O'Neill 1997).

ARCAÑO AND THE MODERN *CHARANGA*

In the late 1930s, the *danzón* was revitalized by the *charanga* of flute player Antonio Arcaño. Perhaps the most popular Cuban band of its time, the Arcaño ensemble prototyped the modern *charanga*. Fired by the creative energy of bass legend Israel "Cachao" Lopez and brother Orestes, the Arcaño *charanga* increased the black quotient in the traditionally staid *danzón*. The Lopez brothers and the Arcaño band are often credited as major influences in the development of the *mambo*[1] and *chachachá*[2] styles. Cachao is also the creator of the *descarga*[3], or Cuban jam session (O'Neill 1997).

The Arcaño orchestra defined the modern *danzón* and *charanga*, drawing on many of the same inherent ideas that simultaneously fired Arsenio Rodríguez's redefinition of *son*. Rodríguez led the way by adding *conga* to the *son conjunto*, but Arcaño soon followed suit in introducing this street-associated percussion instrument into his *charanga*. Cachao and his brother Orestes wrote most of the music for the Arcaño *charanga* and borrowed liberally from the *son* in their reformation of the *danzón*.

Credited as the inventors of the *mambo*, the Lopez brothers incorporated the *montuno* section of the *son* to the *danzón* and added to the rhythmic excitement by introducing figures in the violin and flute parts that emulated the "diablo rhythm" (O'Neill 1997) of Rodríguez's *tres*-driven *montuno*. Another instrumental change that was pioneered by the Arcaño *charanga* was the standard implementation of the fixed cowbell by the *timbale* player. By the 1950s, Pérez Prado had made a jazz-influenced version of the Arcaño *mambo* style an international hit.

At the same time, the Palladium nightclub in New York had ushered in the *mambo* era through the nightclub's rotation of the

bands of Cuban Machito and Puerto Rican bandleaders Tito
Puente and Tito Rodriguez. Because these three bands were more
derivative of the *son/conjunto* tradition than of the *danzón*, the
mambo and its successor *salsa* are in reality a merging of both genres. In the mid-1950s, the *charanga* instrumentation, with its *son*-
influenced *danzón-mambo*, was represented most notably by the
Orquesta Aragón, which was founded in 1939 (Manuel 1991).
When the *chachachá* achieved international popularity in the
1950s, the *charanga* sound became popular throughout the world.

The *charanga* and the *danzón* have continued to be potent forces
in Cuban music. When New York was established as the major ex-
ternal center of Cuban-derived music following the Castro revolution and the consequent emigration of many major Cuban stars, the
charanga style lived in a number of New York–based bands. Perhaps the most important of these groups was the Orquesta Broadway. Formed in New York in 1962 by three brothers from Güines,
Cuba, Orquesta Broadway continued the consolidation of the
danzón and *son*. While groups like Orquesta Broadway continued
to use the violin/flute-driven *charanga* instrumentation, they played
(in addition to the *danzón*) "all the basic genres of Cuban dance
music" (Manuel 1991). Los Van Van, the most popular band to
come out of Cuba in the last thirty years, furthers the *charanga/
conjunto* merging by including both the brass section of the *conjunto* and the flute/violin *charanga* frontline.

The reemergence in the 1990s of Israel "Cachao" Lopez, one of
the most important musicians in Cuban history, illustrates the
son/danzón dichotomy. The Cachao 1995 recordings *Master Sessions*, volumes 1 and 2, feature two distinct configurations. On some
of the selections, the band assumes a *charanga* instrumentation with
a string section and flute. At other times, the band becomes a classic *conjunto* with an all-star horn section, including, among others,
Alfredo "Chocolate" Armenteros on trumpet, Paquito D'Rivera on
woodwinds, and Jimmy Bosch on trombone. Because of the stature
and musical genius of Lopez, these two recordings are an excellent

1990s encapsulation and history of the major Cuban music genres of the twentieth century.

LATIN JAZZ AND THE *MAMBO*

While the Arcaño and Rodríguez groups were helping to define the mature manifestations of the traditional *danzón* and *son* in Cuba, there were simultaneous significant developments taking place in New York City. The 1940s modern jazz-fueled New York music scene was an environment ripe for synthesis with the rhythmic richness of Cuban music. Conversely, the most important influence of jazz on Cuban music at this time was in the area of instrumentation and instrumental arranging.

The seminal ideas leading to the tradition of Cuban/American cross-fertilization and the creation of Latin jazz are often attributed to the friendship that developed in the late 1930s between two members of the Cab Calloway big band trumpet section: Dizzy Gillespie and Mario Bauza, both of whom formed ensembles of their own that fostered a collaboration of Cuban musicians such as Machito, Mario Bauza, and Chano Pozo with jazz musicians like Dizzy Gillespie and Charlie Parker in the 1940s (Boggs 1992).

Gillespie has often credited Cuban trumpet player Mario Bauza with introducing him to Cuban music; many of the ideas that led to the formation of Gillespie's landmark Latin jazz–influenced big band of the late 1940s were initiated by discussions between these two young section mates. While Gillespie's association with Bauza may eventually have influenced the creation of this legendary big band, Bauza is most famous for his role as musical director of the Machito orchestra. Besides being the musical leader of this band (the most important New York–based Cuban ensemble of its time), Bauza, as a trumpet player in the Cuban style, was one of the most important stylists on the instrument in the late 1930s and 1940s (González 1997).

Following the example of the great Machito orchestra, many Latin groups started using large brass and saxophone sections in the North American big band tradition. In addition to the larger number of instruments, many of these ensembles had arrangements that reflected the advanced harmonies and voicings that came out of the modern jazz or bebop movement. Although most of these large bands were from New York and associated with the Palladium *mambo* era, there were also similar groups in the 1950s Havana scene, most notably the Cuban-based orchestra of singing legend Beny Moré (O'Neill 1997). Among the great brass players who spent time in the Moré group were Moré's cousin Armenteros and trombone innovator Generoso "Tojo" Jiménez.

The big band format continues to exist in Latin music as the twenty-first century begins. The Machito band continues to play, now under the leadership of Machito's son, and Tito Puente (who initially gained fame as a performer with Machito) fronted his own large band for over forty years.

SALSA

A schism developed in the world of Afro-Cuban music when Fidel Castro led the communist revolution of Cuba in 1959. Despite how one might view the political consequences of the revolution, there is no doubt about its impact on the development (and future development) of Afro-Cuban music. Although music continued to have a vital presence in Cuba following the revolution, the commercial and international focal point of this musical style became the United States. New York, Miami, and Puerto Rico largely replaced Cuba as the primary commercial centers of the music in the 1960s (Boggs 1992). One result of this displacement was the increased influence and importance of Puerto Rican musicians. Even though many established Cuban musicians defected to the United States following the revolution, the younger generation of

Puerto Rican musicians who were coming of age in the 1960s established themselves as the main agents of change in the new *salsa* scene.

While there were Puerto Ricans who had previously established themselves as stars in Cuban music, such as the two Palladium *mambo* kings, Tito Puente and Tito Rodríguez, the Cuban revolution (and the resulting American embargo) opened the floodgates for musicians of Puerto Rican descent. By the 1970s, Puerto Ricans like Eddie and Charlie Palmieri, Ray Baretto, Hector LaVoe, and Willie Colón were international *salsa* stars. Although these musicians often performed indigenous Puerto Rican genres like the *bomba* and the *plena*, the bulk of the music they performed was Afro-Cuban. Not only did bands like Eddie Palmieri's La Perfecta re-create the Arsenio Rodríguez style of *son/conjunto* (in La Perfecta's case, substituting trombones for trumpets); they also often reprised many of the old songs from Cuba (Roberts 1979).

The commercial peak of this style of music was around the mid-1970s, when all-star concerts sponsored by the Fania record label sold out large venues such as New York's Madison Square Garden. The term *salsa* was created at this time by the Latin music recording industry to refer to Afro-Cuban music, and the term caught on with the public (Gerard and Sheller 1989).

In addition to Puerto Rico, *salsa* musicians came from almost every Spanish-speaking country in the Western Hemisphere. This included a large contingent of expatriate Cubans, such as Celia Cruz, Machito, percussionist Mongo Santamaría, flute player Fajardo, and trumpeter Armenteros. The Dominican Republic, Panama, Venezuela, and Colombia all contributed significantly to the *salsa* pool. Dominican flute player Johnny Pacheco (with attorney Jerry Masucci) was the head of Fania Records and at the time one of the most powerful individuals in *salsa* music. Columbia has produced Grupo Niche, and Oscar D'León is Venezuela's favorite son. One of the biggest singing stars on the New York *salsa* scene since the 1970s is Panamanian Ruben Blades, who began his career as lead singer in Willie Colón's band.

By the late 1970s, the popularity of *salsa* was waning in the United States, due in part to the increased popularity of the Dominican *merengue* with its lively rhythm and simplified dance style. When Cuban-style music did regain some of its popularity in the late 1980s, it was most often in the form of highly produced recordings built around matinee idol–type singing stars (much in the way North American pop music is created). Singers like Frankie Ruiz, Tito Rojas, Tito Nieves, La India, and Marc Anthony have achieved great commercial success with slick, swinging *salsa* music. Although the standardized arranging and romantic singing style have proven to be a formula for economic success, this music is often criticized for lacking the spontaneity and improvisatory qualities of the best of Cuban and *salsa* music. However, there have been other musicians and groups in the United States who have kept the traditional flames burning. Bands like Manny Oquendo's Libre and Wayne Gorbea's Salsa Picante have dedicated themselves to honoring and emulating the *conjunto* tradition of musicians like Arsenio Rodríguez and Eddie Palmieri. Likewise, Johnny Almendros and Los Jovenes del Barrio present a modern-day homage to the *charanga* style.

Latin jazz has also thrived in the last two decades in the United States. Musicians like flute player Dave Valentín, saxophonist Paquito D'Rivera, and brothers Andy and Jerry González (from the Fort Apache band) have achieved worldwide success among Latin and jazz audiences. Finally, as the twenty-first century takes hold, many of the pioneers of Cuban-derived music such as Alfredo "Chocolate" Armenteros and Israel "Cachao" Lopez are still very active in the United States both recording and performing *salsa*.

REVOLUTIONARY CUBA

Even though the importance of New York and other international locations increased tremendously following the Castro revolution, the music tradition of Cuba continued to develop along its own fertile (albeit isolated) path (Manuel 1991). As a result of Cuba's alienation from the United States, musicians in Cuba lacked access to the commercial outlets that fueled the *salsa* movement in New York. While most of the rest of the *salsa* world was privy to events taking place in New York, there was very little direct knowledge about this in Cuba. For the first decade following the communist takeover, many of the musicians and groups from the 1940s and 1950s who didn't emigrate from Cuba continued to assert their influence on the musical environment. Among the legacy groups that continued to flourish in Cuba in the 1960s were Félix Chappottín and his Estrellas, the *charanga* Orquesta Aragón, and the traditional *rumba* group Los Muñequitos de Matanzas. However, thanks to the endurance of Cuba's strong conservatory training system and the direct influence of the homegrown music tradition, several young musicians and groups started making their mark starting in the late 1960s. In 1969, twenty-eight-year-old bassist and composer Juan Formell formed Los Van Van, which became and remains the most popular musical organization in Cuba. This *charanga*-derived group embraces a multitude of traditional music genres and created the *comparsa*-based *songo* style. The jazz-influenced Irakere provides an excellent example of just how successful the Cuban music education system has been in creating virtuoso musicians. Formed in 1973 under the creative leadership of pianist Chucho Valdez and saxophonist Paquito D'Rivera, Irakere has served as a showcase for many of modern-day Cuba's greatest musicians, including the trumpet master Arturo Sandoval (Manuel 1991).

Cuban music in its various manifestations is still alive and thriving. Although the United States and Cuba are still fighting their version of the cold war, there has been a thawing in the musical arena. Several Cuban artists have made regular trips to the United States, and musicians and music writers from the United States have been going to the island with more and more frequency. Besides recent appearances by Los Van Van, Los Muñequitos de

Matanzas, and Chucho Valdez, newer artists like NG La Banda, Issac Delgado, and the a cappella singing group Vocal Sampling have performed with great success outside of Cuba. The older *son* style has reached the peak of its international success with the phenomenon of the Buena Vista Social Club, which provided a reprise to the careers of many Cuban musical elder statesmen. Additionally, several musicians who developed their musical skills in Cuba have emigrated to the United States or Europe in recent years. These include former Irakere trumpeter Arturo Sandoval, trombonist Juan Pablo Torres, and the young trumpet master Jesús Alemañy who, with his group ¡Cubanismo! has demonstrated a solo style that makes him heir apparent to the tradition of Chappottín, Armenteros, and the other renown Cuban trumpet performers.

COMMON CHARACTERISTICS OF CUBAN MUSIC

Harmonically, Cuban music represents tonality in its most direct form. The Cuban style adheres to the most fundamental rendering of the European-defined concept of the dominant-tonic relationship and hardly ever strays from the established key area, as European and North American music is apt to do in harmonic modulation. Cuban musicians typically have an unquestioned allegiance to tonal harmonic laws (much in the tradition of Heinrich Schenker).

In truth, however, the music of Cuba is more interested in adhering to its own immutable approach to rhythm. Instead of having a reverence for harmony, Cuban musicians worship at the altar of the *clave* (figure 1.1).

Figure 1.1.   Clave

The two-measure *clave* rhythmic structure is the fundamental grounding element in Cuban-based music (Gerard and Sheller 1989). While a musician working in the Cuban system is expected to adhere to the established harmonic and melodic elements of the music, a lapse in one of these areas is much more tolerable than a *faux pas* in the rhythmic realm. To cross the *clave* is a cardinal sin in Latin music. The greatest insult to a performer is to be accused of being *cruzar*, or against the *clave*.

One of the most important musical structures in Cuban music is the *montuno*.[4] In its simplest form, the *montuno* combines the *clave* rhythm with a basic two-, four-, or eight-bar harmonic progression.

While there are a variety of formal structures in Cuban music, the *clave* is the ever-present and controlling factor in all of these forms. When analyzing the music of a master soloist in the Cuban tradition such as Armenteros, the primary objective is to determine how the improviser uses melodic, harmonic, rhythmic, and technical elements to interpret the *clave*.

NOTES

1. *Mambo*—in *salsa*, the *mambo* was the section of an arrangement featuring horn lines and new musical material.

2. *Chachachá*—a slow rhythmic dance derived from the *danzón*.

3. *Descarga*—an Afro-Cuban jam session.

4. *Montuno*—a short, repeating, two-, four-, or eight-measure phrase, based on a simple chord progression, which contains the call-and-response portion of a piece. The most common usage of the *montuno* is to support the interchange of *coro* (chorus) and *sonero* (solo singer). However, in many cases the *coro* may exchange *montuno*s with an instrumental soloist. The *montuno* is also commonly used for extended instrumental soloing.

2

THE *SON*

HISTORICAL PERSPECTIVES

The *son* and its place in the music of Cuba have often been compared to the role that the blues plays in the music of North America. Both the blues and the *son* have dual meanings within their respective music systems. Each term can be defined as either a specific concrete formal structure or as a more generic underlying principle. In comparing the *son* to the blues, Robbins, in "The Cuban *Son* as Form, Genre, and Symbol," notes that their meanings "range similarly from the concrete and specific to the nebulous and inclusive" (Robbins 1990). When the *son* came of age in the 1920s, it soon became the essence of mainstream Cuban music. Both in its codifying of the *clave* and in its establishment of standard structural parts such as the *largo* and the *montuno*, the *son* influenced every type of Cuban music, including the previously dominant *danzón*.

The *son* was especially influential in the development of the Cuban trumpet style. Although the trumpet had been used previously in Cuban music, it was its addition to the early *son* ensemble that initiated its formal stylistic development within the Cuban music system. This development reached its peak in the 1940s in the *conjunto* playing of trumpeters such as Félix Chappottín and Alfredo "Chocolate" Armenteros.

Two groups in particular are cited frequently as the epitome of the 1920s *son* style, especially as it relates to the trumpet. Sexteto Habanero and Septeto Nacional[1] both added trumpet players to their ensembles in the late 1920s. Both groups went on to become internationally renowned exponents of the Cuban *son*. Félix Chappottín, who joined the Sexteto Habanero in the late 1920s, is sometimes compared to Louis Armstrong in terms of the importance of each of these innovators to the development of the early solo trumpet style in their respective musical arenas. Chappottín and his lesser-known colleagues from the 1920s and 1930s initiated a *son*-based interpretive system of brass performance that is still practiced by brass players over 70 years later. Following a synopsis of the historical issues and general musical characteristics of the *son* in the following section, a variety of musical examples will be discussed in detail.

THE *SON*

While it is known that the *son* originated in the Oriente province of eastern Cuba, the details surrounding its inception and early development remain murky (Robbins 1990). Claims have been made for an earlier genesis of the *son*, but the developmental cycle actually began in the last two decades of the nineteenth century. Starting in the mountainous rural areas of Oriente, the *son* took on an urban identity by the turn of the century when it started to become popular in the eastern cities of Santiago, Guantanamo, and Baracoa. By 1910 the *son* had spread to Havana.

Two distinct types of ensemble represent the earliest examples of the *son* style in the capital. The earliest groups were trios or quartets of musicians transplanted from the east. In many cases, the musicians were "soldiers of the permanent army" (Robbins 1990) who had been discharged from their army posts in Oriente following the overthrow of Spanish rule. An example is the Trio Oriental, which was one of the most important early *son* groups.

The other type of ensemble was indigenous to Havana and consisted of a choral interpretation of the *son*. Singing by large choral groups had a tradition in Havana predating the introduction of the *son*. The *coros de clave* had been in existence since well before the turn of the century. Usually associated with social clubs, these eighteen- to twenty-member choral groups changed style and became *coros de son* (or sometimes *coros de guaguancó*) shortly after the introduction of the *son* in the capitol. While the importance of these large choral groups waned in the 1920s, they continued to influence the mainstream small *son* bands in Havana. Sexteto Habanero, in particular, placed a strong emphasis on ensemble singing that reflected the musical style of the *coros de son*. The members of Trio Oriente (who later founded Sexteto Habanero) were also members of Los Apaches, one of the most famous of the *coros de son* (Robbins 1990).

The original *son* trios consisted of guitar, *tres*, and vocals. As the groups increased in size, other instruments were added until the ensemble became a sextet. The *son* ensemble became standardized by the 1920s into the instrumentation represented by groups like the Sexteto Habanero and the Septeto Nacional. The typical *sexteto* instrumentation augmented the *tres* and guitar of the trio with bass, *bongó*, and two singers who doubled on percussion instruments like *claves*, *maracas*, or *guiro*; however, the instrumentation sometimes varied slightly. Although the bass violin eventually became the standard bass instrument, the *son* sextet of the early 1920s typically used a *botijo* or a *marimbula*. The *botijo* was fashioned from a large ceramic jug into which the performer directed his airstream to create the sound. (Similar techniques were used at the same time in the United States by jug bands associated with the Mississippi delta blues.) The *botijo* can be heard on early recordings by the Sexteto Habanero and other *son* groups. The *marimbula* has African roots and is built along the architectural designs of the *mbira* or thumb piano; on the *marimbula*, metal strips are fastened to a large, resonating wooden box. The strips are tuned by varying their lengths and the performer sits on the box and plays notes by plucking the metal bars. The *marimbula* is strongly associated with the *coros de son* (Robbins 1990).

The *bongó* was the most controversial addition to the *son* ensemble. Played with the hands, the *bongó* was the *son* instrument most closely related to Cuba's African heritage. At various times the *bongó* and other non-Western instruments of the *son* ensemble were banned from public performance in Havana and other Cuban municipalities because they "resembled instruments used in *santería* and *abukuá* ceremony" (Moore 1997). Before the musical style became widely disseminated in the mid-1920s, *son* musicians faced constant harassment, and "even members of the well-known Sexteto Habanero were thrown into jail on various occasions for playing *sones* at public gatherings" (Moore 1997). In the *son* ensemble, the *bongó* player, as the primary percussionist, played in a free improvisational style while the other percussion instruments (e.g., *clave* and *maracas*) remained within their narrowly defined rhythmic parameters.

The *clave* had an extremely limited but important role. Its task was to strictly perform its two-measure namesake rhythmic pattern, around which all of the other instruments based their own musical input. Likewise, the *maracas* played its own strictly defined eighth note–based pattern, which helped to cement the ensemble performance. The *clave* and *maracas* players in the *son* ensemble were hired primarily as vocalists, as opposed to the *bongosero* (*bongó* player), who was employed for his skills as an instrumentalist.

Although the *tres*, guitar, and bass players supplied the harmonic and (along with the singers and trumpet) the melodic elements of the *son*, they did so in a manner that strictly adhered to and reinforced the *clave* pattern. One of the most characteristic features of the *son* is the so-called anticipated bass. Peter Manuel, in "The Anticipated Bass in Cuban Popular Music," traces the origins of this unique bass style. Rhythmically, the anticipated bass figure occurs only at two points in the measure: on the second half of beat two of the measure and on beat four. While similar to the three-side of the *clave* pattern, this two-note rhythm is played in every measure on the bass. The reason for the name *anticipated bass* is the anticipation of a measure's harmonic progression by one beat. Because the first beat of a measure is never sounded in this bass figure, the harmony actually changes on the fourth beat of the preceding measure. The bassist is not as strictly tied to this rhythm as the *clave* player is to the *clave* pattern and is allowed a narrowly defined latitude in rhythmically varying the bass pattern. The other nonpercussion instruments or vocalists normally resolve on the usual first beat (or perhaps the upbeat of four), which creates a short built-in dissonance factor. An ambiguity of resolution also results, weakening the cadential formula and creating a floating effect (Manuel 1995). When the *conga* was added to the *son* group in the 1940s to create the modern *conjunto*, the *conga*/anticipated bass combination was referred to as the *tumbao*.[2]

The term *guajeo*[3] is used to describe the rhythmic ostinato patterns realized in the *son* ensemble by the *tres* and guitar (and later the piano). In this technique, the chord instrument (typically the *tres*) sounds the harmonic progression using highly syncopated rhythmic patterns based on the *clave*. The pattern is partially based on the *cinquillo* isorhythm that is also a prominent feature of the *timbale cascara*[4] figure, which first came to prominence in the *danzón* (figure 2.1).

Figure 2.1.   The *cascara* figure (played on the sides of the *timbales*)

The main melodic element of the *son* exists in the vocal parts and the *tres* (and later the trumpet). Both *coro* singing and solo singing are main elements in the *son*. In the final or *montuno* section of a piece, the normal practice is an alternation between a two- or four-measure predefined *coro* figure and a more or less improvised solo singer figure. The phrases by the soloist are often "referred to as *inspiraciones*" (Moore 1997).

Like the instruments, the vocal performances are controlled by the rhythmic content. While the *coro* generally stays close to the *clave* rhythm, the *sonero*[5] (or solo singer) has much more leeway in the area of rhythmic placement. Instead of conforming completely to the dictates of *clave*, the best solo singers are noted for their ability to tug against the underlying rhythm. While never committing the unforgivable *faux pas* of "crossing" the *clave*, the singer places notes behind or in front of the beat throughout a phrase, only to snap back into perfect *clave* as the phrase ends or the vocal line moves into a new phrase. By creating rhythmic tension and resolution, a cadential feeling (not dissimilar to the harmonic movement of European classical music) is achieved in the realm of rhythm. As the *son* evolved, this method of rhythmic give and take was applied to the performance style of instrumental soloing as well (González 1997).

When the trumpet was finally introduced to the *son* ensemble around 1927, it quickly emulated this vocal style. In the first part (or *largo*) of a *son* composition, the trumpet player often introduced the melodic material that was then repeated by the *coro* or *sonero*; in the *montuno* section, the trumpet emulated the improvisational style of the *sonero*. The same type of rhythmic give and take discussed earlier was an essential component of the trumpet's improvisational style.

By the 1940s, soloists like singer Miguelito Cuní and trumpeters Chappottín and Armenteros had created a school of rhythmic sophistication that has seldom been equaled in music regardless of style. Because the voice and trumpet share a breath-articulated method of sound production and therefore a similar expressive manner, it was natural that the voice and the trumpet would evolve along similar paths in the development of Cuban music.

FORMAL CHARACTERISTICS OF THE *SON*

An important contribution of the *son* to Cuban music is in the area of formal structure. One of the strengths of the *son* is its ability to adapt to and encompass other musical styles. This versatility expresses itself in the development of a large number of "hybrids such as *bolero-son*, *son-guaguancó*, and numerous other Cuban types" (Robbins 1990). Although the *son* expresses itself in numerous permutations, it consists in most cases of a formal structure divided into two general parts.

The first part is commonly referred to as the *largo* and is usually based on various strophic structures that derive from the European side of the syncretic equation. The *largo* section utilizes an "extended harmonic progression, and a melody often sung in suave bel canto style" (Manuel 1995). In the *son* form, "the first part is like a closed form in itself. . . . [O]ften it uses the thirty-two bar AABA format typical of Euro-American popular songs, in which the B section is a modulating bridge" (Manuel 1995). This section can be realized in a variety of ways. A solo vocalist, a vocal chorus, or a combination of both musical textures can perform the melody.

Early *son* groups like the Sexteto Habanero emphasized a choral approach, which reflected their *coros de son* influence. On the other hand, Septeto Nacional as well as the later *conjuntos* utilized more solo singing in the *largo* section. The earlier groups like Habanero and Nacional often used instruments like the *tres* and trumpet to perform some of the melodic material in the *largo* section. In a typical case, the *tres* or trumpet would precede a vocal melody with a performance of the same material. Material from the initial part would sometimes be recapitulated in a coda section. In some cases, the *largo* part was omitted completely, and the entire piece was a *montuno*.

The second part of the *son* form, the *montuno*, represents the essence of the Cuban style and is more reflective of Cuba's African heritage than the *largo*. The *montuno* expresses the *clave* in its most direct manner and tilts the European/African equilibrium in the African direction. This part of the *son* is directly related to the strongly rhythmic folk music forms such as the various traditional *rumba* types (Robbins 1990).

The *montuno* part consists of a short repetitive harmonic phrase (also called a *montuno*) directly related to the *clave*. The *montuno* phrase generally consists of a harmonic progression built over one or more iterations of the *clave*. Once this section has started, the *montuno* pattern is repeated verbatim (with occasional break figures) until the end of the piece. A contrasting *montuno* pattern is sometimes introduced later in the *montuno* section, but this practice did not occur with any regularity until years after the pieces examined here were recorded.

Because the *clave* is two bars in length, the *montuno* pattern is always an even number of measures (usually two, four, or eight). If a *montuno* is four measures in length, the pattern contains two repetitions of the basic two-measure *clave* figure. Harmonically, there are several common patterns. The *montuno* pattern is based on one of a variety of possible configurations of the tonic-dominant relationship. One typical formula is a movement from the tonic in the first measure of a four-measure *montuno* pattern to the dominant for measures two and three, and a return to tonic in measure four. However, there are variations on this particular progression as well as a myriad of completely different formulae.

There are a number of ways in which the *montuno* section of the *son* reflects African musical values. Because the harmonic framework of the *montuno* is much less complex and extended than the strophic *largo*, the rhythmic element becomes more important. It is common, especially in later decades, for the percussionists to change to more intensive rhythmic patterns when a piece switches from the *largo* to the *montuno*.

A variety of musical events can occur over the *montuno* foundation created by the rhythm section (Mauleón 1993). The most common activity is the African-influenced call-and-response-type alternation between a *coro* (chorus) figure and a solo singer. The *coro* figure is an unvarying and harmonized melodic line, typically the same length as an instance of the *montuno* pattern. The lyric/melodic content is almost always the same with each iteration of the *montuno*; however, it may on occasion be altered or truncated in different parts of the *montuno* section. The solo vocalist or *sonero* sings a freeform, often improvised, melodic statement. The lyrics frequently take the form of commentary on the subject matter introduced in either the *coro* or in the first part of the song. However, the words can be about anything that occurs to the singer at the time of the performance.

Although the call and response in the *montuno* section usually occurs between the *coro* and the lead singer, a solo trumpet often replaces the solo singer. Occasionally, prearranged trumpet section parts will fill in the spaces between *coros*.

SEXTETO HABANERO

During the late 1920s the major Cuban *son* ensembles expanded by adding a trumpet to create a seven-piece group. Since that time the term *septeto trumpet* has been associated with the performance style developed by these early Cuban trumpet players. While Félix Chappottín was the most celebrated of the trumpeters to play with seminal bands like Septeto Habanero and Septeto Nacional in the 1920s, there were several other important trumpet players from the era. Enrique Hernández was the first trumpet player to join the Sexteto Habanero in 1927; Chappottín made his first recordings with the band in 1928 and was replaced by José Interián on the recordings starting in 1930. Because the band was at different times a sextet or a septet, the name Habanero will be used by itself at times when referring to either version of the band. During the same time period that these three brass players were playing with Septeto Habanero, trumpeter Lazaro Herrera began a long-term association with Septeto Nacional. While the analysis in this chapter will be confined to Chappottín and the other Habanero trumpet players, Herrera's work with Septeto Nacional also deserves a systematic investigation.

One of the oldest and most popular of all *son* groups was the Sexteto Habanero. Formed in 1918, the group was made up of members who lived in the outlying Havana barrio of Pueblo Nuevo (Moore 1997). The band was an extension of the Trío Oriental that had moved from the Oriente province to Havana around 1910. The group soon became the Cuarteto Oriental when they added a *bongosero*. When the group expanded to six pieces under the name Sexteto Habanero, both *tres*[6] player Carlos Godínez and guitarist Guillermo Castillo of the original Trío Oriental were members. There are various reasons why Sexteto Habanero became the preeminent *son* ensemble of the 1920s. In 1920 Habanero traveled to New York City to make their first recordings for the Victor Talking Machine Company (Robbins 1990). This was approximately the same time period that the first American jazz recordings were being produced. In addition to making some of the earliest *son* recordings, the band performed live at various North American venues (Moore 1997). These performances were the harbinger of a number of high-profile international tours by Habanero over the next several decades. Another reason for Habanero's success and for the success of *son* in general was the early development of radio broadcasting in Cuba. The music of Habanero and the other *son* groups of the 1920s reached a wider and more diverse audience in Cuba as a result of early radio. Prior to the advent of radio, *son* had been exclusively the province of lower-class working blacks. The inherent color-blindness of radio broadcasting allowed the sounds (if not the actual physical presence in a nonservile role) of black Cubans into the homes of the rich and middle-class white Cubans.

GRABACIONES COMPLETAS 1925–1931

The Tumbao label has provided a number of recent reissues of early recordings by Septeto Habanero and Septeto Nacional in CD format that thoroughly document this period. One of these reissues is *Grabaciones Completas 1925–1931* (Sexteto y Septeto Habanero), a monumental four-CD box set containing all of the Septeto Habanero recordings on the Victor label between 1925 and 1931. This four-volume set includes ninety-eight recordings and purports to contain all of the recordings by Habanero during this time period except for two that are documented in the Victor catalog but were not located by Tumbao. Hernández, Chappottín, and Interián are all amply represented in this box set. In additional recordings reissued by Tumbao, there are numerous examples of Herrera's work with the Septeto Nacional in the late 1920s.

Of the ninety-eight recordings on the four-volume Habanero set, fifty-four are recordings by the sexteto without the added trumpet. According to the liner notes for the album, Enrique Hernández plays on seven of the selections; Chappottín plays on nineteen tracks, and Interián on eighteen. While these credits are accurate for the most part, there are a few occasions where the attributions are questionable. A couple of these discrepancies will be discussed later.

Tumbao's four-CD Habanero collection contains recordings from nine distinct groupings of sessions, which took place between October 29, 1925 and February 28, 1931. Usually each of the groupings contained two or three sessions occurring within the space of a week. On six occasions these session groupings took place in Havana. The other three took place in New York City. The first set of recordings took place in Havana in late October and early November 1925. The four songs and the twelve selections recorded a year later in New York are sextet recordings and predate the addition of the trumpet. "Tres lindas Cubanas" was one of the sides recorded in New York at this time. Because it was one of the band's biggest hits and is typical of their work before and after the appearance of the trumpet, this selection will be analyzed in more detail below.

Although nine of the ten pieces recorded in March 1927 in Havana also feature the sextet, the trumpet was used for the first time on "La chambelona," which is a re-recording of a *comparsa* standard. This piece is very different in character than anything else recorded by Habanero at this time. Tumbao credits Enrique Hernández as the trumpet player on "La chambelona," but this trumpet performance does not sound at all like any of the work by Hernández on the six other pieces he is credited with playing on in this collection. The six Hernández selections, along with seventeen others featuring the trumpet-less sextet, were recorded in New York in October of 1927. Even though Habanero added the trumpet to its instrumentation in 1927, it continued to record prolifically as a sextet *sans* horn in later years.

Twenty-year-old Félix Chappottín makes his recorded debut with Septeto Habanero on five selections recorded on February 1928 in Havana. The sextet recorded five additional trumpet-less songs at these sessions. Of the thirteen selections recorded by Habanero in their next series of sessions (New York, May 1928), eight contain the playing of Chappottín. Chappottín's last attributed work with Habanero on the Tumbao set is on seven of eight numbers recorded in Havana in late November and early December of 1928. The remaining selection featured the sextet.

There was a lapse of over a year before Habanero recorded again for Victor. In February of 1930, the band recorded ten numbers in Havana. By this time the trumpet is present on all of the recordings made by the group. In this case, José Interián is credited as the trumpet player. However, on at least one song ("Lamento esclavo") Chappottín is the trumpeter. Because "Lamento esclavo" represents a very early example of the mature Chappottín style, this selection will be examined in more detail later. The final eight pieces in the Tumbao boxed set were recorded a year later in February 1931 and all feature Interián.

ANALYSIS OF "TRES LINDAS CUBANAS"

In order to better understand the role of the septeto trumpet in the early *son* ensemble, it is useful to analyze at least one piece performed by Sexteto Habanero before the horn was added. One of the most popular of the pre-trumpet songs in the Tumbao collection of Victor recordings is "Tres lindas Cubanas," which was recorded in September of 1926. In addition to being one of the most important of the band's songs, "Tres lindas Cubanas" is a use-

ful candidate for analysis because it is very typical of Sexteto Habanero's music at the time.

The *largo*[7] of "Tres lindas Cubanas" contains two repeated
eight-measure sections. The A section begins with a repeated two-
measure melody module, the first ending on A and the second on
B♭. Following three measures of tonic F major, the B♭ ending of the
second module introduces the dominant harmony in the fourth
measure. A contrasting melodic line fills out the second half of the
A section. The dominant harmony continues for the first three bars
of this phrase before returning to the tonic in bar eight. As an introduction, the *tres* plays the entire eight-measure A section
melody. This was a common practice in *son* band arrangements,
with the trumpet replacing the *tres* in this role after this brass instrument was added to the instrumentation.

After the vocal chorus version of the A section and its repetition,
the chorus immediately proceeds into the B section. In many other
examples of the band's arrangements, the *tres* (or trumpet) would
also introduce this section with an iteration of its melody. The B
section of the *largo* is also eight measures in length and is repeated. In this case, the melody begins with a two-measure module consisting of a syncopated descending line in the first measure
connected to a whole note in the second. Measures three and four
of B contain a sequence of this module a diatonic step higher. As
in the A section, the second half of B contains contrasting melodic
material. The B section also closely resembles A in its harmonic
progression. The entire *largo* is sung chorally with a solo singer
providing a fill-in commentary in the eighth measure of each section except for the final B section, which leads to the *montuno*.

"Tres lindas Cubanas" has an unusual *coro*[8] for a *montuno* section
in that it extends to sixteen measures before the solo voice enters
and resembles a *largo* in its melodic development, albeit with a typical *montuno* harmonic progression. The *tres* starts the *montuno* section off with a statement of the first four measures of the *coro*. This
phrase is a repeated, four-measure melodic module containing the

title lyrics. At this point the *coro* is very *montuno*-like in character. However, the second half of the *coro* is an eight-measure through-composed melody that gives the entire *coro* its *largo*-like nature. A twelve-measure solo voice section follows the sixteen-bar *coro*. This entire twenty-eight-measure *coro*/solo part is repeated twice before the recording ends with a final iteration of the sixteen-bar *coro*.

ENRIQUE HERNÁNDEZ

Although Enrique Hernández did not achieve the renown of his successor Chappottín, he was charged with the important duty of initiating and establishing the role of the trumpet in the early Habanero. On the six pieces recorded with Septeto Habanero during the October 1927 sessions, Hernández demonstrates little in the way of improvisational skill and in most cases simply states the melodic content of a piece prior to the entrance of the singers. This was a duty that the trumpet inherited from the *tres*. In the same way that the *tres* introduces the thematic material in "Tres lindas Cubanas," Hernández introduces the theme with his trumpet on all of the pieces he plays on.

"Como está Miguel" is the first piece listed in the Victor catalog that indisputably features Hernández. Like virtually all *son* songs (including "Tres lindas Cubanas"), "Como está Miguel" contains both *largo* and *montuno* sections. In this case the *largo* is sixteen measures in length and is performed four times. The trumpet states the *largo* melody the first and third times and the vocal chorus performs it the second and fourth times. Although Hernández is completely faithful to the *largo* melodically, he uses a rhythmic approach that foreshadows later developments by trumpeters like Chappottín as well as by a number of solo singers. In stretching the time of eighth note syncopation in the direction of quarter note triplets, Hernández might not be improvising per se on these recordings, but he is helping to establish a uniquely Afro-Cuban style of melodic interpretation.

The only playing Hernández does in the *montuno* section of "Como está Miguel" is the doubling of the *coro* response to the solo singer. All of the other recordings from this session follow the same pattern, with the trumpet playing the melody before the vocalists perform lyrics using the same melody. In most cases this material is repeated at least once.

FÉLIX CHAPPOTTÍN

Chappottín's first sessions with Habanero on February 4th and 8th of 1928 are performed for the most part in the conservative mode of his predecessor Hernández. However, even on these five songs Chappottín displays a continuous pull in the improvisational direction. On these recordings the improvisation impulse shows itself in discrete variations of the various melodic figures. These changes usually occur at the beginning or end of a particular figure. While Hernández hints at the rhythmic possibilities of interpreting a melody, Chappottín bends and stretches the time in a number of different ways.

The form of "El bongo del Habanero" is on the simple side. After an almost mandatory (for Habanero) *tres* introduction, the *largo* contains three sets of repetitions of eight-measure melodies between the trumpet and the *coro*. In this case the first two sets are one melody and the last set contains a contrasting theme. The second trumpet version of the first melody is preceded by a long, syncopated pickup note, which was a standard practice used by all of the Habanero trumpeters. This possibly explains why, later on, the first part of a melodic figure performed by the trumpet usually contains the most improvisational material. In case after case on these recordings the beginning of one of these melodic sections will diverge significantly from the original figure only to end up exactly like the original by the last few notes of the section.

Following the *coro* repetition of the second theme, the *montuno* section starts with a *tres* introduction of the melody. This melody consists of a seven-note figure performed by either the trumpet or the solo singer, which is followed by a two-note *coro* response. A pattern is set up with the trumpet taking the lead for two repetitions followed by the solo singer for four repetitions. This pattern occurs three times, with a *bongó* solo taking place between each of these extended patterns. The *coro* begins the second and third iterations of this pattern set. The solo singer is much freer and improvisational in his treatment of the seven-note melody than Chappottín. However, the trumpeter does vary the melody slightly in his last few repetitions.

"Alza los pies congo" is much more complicated formally than "El bongo del Habanero." In this case the formal sections are longer and there are short two- or three-measure interludes between each section. As in most of the recordings in this collection, the trumpet performs the initial melodic material as an introduction to the vocalists. In this case it is a shorter subset of the vocal melody that follows. The trumpet version contains a four-measure phrase and an eight-measure phrase followed by a two-bar interlude. The vocalists then extend this melody to twenty-four measures in length by repetitions of each of the phrases. After another two-measure interlude the whole process repeats itself. Following this second repetition, the interlude is extended to three measures, which changes the *clave* from two-three to three-two and introduces the *montuno* section.

The *montuno* contains a number of call-and-response sections between a four-bar trumpet melody and a *coro* of the same length. For the first two times through these alternations Chappottín plays his melody exactly. However, during the second *coro* he starts to play single-note syncopated figuration behind the singers, which continue into the first part of his next melody section, creating a brief amount of improvisation which quickly reverts to the written melody. He continues to use this technique during the next call-and-response section. Although he keeps playing the single-note syncopated figures behind this chorus, he lays out entirely in his last solo section (except for the last two notes). The following *coro* section (with his background figurations) brings the song to a conclusion. Even within its very limited scope, the improvisational devices used by Chappottín in his solo sections on this song are already much more advanced than in the work of his predecessor Hernández. An interesting side note on both "Alza los pies congo" and "El bongo del Habanero" is that the *clave* player begins both pieces on the wrong side of the *clave* but immediately adjusts when the melody starts.

"Amparo" has a simple formal structure. The *largo* section consists of four repetitions of a twelve-measure melody separated by two-measure interludes. In the standard manner, the trumpet plays the first and third repetitions of the melody, alternating with the *coro*. Simplicity of form also characterizes the *montuno* of "Amparo." Here trumpet and *coro* trade four-bar melodies five times each to the end. Chappottín performs his assigned melody as written all five times. There is little improvisation by the trumpet in this song.

"Dora" on the other hand contains some of the most expressive work by Chappottín on his first recording sessions with the band. Formally it is identical to "Amparo," with an added eight-measure call-and-response section between Chappottín and the *coro* in the *montuno* section. While he plays most of his melodies straight, he adds anticipation and rhythmic manipulation to his renderings of these themes with a highly personal and forceful character.

The *largo* of "Por un beso de tu boca" contains four alternating sixteen-measure sections between the trumpet and the *coro*. After a two-measure break, the *montuno* contains typical four-measure call-and-response sections between the trumpet and the *coro*. Chappottín's playing on this song is the most improvisatory of his initial sessions with Habanero. Although his first four-bar solo stays faithful to the melody, he takes many liberties on his other solos and provides single-note rhythmic commentaries behind the *coro* sections throughout.

Chappottín's creative abilities as an improvising trumpeter are used to greater effect on his second set of recordings with Habanero. These eight selections were recorded in New York at the end of May in 1928. On most of these songs, Chappottín shows many of the elements that characterize the celebrated soloing style he developed in the decades following his stint with Habanero.

An eighteen-measure melody is alternated twice each by the trumpet and *coro* in the *largo* of "Olvido." In the *montuno* section of "Olvido" (written by the famous *son* musician Miguel Mata-moros) Chappottín plays three versions of the *coro* melody alter-nating with the vocal renditions. Initially the trumpeter remains (for the most part) faithful to the original melody. The two succes-sive versions are liberally altered paraphrases, which are changed primarily though rhythmic manipulation.

"Tribilín cantore" contains a two-measure I-V-I *montuno* pattern throughout the song. Following an out-of-time opening figure, a trumpet/*tres* duet initiates the tempo with the first of several iter-ations of a two-bar melody. The *coro* takes over this melody with contrapuntal bass voice and trumpet accompaniment figures. Fol-lowing several coros the solo voice comes in and the remainder of the song consists of alternating *coro* and *sonero* sections. Chappot-tín's participation in this song is confined to the introduction and his counterpoint figures behind the coros. "Tribilín cantore" sounds very different than the other songs at these sessions. In ad-dition to the continuous two-bar *montuno*, unusual aspects are the highly rhythmic percussion parts and a rare use of the cowbell.

After four measures of *tres*, the trumpet plays his version of the twenty-bar minor key *largo* of "Mi guitarra." A two-measure inter-lude introduces the *coro* version, which is the same except for a two-measure insertion following the first eight measures of the melody. After the *coro* version, an interlude leads to the *montuno,* which contains several alternating eight-bar sections between solo trumpet and *coro*. Only the first of Chappottín's four solo sections remains faithful to the *coro* melody. In the other three solos, he does some of his most adventurous improvising yet. In the third solo he even plays a brief double-time figure. He demonstrates a good sense of form by returning to a closer reference to the *coro* theme in his last solo.

A trumpet statement of the sixteen-measure theme follows the usual short introduction in "Romerillo." A two-bar interlude leads to the *coro* version of the *largo* theme. It differs from the trumpet version in that the second half of the theme is repeated and lengthens the form to twenty-four measures. A two-bar interlude leads to a repetition of the entire twenty-four-measure *coro* section. A simple V-I two-measure progression provides the *montuno* pattern. Presaging a device that became common in the 1940s *conjunto* era, Chappottín plays the first two-measure section in the call and response with the *coro* before turning it over to the *sonero*. After two *soneos*, the floor is returned to the trumpet for one turn before returning to the *sonero*. This pattern continues to the end of the piece. In his short solos Chappottín is almost totally improvising.

Félix Chappottín doesn't come in on "La campana" until the *montuno* section. The *largo* consists of a long theme sung by the *coro*, which is repeated immediately. In the *montuno*, the trumpet and then the *sonero* trade off eight-measure sections with the *coro*. In this case, Chappottín plays the *coro* melody faithfully in his two solo sections. In apparent tribute to the song title "La campana" (the bell), a cowbell is featured prominently in the *montuno* section.

"Coralia" contains some of the most adventurous soloing by Chappottín on these sessions and will be discussed in detail below.

"Mujer mariposa" is another tour-de-force of the developing solo style of the young Félix Chappottín. Following four iterations of the simple eight-measure *largo* melody, "Mujer mariposa" contains one of the longest *montuno* call-and-response sections on these recordings. The four-bar pattern is repeated eighteen times with nine trumpet solos alternating with nine coros. Chappottín plays some of his best early solos here and at times does some interesting duet playing with the *bongocero*, Agustín Gutiérrez, who is on fire throughout this recording. Gutiérrez switches to cowbell during the last few measures of this piece.

The *largo* of "No me maltrates nena" consists of two sixteen-measure themes, each of which is performed by the trumpet and the *coro*. After these sixty-four measures, the piece continues with ten four-measure call-and-response sections between trumpet and *coro*. There is little of interest in Chappottín's work here because he doesn't deviate from the melody in any of his solos.

Félix Chappottín's last regular sessions with Habanero in the Tumbao collection occurred in Havana at the end of November and beginning of December in 1928. Chappottín plays on seven of the eight numbers at these sessions.

"Gloria a mis claves" has an A-A-B-B *largo* with a sixteen-measure A section played once each by the trumpet and *coro*. On the first B section Chappottín starts on the last bar of the previous *coro*, which turns the *clave* around to two-three (where it remains for the rest of the piece). The *montuno* is built on a four-measure pattern with the usual call and response between trumpet and *coro*. There are five trumpet solos sections and most of them contain a generous amount improvisation by Chappottín. Trumpet/*bongó* interplay is particularly impressive in the third solo section.

"Bun bun pa'mi china" has a very interesting formal structure. After a short introduction the trumpet version of the *largo* is thirty-four measures in length, while the *coro* version extends to forty-two bars. The form of this *largo* can be described as A-A-B-B-C. A is six measures long with the fourth bar of the melody elongated for two measures. This technique is also used in the contrasting B section. In C the rhythm section breaks for three measures starting on the second measure of the eight-measure part. After the trumpet *largo* there is a two-measure extension before the *coro largo* begins. Except for a repetition of the C section, the *coro largo* is the same as the trumpet version. In this case, the solo singer replaces the *coro* in the break part in both of the vocal C sections. The final part of the *largo* coincides with the beginning of the *montuno*. The *coro* melody from the fifth and sixth measures of the C section becomes the *coro* of the *montuno*, with the trumpet echoing this figure in measures seven and eight of the last C. There are an additional four-trumpet and five-*coro* two-measure sections before the piece closes. Except for on his first solo, Chappottín is given free rein to improvise.

"Las maracas de neri" consists of a number of long sections and can be described as an extended *largo* without a *montuno* section. After the four-measure introduction, the trumpet plays the first half of the initial sixteen-measure theme. This is followed by two repetitions of the entire sixteen bars by the *coro*. A secondary twelve-measure theme is alternated twice by the trumpet and the *coro*, leading to the end of the song. Chappottín states all of his melodies straight with very little elaboration.

"Debajo de la mata" has one of the most complex formal structures used by Habanero at this time. In addition to having a lengthy *largo* theme both the trumpet and *coro* (slighty longer) versions change *clave* direction in the final section. Both *largo* themes change from three-two to two-three in the final two phrases of the melody. In the case of the trumpet version the *clave* switches back to three-two for the entry of the *coro largo*. Due to a repetition of the first eight measures, the *coro largo* is therefore that much longer than the trumpet version. After the solo singer begins the *montuno* with the first of three two-measure call-and-response sections with the *coro*, Chappottín takes over from the *sonero* for four additional tradeoffs with the *coro*. In his solos in "Debajo de la mata," the trumpeter shows that he has started to consolidate many of his ideas into recurring motives, albeit with a certain lack of spontaneity. One interesting feature of the trumpet in these short solos is the rare use on these recordings of the muteless open horn.

Tresero Carlos Godinez is the featured soloist on "Preludio de Godinez." Following three repetitions of the eight-bar *largo* (one by the trumpet and two *coro* versions), Godinez performs a rare extended *tres* solo in a very rhythmic chordal style. Although inventive, the eight-measure trumpet solos that trade with the *coro* in the *montuno* section again lack the improvisational fire of his work on the mid-1928 New York sessions.

"De la boca al corazon" begins with a six-measure rhythm introduction before the trumpeter plays the first iteration of the eighteen-measure *largo* melody, which is firmly entrenched in three-two *clave*. This melody is repeated three more times by

coro, trumpet, and final *coro*. Coming in on the sixteenth measure
of the final *coro largo* section, the *montuno* reverses the *clave* to
two-three. In this case, the *montuno* pattern is four measures in
length, with the trumpet alternating with the *coro* for the first sixteen measures. *Sonero* and *coro* trade patterns for the final sixteen
measures of the recording. In his two sections here, Chappottín
demonstrates a firmer command of his solo statements. He is
starting to develop a distinctive personal style. There is a tradeoff
in terms of spontaneity when comparing these solos with his work
on the earlier New York City sessions.

"La diosa" consists entirely of alternating sixteen-measure sections. There are different ways of looking at the form of this composition. One would be to consider the entire piece as a two-theme
largo with the A theme being performed three times (once by the
trumpet and twice by the *coro*). Theme B is then performed four
times. Chappottín plays this theme the first time, followed by *coro*
and *sonero* versions. In the final iteration, the *coro* sings the theme
with commentary by the *sonero* and the solo trumpet. Except for
in the final chorus, Chappottín does not improvise on this piece.

ANALYSIS OF "CORALIA"

In the set of recordings made in May of 1928 in New York City, Félix
Chappottín performs the most significant of his earliest work with
Habanero. Although not as developed and exciting as his remarkable
playing on "Lamento esclavo" (recorded almost two years later when
the trumpeter was no longer a regular member of the group), in the
New York sessions Chappottín's soloing contains a balanced mixture
of spontaneity and technical assuredness. While his prior sessions
with the group demonstrated a lack of maturity, Chappottín had put
together most of the elements of his celebrated style by the time of
the May 1928 recordings. Conversely, the recordings he made later
in 1928 in Havana show a complete command of his performance
style but lack the daring and inventiveness of his soloing on the eight
New York pieces. While there are several significant examples of

improvisatory playing by Chappottín in these selections, "Coralia" contains some of his best early solo work.

"Coralia" was written by bassist Gerardo Martínez and contains a relatively short *largo* form in F minor and a four-measure *montuno* pattern in the relative major. The *montuno* section contains five trumpet solos over this pattern alternating with five *coros* (the last *coro* bringing the piece to a close). The structure of "Coralia" is indicated in table 1. From m. 1 to m. 65, part A contains the entire *largo,* including the introductions and the transition to the *montuno*. The *montuno* section is described by part B (mm. 66–105).

Table 2.1. Time Line of "Coralia"

Time-(min./sec.)	Section	Description
	Part A	
	(*Largo*)	
0:00	1. mm. 1–2	*Tres* introduction.
0:04	2. mm. 3–4	Entrance of remaining rhythm section.
0:08	3. mm. 5–16	12-measure version of *largo* melody in trumpet.
0:29	4. mm. 17–18	Rhythm section interlude.
0:33	5. mm. 19–32	16-measure version of *largo* melody in chorus.
0:58	6. mm. 33–34	Rhythm section interlude.
1:02	7. mm. 35–46	Repeat of 12-measure version of *largo* melody in trumpet.
1:23	8. mm. 47–48	Rhythm section interlude.
1:27	9. mm. 49–62	Repeat of 16-measure version of *largo* melody in chorus.
1:52	10. mm. 63–65	Transition to *montuno*
	Part B	
	(*Montuno*)	
1:57	1. m. 66–69	Trumpet solo 1.
2:04	2. mm. 70–73	First *coro*.
2:10	3. mm. 74–77	Trumpet solo 2.
2:17	4. mm. 78–81	Second *coro*.
2:24	5. mm. 82–85	Trumpet solo 3.
2:30	6. mm. 86–89	Third *coro*.
2:36	6. mm. 90–93	Trumpet solo 4.
2:42	6. mm. 94–97	Fourth *coro* with trumpet figures.
2:49	6. mm. 98–101	Trumpet solo 5.
2:55	6. mm. 102–105	Fifth *coro* and ending.

The *largo* of "Coralia" can be described as A-A' and its repetition. A is twelve measures in length and is performed in both cases by the trumpet (figure 2.2). An additional two measures are inserted into the beginning of the A' section. Both of these fourteen-measure sections are performed by the *coro*. There are two-measure rhythm section interludes between all of the sections. In the following analysis the trumpet version of the *largo* melody will be used with the variations in the *coro* version indicated when appropriate.

Figure 2.2.   "Coralia": The *largo* A section—trumpet version

"Coralia" begins with a four-measure introduction over an F minor tonality starting with the solo *tres*, which is joined by the rest of the rhythm section in m. 3. The twelve-bar melody is through composed over a complex harmonic structure. In the first measure of the A section, the trumpet begins a two-bar module with a five-note figure that embellishes a C5 starting on the upbeat of two. The module continues in the next measure with a syncopated ascending G diminished triad ending on an extended Db 5 over the change from the tonic F minor to the underlying dominant tonality, which persists for the rest of the four-bar phrase. In the second half of the phrase, the melody begins with an embellished F4 before leaping again to a Db 5 that descends to C5 a beat and a half later. This two-note rhythmic device of a dotted quarter note followed by an eighth note tied to a half note in the fourth bar of a phrase presages the *montuno* section, where it occurs in every trumpet solo and *coro*.

A modulation to Bb minor is the main feature of the second phrase in the *largo* melody. Emphasizing the dominant harmony of the new key, the melody in the first module is an ascending F dominant seventh arpeggio beginning on F4 and returning from the seventh (Eb) to A4 in the second measure of the phrase. The melody becomes linear again in the next module, when a six-note line rises from A4 to Db5 and returns to Bb4 and the resolution of the Bb minor harmony in the next measure. This harmony sustains into the following bar (and phrase), which contains a slightly altered repetition of the melodic line in the first measure in the previous module. A descending line from Db5 to E4 accompanies the return of the F minor tonality in the second measure of this final phrase. This final module of the *largo* melody contains a dominant-tonic cadence that begins with an ascending arpeggio to C5 and then a descending eighth note line to the tonic in the final bar.

"Coralia" switches to the major tonality for the *montuno* section. In the first of his five four-measure solo sections, Chappottín performs the same melody (figure 2.3) that the *coro* sings between each of the trumpet solos. The *montuno* pattern is based on a standard I-V-V-I chord progression; with the melody starting on F4 (repeated four times) followed by an ascending eighth note line, which ends on a half note C5 in the following measure. Starting on the upbeat of three, the last four notes of this module are repeated. However, instead of sustaining the C5 the *montuno* continues the string of eighth notes by descending to A4 and then linearly to the F. Changing to quarter notes, the A-to-F figure is played again with the F repeated a beat and a half later. This syncopated pair of Fs is performed in the final measure of every solo and *coro* in the *montuno* section.

Figure 2.3.   "Coralia": Trumpet solo one

In the next three trumpet solos, Chappottín deviates significantly from the *coro* melody. The first of these solos (figure 2.4) begins on the upbeat of three in the final bar of the previous *coro* section. This D5 sustains through the third beat of the next measure. A C5 eighth note on the last half beat of the bar introduces a pair of quarter note triplet groupings, each containing lower and upper neighbor tones preceding a C5. The C5 ending the second triplet sustains for an extra three beats before two eighth notes on the fourth beat (G4 and A4) lead to the final syncopated pair of F4s.

Figure 2.4. "Coralia": Trumpet solo two

Although the second half of the third trumpet solo is identical to the *coro* melody, the first half is for the most part a heavily syncopated series of C4s, which are again embellished with a number of neighbor tones (figure 2.5). Like the previous solo the lower neighbors are half-step B5s rather than the diatonic Bb. A ghosted E4 eighth note on the second beat of the last measure in the solo varies this instance of the characteristic F4 pair slightly.

Figure 2.5. "Coralia": Trumpet solo three

In the fourth solo (figure 2.6) the repeated C5 motif is used again with the embellishing tones stripped away. Except for a single B5 inserted before the final C5 in the third measure of the phrase, rhythmic syncopation is the only means used to develop the solo until the final four-note figure. In these repeated figures, Chappottín uses very sophisticated time manipulation.

Figure 2.6. "Coralia": Trumpet solo four

A return to the *coro* melody in the final trumpet solo (figure 2.7) gives the *montuno* section a strong sense of unity. In this case, the melody is played more simply than in the first trumpet solo, has a more relaxed feel, and seems to indicate that the end of the song is approaching.

Figure 2.7. "Coralia": Trumpet solo five

Although they seem tame by today's standards, the improvisational elements in these short solos by Félix Chappottín on early Habanero recordings such as "Coralia" were revolutionary and forever changed the way the trumpet is played in Afro-Cuban music.

ANALYSIS OF "LAMENTO ESCLAVO"

Although credited to Interián in the liner notes of the boxed set, the trumpet playing on "Lamento esclavo" is unquestionably the work of a surprisingly mature Félix Chappottín. It was recorded just a little over a year after his previous recordings with Habanero, and Chappottín's playing had changed dramatically in the interim. On "Lamento esclavo," he displays many of the characteristic figures and phrases that became trademarks of his style throughout his long career.

"Lamento esclavo" is an unusual number in this collection. While almost all of the selections are standard *son* songs, "Lamento esclavo" is labeled as a *canto negro*. In addition to having a different rhythmic feel (with the bass playing on beats one and three) than most of the material played by Habanero at this time, the song's *largo* section has a more complex formal structure than usual. As in the other songs, the trumpet performs the melodic line as an introduction to the vocal version. In this case, only the first eight measures of the vocal melody are quoted. A solo voice with chorus counterpoint comes in following the trumpet introduction. After four measures, the chorus completes an eight-measure section. This eight-bar period is built over a chord progression containing four measures of tonic going to the dominant harmony for two measures before returning to the Bb tonic chord in the final two bars. This eight-measure section is then repeated. Following this repetition the second half of the same section is performed twice. At this point a new eight-measure section is introduced. The first four measures of the new section are contrasting, with a double-time feel and a cowbell figure.

Although the cowbell (*campana*) became a familiar instrument in Afro-Cuban music, it was only occasionally used by Habanero at this time. The cowbell is found on only a few selections in this collection. The second half of this section is the same as the end of the original section. A two-measure transition featuring a growling trumpet figure leads to a repetition of the entire *largo*. Chappottín supplies fill-in commentary throughout the *largo* using the smears, growls, and half-valvings that became signal features of his style in later years.

A three-note ensemble break brings the *largo* repetition to a close and a three eighth-note *coro* pickup figure introduces the *montuno* section. One feature here is the change of *clave* from three-two to two-three. Chappottín plays three initial solos alternating with the *coro*, which is built over a simple two-measure V-I *montuno* pattern. His first solo begins with two quarter-note triplet groupings and ends with offset eighth-note figures, all played with a subtle sense of rhythmic placement. One of Chappottín's most familiar devices is the high-range syncopated trill and it is the primary feature of his second solo. Arpeggiated pentatonic figures dominate the third solo and are very similar to what he used two decades later in the classic Arsenio Rodríguez recording of "Dundunbanza." After the three solos the lead singer replaces the trumpet for two call-and-response sections with the *coro*. Chappottín then returns with two more solo sections, which are less virtuosic and more rhythmically stable than his previous three solos. A final *coro* brings the piece to an end.

JOSÉ INTERIÁN

The septeto trumpet style had evolved considerably by the time José Interián joined Habanero in 1930. While the trumpet still introduced the melody in almost all of the pieces, there was far more flexibility in what he could play during the rest of the tune. It was common for the player to fill in behind the singers and much of what was performed during the *montuno* section was pure improvisation. Whereas Hernández in the early years had stuck strictly to the melody, with only slight rhythmic shifting on occasion, both Chappottín and Interián took more and more liberties, first with greater rhythmic shifting and finally with completely new melodic and rhythmic content.

Like Chappottín, Interián is a master of the Afro-Cuban style and his work with Habanero in this collection shows an inventive sense of melodic development. However, he doesn't possess as keen a sense of rhythmic give and take as the brilliant Chappottín. A typical example of Interián's playing is on "Criollo haragan." A detailed analysis of this piece and Interián's style will complete this examination of the early *son*.

ANALYSIS OF "CRIOLLO HARAGAN"

"Criollo haragan" (Sexteto y Septeto Habanero, *Grabaciones Completas 1925—1931*, vol. 4) was recorded by Sexteto Habanero in February of 1931 and features the trumpet playing of José Interián.

"Criollo haragan" is a typical example of the *son* form, with fully developed *largo* and *montuno* sections. In the analysis of "Criollo haragan" that follows, reference will be made to table 2.2, which contains two divisions. Part A includes the introduction and *largo* from m. 1 through m. 54. Part B includes the entire *montuno* section from m. 55 to the end of the recording.

Table 2.2.   Time Line of "Criollo haragan"

Time-(min./sec.)	Section	Description
	Part A	
	(*Largo*)	
0:00	I. mm. 1–2	*Tres* pickup to rhythm section.
0:04	2. mm. 3–4	Entrance of remaining rhythm section.
0:07	3. mm. 5–20	A section of melody in trumpet.
0:38	4. mm. 21–22	Interlude.
0:41	5. mm. 23–38	A section of melody in chorus.
1:12	6. mm. 39–46	B section of melody in trumpet.
1:26	7. mm. 47–54	B section of melody in chorus.
	Part B	
	(*Montuno*)	
1:41	I. m. 55	Rhythm transition of *clave*
1:43	2. mm. 56–61	Trumpet solo I with pickup.
1:54	3. mm. 62–65	*Coro* one (long *coro*)—1st time.
2:01	4. mm. 66–69	Trumpet solo 2.
2:08	5. mm. 70–73	*Coro* one—2nd time.
2:15	6. mm. 74–77	Trumpet solo 3.
2:21	7. m. 77	Solo voice.
2:23	8. mm. 78–81	*Coro* two (short *coro*)—1st time.
2:30	9. mm. 82–85	*Coro* two—2nd time.
2:37	10. mm. 86–89	*Coro* two—3rd time.
2:44	11. mm. 90–93	*Coro* two—4th time.
2:51	12. mm. 94–97	*Coro* two—5th time.
2:59	13. mm. 98–101	*Coro* two—6th time.

The piece opens with the *tres* and guitar establishing the rhythm; the remainder of the rhythm section enters in m. 3. This *tres* figure varies melodically, as the harmony changes or disappears completely when the texture of the music becomes more complex. The guitar player strums throughout the chord progression, usually in continuous eighth-note rhythms with the downbeats of beats one and three silent. When the rhythm section enters in m. 3, the two-three *clave* is firmly established before the trumpet player enters with an eighth-note pickup to m. 5. For the next sixteen measures, the trumpet performs the initial melody: the first A section of the *largo*. This is followed by a short interlude and then by a harmonized vocal version of this same section.

The initial presentation of the vocal melody by the trumpet is a common feature of the early *septeto*. Prior to the addition of the trumpet to the *son* ensemble, the *tres* would play this melodic material.

The *largo* section of "Criollo haragan" can be described formally as A-A-B-B. The melodic material in both the first A section and first B section is performed by the trumpet. In both instances, the vocal chorus repeats the material. The trumpet version of the melody will be the primary musical material used in the following analysis of the *largo* section.

The A section is sixteen measures in length and consists of two eight-measure parts, both of which contain repetitions of four-measure phrases (figure 2.8). The four-measure chord progression that makes up the first half of the A section is unusual in that it harmonically ends with a deceptive cadence. The ending of the progression on C♯ minor hints at the modulation to the relative minor that takes place in the B section. In the initial phrase of the A section, the tonic E major of the first measure is followed by two measures of dominant harmony before the deceptive resolution to the C♯ minor chord, which moves immediately to the tonic chord of the phrase repetition.

Figure 2.8. "Criollo haragan": The *largo* A section

At the end of the phrase repetition, the C♯ minor again moves to E major at the beginning of the second half of section A. The repeated four-measure phrase in this part is over the more standard I-IV-V-I harmonic progression.

Both of the four-measure phrases of the first eight-measure part of the A section are the same melodically, except for slight interpretive variations in the performance. The A section is also based on the technique of repetition on both smaller and larger formal levels. The four-measure phrase itself is made up of two two-measure modules. The second module is a sequential repetition of the first module a step lower. Linearly, the first module consists of an ascending movement from an eighth-note G♯4 on the upbeat of beat four in m. 4 to D♯5, which starts on the upbeat preceding m. 6 and sustains for the following three beats. The first part of m. 5 consists of two repetitions of B4 and a return briefly to the G♯4. The B4 is then reiterated twice before the line ends on the D♯5. The second module in the phrase is identical except for the whole-step displacement, which causes the line to move from F♯4 through A4 to C♯5.

The second half of the A section (see figure 2.8) also consists of two melodically identical four-measure phrases. In this case, however, each of the two four-measure phrases contains contrasting modules. The first module starts with C♯5 on beat four of m. 12, descends to F4 on the upbeat of three in m. 13, and concludes on F♯4 on the first beat of m. 14. There is a break by the entire ensemble at this point with the exception of the *maracas*. The rest of the rhythm section returns in the following measure. The second module starts with B4 on the third beat of m. 14. On the fourth beat, a lower neighbor tone, A♯4, and another B4 lead to D♯5 at the start of m. 15. The melody then descends step-wise to A4 and skips downward to C♯4 before resolving with two ascending minor thirds to E4 in m. 16. A B4 and C5 in the second half of the measure lead to the phrase repetition. While the second version of the phrase is almost exactly the same melodically as the initial one, quarter-note triplets instead

of syncopated eighth-note figures rhythmically articulate the beginning of the second module.

The vocal rendition of the A section follows the same basic linear shape as the trumpet version. However, the melody is simpler
in the *coro* treatment and does not include the extensive orna-
mentation of the trumpet interpretation. Texturally, the vocal chorus is a rhythmically freewheeling improvisatory harmonization of
the basic melodic line.

In general, the chorus parts in the early *son* groups do not line
up with the rhythmic precision of ensemble singing in bands from
the *conjunto* and *salsa* eras. In addition to being a cruder prototype
of the later styles, the Sexteto Habanero chorus directly reflects its
coros de son heritage.

In addition to modulating to C♯ minor, the B section melody encompasses a larger range than the A section (figure 2.9).

Figure 2.9. "Criollo haragan": The *largo* B section

While the A section melody is contained within the major ninth
C♯4 to D♯5, the B section extends downward to cover an octave and
a fifth from G♯3 to D♯5. The B section is eight measures in length
and, like the second half of section A, consists of a four-bar phrase
(with contrasting modules) and its slightly modified repetition. Following an eighth-note G♯3 pickup note on the last half beat of m. 38,
the quarter-note C♯4s on beats one and two of m. 39 and beat one of
m. 40 (along with the E4-G♯4-E4 arpeggiation in the second half of
m. 39) establish the modulation to C♯ minor. This seven-note figure
is the first (and shortest) module in the phrase. The second module
begins on the second half of beat two in m. 40 and represents an octave register transfer of the initial melodic movement of the phrase
(in this case G♯4 to C♯5). Like the first module of the phrase, the C♯

occurs on consecutive beats; however, in this case, there is a D♯5 upper neighbor tone during the second half of beat three and a B4 on the upbeat of beat four which then moves on to a G♯4 half note on the dominant harmony in m. 41. The second half of m. 41 is an eighth-note step-wise linear movement back to C♯4 and a harmonic return to the tonic.

The phrase repetition in the trumpet rendition of section B is identical to the first instance, save for the addition of embellishing neighbor and passing tones at various points. The vocal rendition of the B section, as in the A section, follows the same basic linear shape of the trumpet version.

Following the vocal repetition of the *largo* B section, there is a one-measure transition (m. 55) in which the *clave* is switched from the two-three *clave* of the *largo* to the three-two *clave*, which prevails for the remainder of the recording. This measure also reestablishes the key of E major and, along with the two measures following it, begins the *montuno* section of the piece.

The *montuno* section of "Criollo haragan" is based on two *coros*: each a four-measure I-V-V-I chord progression, one chord per measure. *Coro* one (see figure 2.10) is a four-bar phrase that alternates with the solo trumpet.

Starting on the third beat of the transition measure (m. 55) to the *montuno* section, the trumpet begins a six-and-a-half-measure solo that leads to the first instance of *coro* one. The first three measures (mm. 55–57) of solo one can be considered a pickup to the main four measures of the *montuno* pattern of the solo (see figure 2.11). Because all three of the initial trumpet solos and both versions of the first *coro* pattern contain large one- or two-measure pickup figures, a certain ambiguity of form is created that can be likened to the effect the anticipated bass has at the cell level. In the same way that the anticipated bass lets the rhythm flow across the *clave*, the use of large-scale anacrusis figures creates a resistance to the tendency of the *montuno* figure to divide the music into overly delineated four-measure segments. This technique of linear elision helps to deregulate and redirect the rhythmic impetus of the music.

Conversely, the three solos and two *coro* sections of *coro* one are
unified by the fact that all five phrases end with the same melodic
movement. All three of the trumpet solos are exactly the same for
the last six and a half beats. This figure begins with two eighth-note
C♯4s on the second half of beats two and three in the penultimate
measure of the *montuno* phrase. These two syncopated notes then
lead to a quarter-note E4 on beat four and a reiteration of the E4
on the first beat of the following measure.

Although the *montuno* section of "Criollo haragan" begins with
Interián's trumpet solo, the *coro* is usually the most important factor in defining the character of a *montuno*. For this reason, the first
coro will be described prior to the analysis of the three initial trumpet solos (figure 2.10).

Figure 2.10. "Criollo haragan": *Coro* one

The *coro* of the early *son* group is, in many ways, more problematic than examining the *coro* of later generations of Cuban music. The early *coro* is improvisatory and is seldom, if ever, succes-
sively performed in exactly the same way. Consequently, a
transcription can only represent either one particular instance of
the *coro* or a composite of different versions. Since the voices often cross in these *coros*, the actual main melodic line can only be
approximated.

In the version of the *coro* notated in figure 2.10, the line begins
with an E4 on the upbeat of two in the anacrusis measure. Following B3 on the second part of beat four, the main part of the
phrase begins on a dotted quarter E3. A B3 eighth note on the upbeat of two and two quarter notes (F♯4 and D♯4) on beats three and
four lead to a B3 dotted quarter and the dominant harmony in the
second bar of the phrase. A sequence of the *coro* pickup figure
starts on D♯4 on the second half of beat two. The remaining part of
the *coro* is a rhythmic repetition of the first module with a con-

trasting melodic line. The final three notes of this line (C#4, E4, E4) contribute to the unity of the piece in that they are melodically the same as the final figure in the first three trumpet solos.

As stated earlier, the first trumpet solo begins in the transition bar that starts the *montuno* section (figure 2.11).

Figure 2.11. "Criollo haragan": First trumpet solo

The initial three notes (B3, A#3, B3) are a reprise of the three pickup notes to module two of the phrase that starts the second part of the *largo* A section. In this case, the three-note figure leads to E4 on beat one of m. 56. Following three beats of rest, the solo resumes on a G#4 on the second half of beat one in m. 57. For the next three measures, the melodic line revolves around G#4 in a vacillating motion through the range of E4 and C#5 before the phrase ends on the aforementioned four-note cell that finishes each solo. A melodic figure that creates unity between the first and second trumpet solos is the eighth-note figure on beats two and three of m. 58. This G#4-C#5-B4-G#4 line is repeated at a one-beat displacement on beats three and four in m. 66 (see figure 2.12). The first two beats in m. 66 can be seen as a rhythmic inversion of beat four of m. 57 and beat one of m. 58 with the addition of an F#4 passing tone.

The first trumpet solo is an excellent example of performing over the *clave*. In m. 55, the two-side of the *clave* is represented by the B3 on beat three. The E4 on beat one in m. 56 is the first note of the three-side, and the emphasis on beats two and three in m. 57 is a direct representation of the *clave* two-side. M. 58 uses a subtle but ingenious method of presenting the three-side of the *clave*. While the E4 on the first beat concretely emphasizes the first note of the three-side, the other two notes of this figure are indicated using a subtler technique which combines linear redirection and intervallic movement. The G#5 on the second part of the three-side (the upbeat of two) is emphasized in m. 58 by the isolating effect of being approached by the ascending leap of a fourth and then reversing the linear direction which descends to E4 on beat four (the third part of the three-side). This E4 is further reinforced by a linear redirection to G#4. The two-side of m. 59 is indicated by the B4 on beat three.

A typical Cuban method of presenting a three-side is used in m. 60. In a melodic version of the *timbale cascara* rhythm, the F#4 on beat one, the C#4 on the upbeat of two, and the E4 on beat four neatly outline the final three-side of this solo section. While the melodic displacement in m. 66 of solo two creates a momentary rhythmic ambiguity, the rest of the solo is firmly entrenched in the *clave* (figure 2.12).

Figure 2.12. "Criollo haragan": Second trumpet solo

Except for starting on the E5, which is an octave higher than the E4 in m. 56, the second trumpet solo follows the same linear shape as solo one in that it revolves around G#4 and ends on the identical C#4-E4 final module.

Although the third solo ends exactly the same way as the other two solos and follows the same general shape, this solo is higher in register than the others (figure 2.13).

Figure 2.13. "Criollo haragan": Third trumpet solo

Like the first solo, solo three starts on a B pickup. However, instead of skipping to an E4, this B4 moves stepwise to a two-and-a-half-beat F♯5 starting on the upbeat of beat four of m. 72 (figure 2.13). In this case, B4 provides the fulcrum of the melodic movement of the middle part of the phrase instead of G♯4, which serves in that role in the first two solos.

Following a short solo vocal lead-in in m. 77, the new *coro* begins on the *montuno* pattern that begins on m. 78 (figure 2.14). From this point until the end of the recording, there are six four-measure *montunos*, all of which contain both versions of the abbreviated *coro*. Simultaneously, there is musical material by both the trumpet and the solo vocalist inserted between and over the *coro* patterns, also throughout the final part of the recording. Aside from the lead-in to m. 78, the solo vocal material is confined to the three *montuno* patterns between mm. 82 and 93.

Figure 2.14.   "Criollo haragan": Coro two

This early example of solo singing is a crude but interesting prototype of the *sonero* vocal style that reached its zenith two decades later in the work of master singers like Miguelito Cuní and Beny Moré.

A number of factors make the accurate transcription of the solo trumpet material in this final section of "Criollo haragan" virtually impossible. The poor quality of this 1927 recording and the use of a mute by the trumpet player (a common practice in early recording) make the transcription process difficult, and the final section of the piece is even more problematic in that the trumpet often performs simultaneously with the vocal chorus, in many cases being absorbed into and obliterated by the musical texture. Thus, the performance of the trumpet in the last twenty-four measures of the recording will be described discursively.

During the first of the final *montuno* patterns, the trumpet improvises between and over the short *coro* figures. In this instance, the trumpet starts with eighth-note figures leading to short syncopated notes at the end of this *montuno*, many of which are indecipherable. Briefly overlapped by the entrance of the solo singer, the trumpet solo continues into the first half of the following *montuno*. The trumpet is silent in the next *montuno* section as the solo singer takes over. There is an overlapping again in the third-to-last *montuno* as the trumpet returns in m. 91 to relieve the *sonero* for the final two *montuno* sections. Using a mixture of quarter-note triplet- and eighth-note figures, the trumpet player performs a constant obbligato over the *coro* for the final sixteen measures of the piece. This practice of the trumpet soloist commenting over the *coro* (or over the rest of the horn section in later years) at the end of a piece has become a common practice in the modern *son/conjunto* era.

A TRUMPET LEGACY

A great and ongoing performance tradition was created when Hernández, Chappottín, Interián, and their ilk established the early Afro-Cuban trumpet style. Several generations of trumpet players have continued to keep this style alive and flourishing. Félix Chappottín had a long and illustrious career as the king of Afro-Cuban trumpet players and led one of the most popular orchestras in Cuba until his death in the 1970s.

Among the descendants of the early masters is Alfredo "Chocolate" Armenteros, who became the most celebrated Cuban trumpeter of his generation and is still musically active in his seventies. Jesús Alemañy is considered by many to be the current generation's most important successor to the mainstream Afro-Cuban trumpet tradition as exemplified by Chappottín. Alemañy and his group Cubanismo are popular throughout the world and demonstrate the continuing vitality of a tradition that began more than seventy years ago in Cuba.

NOTES

1. Although the size of these two groups varied at different times, in this document the term *sexteto* will always be used when referring to the Habanero group and *septeto* will be used when referring to Septeto Nacional.

2. *Tumbao*—a repeated pattern played by the bass and the *congas*.

3. *Guajeo*—a repeated rhythmic vamp typically played by the *tres* or the piano.

4. *Cascara*—a drum-shell tapping rhythm.

5. *Sonero*—the solo singer, especially referring to the singing in the *montuno* section of a song. The music sung by the singer is called a *soneo*.

6. *Tres*—a guitar-like instrument that holds three sets of double strings. It is the primary chordal instrument in the *son* ensemble.

7. *Largo*—the initial part of an Afro-Cuban song form. The *largo* is in most cases more complex in structure than the second part, or *montuno*.

8. *Coro*—The *coro* is a repeating phrase sung by a chorus of two or more singers. The phrase will occupy all or part of a recurring *montuno* pattern. Normally, the *coro* alternates *montunos* with a solo singer or instrumentalist.

3

THE *CONJUNTO* TRUMPET STYLE

ORIGINS: THE *SEPTETO* TRUMPET

When the *septeto* trumpet style developed in the late 1920s, a great tradition of brass performance was established. Landmark *son* bands like the Sexteto Habanero and the Septeto Nacional continued to perform throughout the 1930s and later decades. These bands became useful training vehicles for later generations of Cuban trumpet players. One of the most famous and significant of the trumpet players to emerge from these groups in the late 1920s was Félix Chappottín.

In many ways, Chappottín's role in Cuban music can be compared to the position that Louis Armstrong occupies in defining the trumpet style in jazz. Neither of these masters was the first trumpet player in his respective music tradition. However, in the same way that Armstrong took the music of predecessors like Buddy Bolden and King Oliver and redefined the mainstream jazz trumpet style, Chappottín crystallized the Cuban trumpet style from the work of his *septeto* trumpet forbearers and contemporaries (González 1997). As Roy Eldridge, Dizzy Gillespie, and other successors built on the foundation that Armstrong wrought, later Cuban trumpeters such as Armenteros took the baton from Chappottín and created their own interpretations of the *son* tradition.

Many of the earliest *septeto* trumpet players have been forgotten; however, they created a style of playing that has endured, reaching its maturity in the 1940s with the work of trumpet players like Félix Chappottín, Enrique "Florecita" Velazco, and Alfredo "Chocolate" Armenteros.

The *conjunto* ensemble continued the *son* tradition and was the framework within which the Cuban trumpet style evolved, representing, along with the modern *charanga,* the most important manifestation of modern Cuban music.[1] The instrumentation of the *conjunto* merits discussion here, with an emphasis on the role of the trumpet, in order to provide a context for the continuing development of the *septeto* trumpet style. Arsenio Rodríguez' group is the most important of the *conjunto's* golden age.

THE *CONJUNTO*

Arsenio Rodríguez, the blind *tres* player who led the most famous *conjunto* in Cuba in the 1940s, is generally considered the father of modern *conjunto* (O'Neill 1997). His ensemble synthesized and transformed elements of traditional Cuban genres (the *son* and *rumba*) that were performed in the 1920s and 1930s by such groups as Ignacio Piñeiro's Septeto Nacional and Sexteto Habanero. This synthesis represents the mainstream codification of the style created by the traditional *son* ensembles, a finalized *conjunto* form that other groups began to duplicate in terms of instrumentation. Additionally, the style of the Rodríguez ensemble is regarded as having contributed significantly to the development of the modern *salsa* style in New York from the 1950s through the 1970s.

In codifying the instrumentation of the *conjunto* style, Rodríguez incorporated the old and the new. As a *tres* player, he continued to feature that instrument as it had functioned in the traditional *son*. However, the piano assumed the role that the rhythm guitar played in the traditional *son*, taking over the chordal role (or *guajeo*) and becoming one of the primary solo instruments in the Rodríguez *conjunto* (Gerard and Sheller 1989).

Rodríguez also continued to utilize the *bongó* but in a different role. While the *bongosero* remained a main feature in the *conjunto*, "this modernized *son* gave up some of the informal, collective looseness of the traditional *son*, in which, for example, the *bongó* player improvised throughout the son" (Manuel 1995).

Two other modifications by Rodríguez were the addition of the *conga* and the creation of a trumpet section (as opposed to a solo trumpet). *Conga* drums had been used in other venues (mainly outdoor *comparsa* and *rumba* performances), but prior to Rodríguez, the *conga* was viewed as déclassé. Now, it added a new element of vitality that matched the energy of the horn section. (In a parallel move, flautist/bandleader Arcaño added the *conga* to his *charanga*, originating the basic forms of the *mambo* and *chachachá*.)

THE *CONJUNTO* TRUMPET

Although the trumpet was featured with early *son* groups before the modern *conjunto*'s development, it functioned at that point as a solo instrument. The Rodríguez *conjunto* used two or more trumpets (typically three), thus adding the role of section member to the scope of the instrument. This development necessitated the creation of horn arrangements. There were two types of trumpet-section arrangement used in the Arsenio Rodríguez *conjunto*. One type of arrangement was a setting of a typical *septeto* trumpet solo melody for the three trumpets of the *conjunto* using a mixture of unison and harmonized lines. This type of orchestration more closely reflected the *son* tradition than the alternative and more complex arranging style, which was influenced by the slick big band jazz scene of 1940s New York City. The famous Machito Afro-Cubans, directed by Mario Bauza, and the Dizzy Gillespie jazz big band (which featured the Afro-Cuban compositions and *conga* playing of Cuban Chano Pozo) exemplified this second type of arranging influenced by North American jazz. The Arsenio Rodríguez *conjunto* utilized both types of arranging on their various recordings from the late 1940s.

As inventive as the addition of the trumpet section was, the maturation of the solo trumpet style remains the most significant contribution by Rodríguez and his trumpet stars to the Cuban brass-performing legacy. Just as Charlie Parker and Louis Armstrong forged their own styles that set them apart from their predecessors, so did a number of Cuban trumpet players of the *conjunto* movement in the 1940s shape their own unique improvisational styles that grew out of the musical language of earlier *septeto* trumpet performers. The improvisational styles of three trumpet players stand out: Félix Chappottín, Enrique "Florecita" Velazco, and Alfredo "Chocolate" Armenteros.

A unique opportunity exists to examine the development of *conjunto* trumpet soloing: within a two-year period in the late 1940s and early 1950s, these three players were featured on various recordings by the Rodríguez *conjunto*. *Dundunbanza*, a recently released CD, is a reissue of nineteen recordings by Arsenio Rodríguez from the period 1946–1951. Most of the pieces feature Chappottín, but his lesser-known contemporary Velazco and a powerful young Armenteros are also prominent on the CD.

By analyzing in detail one piece by Chappottín and briefly discussing the work of Velazco and Armenteros on *Dundunbanza*, the general elements of the Cuban brass solo style as it attains its full maturity can be observed. "Dundunbanza" (a *guaguancó*), originally recorded on January 12, 1949, features Chappottín and is discussed at the end of this chapter; "No puedo comer vistagacha" (an example of *son montuno* form), originally recorded in January of 1950, features the twenty-one-year-old Armenteros; and "Guaranguí" (another example of the predominant *son montuno* form), originally recorded in October of 1951, features the rhythmically nuanced playing of Velazco.

Before a discussion of each of the trumpet players and pieces, the formal characteristics of the *conjunto* style in general merit discussion.

FORMAL CHARACTERISTICS

In this discussion, the term *montuno* can refer (depending on the context) either to an entire section of a song or to an individual pattern within a song.

The *son montuno* is comprised of two parts. The first section, the *largo*, is self-contained and usually based on a standard extended song form similar to the structures of Tin Pan Alley or music theater composers in the United States. The second section, the *montuno* section, is the continual repetition of a chord progression that is typically (but not always) four measures in length. The two fundamental elements of the *montuno* pattern are the *clave* and the harmonic progression.

More than other forms, the Rodríguez *conjunto* used the *son montuno*, which synthesized structures that evolved during the *son* era: following the *son*'s original, basic, two-part form but placing more emphasis on the second (or *montuno*) part.

With the Rodríguez ensemble, as with the earlier *son* groups, the sections between the *coros* during the *montuno* gave room for the solo trumpet style to finds its primary expression. Extended trumpet improvisations were not yet common practice; in the 1940s, solo improvisation consisted of a series of short solos alternating with *coros*. Typically, these solos were placed at the beginning and end of the *montuno* section. Live performance in a dance or concert venue allowed for extended *coros* and solos, but that luxury was not afforded in the recording studios of the time, and most of the Rodríguez recordings have only two or three consecutive solos.

"Dundunbanza," "No puedo comer vistagacha," and "Guarang í" all contain trumpet solos at the beginning of the *montuno* sections. In "Dundunbanza" and "No puedo comer vistagacha," they begin with two four-bar solos; in "Guaranguí," the *montuno* starts with three Velazco solos, but the *montuno* pattern here is two measures in length instead of the usual four.

FÉLIX CHAPPOTTÍN

Along with fellow U.S. emigré Mario Bauza, Félix Chappottín (born in 1909) is the most renowned trumpeter of early modern Cuban music (González 1997). After honing his performance skills in the early 1930s with innovative *son* ensembles such as the Sexteto Habanero, Chappottín went on to become a star Cuban bandleader in the 1950s. He assumed leadership of the Rodríguez ensemble (renaming it Chappottín y Sus Estrellas) when Rodríguez, seeking a cure for his blindness, relocated to the United States.

Chappottín's work on the title tune of *Dundunbanza* establishes him as the dean of early *conjunto* trumpet players. His solo work reveals a synthesis of his *septeto* background with an exuberant and rhythmically sophisticated solo style. A detailed analysis of the two four-measure trumpet solos from the beginning of "Dundunbanza" will occur at the end of this chapter.

ENRIQUE "FLORECITA" VELAZCO

Enrique Velazco, the least well known of the three players, is consequently also the least documented. Though he seldom displayed the more obvious technical attributes of his two colleagues, his rhythmic subtlety and sophistication is unequaled. Velazco is best known for his work in traditional *rumba* and *comparsa* forms with specialized vocal and percussion groups.

When asked about Velazco, Armenteros responded: "Aah, that's my idol. . . . They called him Florecita because he took tunes, and he 'flowered' them" (Armenteros 1998). Early in his career, Armenteros replaced the older Velazco in the *comparsa* group La Jardinera. For Armenteros, there was no "bigger privilege" (Armenteros 1998) than to replace his idol in this traditional *comparsa*. Although personal information about the little-known Velazco is difficult to find, Armenteros estimates that by the time Armenteros was twenty-one, "[Velazco] must have been forty-seven or forty-eight" (Armenteros 1998). Armenteros has always had the deepest respect for his trumpet-playing forebears, and when asked about the main influences on his playing, he remarked: "Between the two of them [Florecita and Chappottín], I did the following: I said, 'If Florecita does it like this and Chappottín like that, why can't I do something in the middle?' And that's how I got my style" (Armenteros 1998).

This reissue of the November 1950 recording "Guaranguí" reveals Velazco's powerful command of rhythm.

"GUARANGUÍ"

The *son montuno* form of "Guaranguí" (Rodríguez, *Dundunbanza*) makes it slightly more sophisticated in structure than the folk-like *guaguancó* form of "Dundunbanza." The *largo* section, although more complicated structurally than the *montuno* section, still uses a simple, four-measure, *montuno*-like chord pattern. The *montuno* section itself is built over a two-measure *montuno* pattern, with a traditional I-IV-V harmonic progression firmly establishing a tonal center of G major. As in "Dundunbanza," the *montuno* section in "Guaranguí" begins with a call and response between trumpet soloist and the *coro*, with Velazco playing three two-measure solos.

Velazco approached solo performance differently than his contemporary Chappottín, whose ebullience can be likened to that of Louis Armstrong. Velazco more closely connects to the understated world of a Bix Beiderbecke or a Miles Davis. Relinquishing ornament in favor of line, Velazco played his simple and pure melodic ideas over the *clave* with a sense of nuance and sophistication in rhythmic conception that has rarely been equaled. His solos at the beginning of "Guangui" cannot be notated rhythmically with any degree of accuracy using standard Western European music notation. It is the seeming contradiction of rhythmic ambiguity mixed with teleological impetus that defines Velazco's solo style.

ALFREDO "CHOCOLATE" ARMENTEROS

Alfredo "Chocolate" Armenteros, then twenty-one years old, recorded a series of solos on "No puedo comer vistagacha" (Rodríguez, *Dundunbanza*) in January 1950. His mastery of rhythmic phrasing demonstrates, even at that age (as it still does today), why Armenteros is viewed by many as the greatest Cuban trumpet player (Roberts 1979).

Armenteros was born in April of 1928 in the Las Villas province of Cuba. He moved to Havana in 1948 and shortly thereafter joined René Alvarez' Conjunto Astros. During the 1950s, Armenteros played with a number of groups, including the Alvarez and Rodríguez ensembles; in the mid-1950s, he led the brass section of the backup band of his cousin, famed singer Beny Moré. He achieved prominence as a studio musician in radio as well as in the recording studios of 1950s Havana.

Shortly after Fidel Castro took power in Cuba in 1960, Armenteros immigrated to New York City. For the past thirty-nine years, he has performed with every significant *salsa* bandleader on the New York scene. Armenteros is firmly established as one the most important and influential trumpet players in the history of Cuban music. A more detailed biography of Armenteros will occur in chapter 7.

"NO PUEDO COMER VISTAGACHA"

An example of New York–style arranging is "No puedo comer vistagacha" (Rodríguez, *Dundunbanza*), which was recorded in January of 1950 and features impressive trumpet soloing by a twenty-two-year-old Armenteros. Although this composition is closer to the New York style of arranging than other songs recorded by Rodríguez at the same time, this comparatively modern arrangement still reflects the *son* roots of the band as much as they emulate slicker New York influences (such as Machito). "No puedo comer vistagacha" contains excellent examples of the early Armenteros playing style. In order to provide a context for examining contemporary and later developments in the solo performance work of Armenteros, it is useful to examine this piece in some detail.

Structurally, "No puedo comer vistagacha" is more complex than many of the Rodríguez compositions of the time. The *largo* section contains a relatively long form, and the *montuno* section is based on a four-measure pattern. This arrangement borrows modern New York–style elements in its brass orchestration.

An introduction of three bars leads into a *largo* section (figure 3.1) that, although short in length, demonstrates the basic difference between a relatively complex *largo* and the repetitive short form of the *montuno*.

Figure 3.1. **"No puedo comer vistagacha": Largo section**

Instead of repeating a short harmonic pattern as in a *montuno* section, this *largo* uses a twelve-measure song form, starting with a two-measure melodic figure over the tonic harmony, which sequences in the third measure to start a whole step higher over the subdominant. The melody reaches the dominant harmony in the fifth measure of the form and is linearly contrasting while keeping the same rhythmic configuration. The dominant harmony extends over the next five measures, which include an extension of the last note of the figure in the fifth measure for two measures and a repetition of the fifth measure figure in mm. 8–9. The harmony finally resolves in the eleventh measure of this section with a variation on the initial melodic module. The whole twelve-measure section is repeated, with brass replacing vocals during the first four bars.

The brass parts in the *largo* section use sophisticated jazz-like arranging techniques, similar to those used at the time by the Machito band in New York City (Roberts 1979). In "No puedo comer vistagacha," there are sophisticated ensemble trumpet parts supporting the vocalists when the trumpets are not in a leading role, which would rarely occur in a *septeto*-derived horn section arrangement (like "Dundunbanza"). Besides using a variety of harmonic voicings, the three trumpets at times play a unison countermelody, most notably behind the vocal notes that are sustained in the sixth and seventh measures of the *largo* section. The final measure of the *largo* section's repetition uses a rhythmic break to lead into the *montuno* section of the piece.

The pattern of the *montuno* (and its associated *coro*) is based on a four-measure harmonic progression in B major (figure 3.2).

Figure 3.2.   **"No puedo comer vistagacha":** *Coro/montuno* **pattern**

This section begins with a call and response (two alternations of *montuno* sections between the trumpet soloist and *coro*). The first of these two trumpet solos will be discussed below. The solo singer later replaces the trumpet for two more iterations of this call and response.

An intriguing variation of the typical practice for the *montuno* part is the expansion of the four-bar pattern to six measures during the *sonero*; the first four measures during the solo voice part are over a tonic pedal point and lead to a cadence in the fifth and sixth measures. A twelve-measure *tres* solo by Arsenio Rodríguez follows the final *coro*. The *tres* solo explains the choice of B major; it is a characteristic key for this stringed instrument. A six-measure ensemble break follows the twelve-measure solo.

The next part of the recording consists of a series of two-measure call-and-response sections. Built over a tonic pedal, these two-measure sections are performed alternately by the *coro* singing the title phrase "No puedo comer vistagacha" (which is adapted from the longer original *coro*) and either the trumpet section or a solo Armenteros. The trumpet section responds to the *coro* in the first two instances. Armenteros begins soloing over the third iteration of the shortened *coro* and continues until the beginning of the fourth *coro*. The final iteration of the abbreviated *coro* is followed by the original four-measure *coro*, which serves as the ending phrase of the piece.

In his early solos with Rodríguez, Armenteros' instrumental virtuosity already surpasses the technique of older colleagues such as Chappottín and Velazco, who recorded with the bandleader at the same time. Armenteros' fluid linear style contains a high percentage of sixteenth-note figures as well as the mastery of an impressive trumpet range. Armenteros' first solo in "No puedo comer vistagacha" includes a high C♯6 (concert), a major third higher than any note in the Velasco solos and an augmented fourth higher than Chappottín's highest notes in "Dundunbanza." Armenteros' lines display a rhythmic subtlety that defies notational representation and belies the youth of the twenty-two year old (figure 3.3).

Figure 3.3. "No puedo comer vistagacha": First trumpet solo

Armenteros precedes the *montuno* pattern of his first solo with a three eighth-note pickup figure, and the final part of this solo extends into the first two beats of the following *coro* section. This short solo is a masterpiece in the Afro-Cuban art of stretching and compressing a melodic line over the underlying rhythm. Andy González compares this effect to the stretching and releasing of a rubber band (González 1997). While the three pickup notes coincide with the underlying eighth-note rhythms, the following measure stretches the eighth notes of the figures almost into quarter-note triplets. In the last beat and a half of the second measure of the *montuno* pattern, six ascending sixteenth notes reestablish the melodic line to the center part of the pulse. This return to rhythmic equilibrium is disturbed a beat later when the first of four one-and-a-half-beat motives again stretches behind the rhythmic underpinning. Each of these motives consists of four sixteenth notes and an eighth rest. Following the time stretch of the first motive, the time compresses gradually during the succeeding three motives until, by the second beat of the fourth bar of the *montuno* pattern, Armenteros is playing on the front part of the beat. Finally, Armenteros introduces the next *coro* with yet another delaying action on the final three notes of this solo. This short trumpet solo demonstrates an incredible mastery of both trumpet technique and rhythmic manipulation, which is even more impressive when the youthful age of this trumpet prodigy is considered.

"DUNDUNBANZA"

"Dundunbanza" (Rodríguez, *Dundunbanza)* is a "dance hall" version of the *guaguancó*, a variation on the folkloric *guaguancó* type of *rumba*. The *guaguancó* has maintained its own identity as a *rumba* form (with an emphasis on drums and voices), but in the 1940s it also melded with the *son montuno* format of that time. This new *guaguancó* incorporated elements of the *son montuno* (as rendered by the *conjunto*), including an extended *montuno* section (Moore 1995).

The performance of "Dundunbanza" examined here (see table 3.1.) reflects the folklore of the *guaguancó's* heritage as well as elements of the *son montuno*.

The modal harmonic structure reveals the *son's rumba* roots; alternating loosely between an A minor chord and a G major harmony, the dominant-tonic tonal relationship normally used in the *montuno* section of a *son montuno* is never firmly established in this work. This ambiguity of harmonic movement is indicative of the melodic and rhythmic nature of the traditional *guaguancó*, which originally was performed using only percussion instruments and vocals.

"Dundunbanza" is a superb illustration—a "case study" (Moore 1995)—of a *montuno* section's organization. In this case,

Table 3.1.   Time Line of "Dundunbanza"

Time-(min./sec.)	Section	Description
0:00	1. mm. 1-4	*Tres* on first measure, rhythm section enters in m.2.
0:06	2. mm. 5–8	1st *coro*.
0:12	3. mm. 9–12	1st trumpet section part.
0:18	4. mm. 13–16	2nd *coro*.
0:24	5. mm. 17–20	2nd trumpet section part.
0:30	6. mm. 21–24	3rd *coro*.
0:36	7. mm. 25–28	3rd trumpet section part.
0:42	8. mm. 29–32	4th *coro*.
0:48	9. mm. 33–36	1st trumpet solo.
0:54	10. mm. 37–40	5th *coro*.
0:59	11. mm. 41–44	2nd trumpet solo.
1:05	12. mm. 45–48	6th *coro*.
1:11	13. mm. 49–52	1st *sonero*.
1:17	14. mm. 53–56	7th *coro*.
1:23	15. mm. 57–60	2nd *sonero*.
1:29	16. mm. 61–64	8th *coro*.
1:35	17. mm. 65–79	Piano.
1:57	18. m. 80	Break
1:58	19. mm. 81–84	*Coro*.
2:04	20. mm. 85–100	Trumpet section with solo on top.
2:28	21. mm. 101–106	*Coro* and ending.

the *montuno* pattern is four measures in length and the entire recording, two minutes and thirty-seven seconds long, consists of consecutive multiple repetitions of this four-measure pattern. The first four measures of the piece are a statement of the *montuno* pattern by the rhythm section. Rodríguez performs the first measure of the pattern on solo *tres*; the rest of the rhythm section joins in for the final three measures.

The *coro* enters on the second *montuno* pattern (figure 3.4).

Figure 3.4. "Dundunbanza": The *montuno* and *coro* pattern

The *coro* figure is contained within the range of a perfect fifth between F4 and C5. This four-measure melody consists of two one-measure rhythmic cells that are repeated. The first cell consists of a quarter note on the first beat followed by two eighth notes on beat two and an eighth note on the upbeat of three. The first instance of this cell moves melodically from A4 on the first two notes to C5 on the third and fourth notes. The second cell is introduced in measure two of the *coro* and begins the same as the first cell, with a quarter note and two eighth notes (in this case two A4s and an F4). However, in this case, the fourth note of the cell is on the downbeat of beat three (G4) instead of the upbeat. This is significant in that the first cell (with its two upbeats) indicates the three-side of the *clave*. The two-side is indicated in the second cell by the notes on beats two and three. The upbeat of beat two in the first cell takes on greater significance than the same note in the second cell because it is followed by a rest and therefore has a distinctly syncopated sound. Because the same upbeat in the second cell is preceded and followed by notes on the downbeats, it sounds rhythmically weaker. The repetition of the second cell in the fourth measure of the solo is exactly the same melodically as its predecessor, with the addition of a G4 on beat four. The first cell changes melodically in its measure three repetition. As in the first measure, there is an initial leap of a third. In this case, it is a major third from F4 to A4, and there is no repetition of the first note preceding this movement. Instead of continuing to ascend as in m. 1, the melodic line descends from the A4 to G4, which is repeated on the upbeat of three and again on the upbeat of four, which serves as a pickup to the final measure. The *coro* is repeated every other *montuno* another seven times.

The alternate *montunos* provide rich variation. The first three *coros* are followed by trumpet section figures that are harmonized in three parts. The brass parts in "Dundunbanza" are closest in flavor to the *septeto* solo trumpet style. The arranging technique is a simple three-part harmonization of lines that could easily have been improvised trumpet solos in an early *son* ensemble like the Sexteto Habanero. Following the fourth and fifth *coro* sections are two trumpet solos by Félix Chappottín. The sixth and seventh *coros* are followed by solo vocal performances by lead singer René Scull. The eighth and final *coro* of this section is followed by a sixteen-measure (four-*montuno*) piano solo. The last four measures of the piano solo reestablish the melodic elements of the original *montuno*, with the last measure containing a break figure played by the entire band and leading into the final part of the recording.

The *montuno* following the break contains a reprise of the *coro* accompanied by the trumpet section. Two of the trumpet players play rhythmic figures in thirds while Chappottín plays sustained syncopated figures that change register in a quick and dramatic manner. In the following four *montuno* patterns, only the final phrase of the *coro* lyric is sung. The first of these four *montuno* patterns continues with the same trumpet parts. In the next *montuno*, Chappottín continues playing the same part while the other two trumpet players change to a repetitive, three-note, eighth-note figure that increases the density of the rhythmic texture. This figure is performed for two *montunos*. The next and penultimate *montuno* contains a short Chappottín solo; the final *montuno* is a recapitulation of the entire *coro*, which leads to a two-bar coda consisting of the first measure of the *coro* and a four-note rhythmic figure.

Chappottín's trumpet solos reflect techniques that were used by early jazz and swing trumpeters in the United States: a large and expressive sound, and trills and growls that reveal the instrument's power. His first solo on "Dundunbanza" begins with a broad growl on a four-beat G5 that starts on beat three of the fourth measure of the preceding *coro*'s *montuno* pattern (figure 3.5).

Figure 3.5.   "Dundunbanza":Trumpet solo one

Following the G5, the line descends and ends on the eighth notes C5 and D5 on beat three of m. 34. This line features two sequences of a melodic module. The first module starts on an F5 eighth note on the upbeat of three in m. 33. Both halves of beat four in m. 33 and the downbeat of m. 34 are E5s, which are embellished by upper and lower sixteenth-note neighbor tones. The second sequence starts with a D5 eighth note on the second half of beat one in m. 34. In this case, C5 is the note that is embellished. The third of the C5s is followed by an eighth-note D5 on the upbeat of three.

The third measure of the solo (m. 35) is a variation of the previous sequence. The sixteenth-note figure in this case is approached from below by two eighth notes, A4 and B4, on beat one. Instead of the main tone C4s being surrounded by neighbor tones, they surround an escape tone sequence that leaps from D5 to B4. This leap helps to emphasize the second rhythmic part of the three-side of the *clave*. The sixteenth-note figure moves to A4 on the third beat, which leaps to D5 a half beat later and sustains for the remainder of the measure. Chappottín performs this D5 with a trumpet trill similar in style to that which a swing era American player like Roy Eldridge might produce. The first solo ends with an unadorned eighth-note movement from C5 back to A4. This figure starts on the upbeat of one in m. 36 and sustains on the final A4 to end the solo.

Chappottín plays the figures in this solo with subtle variations in timing. For instance, in this solo, the sequenced line in m. 33 and m. 44 starts behind the prevailing pulse in the first sequence before quickly catching up in the second sequence and then going behind the beat again on the final eighth-note D5. While m. 35 is on or ahead of the tempo, the final three notes of the solo are played slightly behind the beat. This solo uses a modal melodic structure that reflects the *rumba* heritage of the dance band *guaguancó*.

The beginning of the second solo illustrates the rhythmic sophistication that is a trademark of the great Cuban musicians (figure 3.6).

Figure 3.6.   "Dundunbanza": Trumpet solo two

This entire solo is built around D5. A series of descending and ascending lines between the prevailing D5 and A4 or A♭4 characterizes this four-measure solo. The pitch range of the solo is established immediately with the two-note pickup G4 and D5. Four D5s occupy the first three beats of m. 41. The line makes its initial descent to A4 with the C5 and B4 eighth notes on beat four of m. 41. The line quickly steps back to the D5 on beat two of m. 42. The sixteenth-note figure beginning on the second quarter of the third beat is again centered on D5 but is unusual in that it is based on a whole tone scale between A♭4 and D5 and might be influenced by the harmony of modern jazz.

Chappottín plays a salute to modernism in the second and third measures of this solo: a sixteenth-note melodic figure that is based on bebop-like harmonic alteration, utilizing a dissonant whole-tone scale. Following this, Chappottín ends his solo with two trills, demonstrating his familiarity with the Louis Armstrong tradition.

CONCLUSION

By studying the solo performance style of these three trumpet masters, classical Cuban solo brass playing can be appreciated at its most sophisticated level. The grand brass tradition that originated with the legendary *son* ensembles of the 1920s and matured in the *conjuntos* of the 1940s can be traced in the playing of this trumpet triumvirate. Félix Chappottín carried the torch from the *septeto* era, Enrique "Florecita" Velazco crystallized the rhythmic style, and Alfredo "Chocolate" Armenteros has brought this unique and important solo trumpet tradition into the twenty-first century.

NOTES

1. Portions of this chapter were originally published by the author in "The Conjunto Trumpet Style: Chappottín, Florecita, and Chocolate" (Davies 1998).

④

CHAPPOTTÍN Y SUS ESTRELLAS

FÉLIX CHAPPOTTÍN

Félix Chappottín was born on March 31, 1907, in Cayo Hueso, which is a district of Havana (Hernández 1986). His first musical experiences involved using a comb and tissue paper to emulate the sounds around him and his talent was recognized early on by his godfather, musician Venario González. At the age of nine Chappottín moved in with González in Guanabay and began his formal study of music. By the age of eleven, young Félix was playing tuba in the children's band of Guanabay. He was soon given a trumpet by the Liberal political party based in Guanabay and began his professional career performing the party's theme song "La chambelona" at various political events, including rallies and parades. After playing "La chambelona" for two years, Chappottín returned to the Havana area and began playing with groups there. Soon after, he began his relationship with Septeto Habanero. It was with this seminal group (and on the numerous recordings he made with them) that Chappottín initially established his reputation as the first major trumpet innovator in Cuban music. The details of his work with Habanero are given in chapter 2.

In the decade between departing from Habanero and joining the equally influential *conjunto* led by Arsenio Rodríguez, Chappottín was associated with various groups. One of the first groups he played with shortly after leaving Habanero was the Septeto Muñamar. This band was formed by a group of dock-workers and included the father of singer Roberto Faz. The younger Faz also played bass with the band on occasion. Another group he played with in the early 1930s was Septeto Agabana, which was fronted by singer Abelardo Barroso, who, like Chappottín, was an alumnus of Habanero. Chappottín also traveled extensively with Septeto Universo, which backed up the performers Pancho and Ramona.

In 1935 he joined the Septeto Bolero (later Carabina de Ases), which included the great *tresero* Niño Rivera. Other groups he played with at the time were Conjunto América and Conjunto Jovenes del Cayo. In 1940 he formed (with his cousin Chano Pozo) Conjunto Azul, which was the house band for Radio Cadena Azul. It was around this time that Chappottín began his historic association with Arsenio Rodríguez. The Rodríguez ensemble is discussed in more detail in chapter 3.

Félix Chappottín y sus Estrellas formed in 1950 and the trumpeter continued to lead and record with this popular group until his death in 1983.

CHAPPOTTÍN Y SUS ESTRELLAS

As the cold war 1950s began, a transition of power took place in Afro-Cuban music that was as significant in its own limited way as the more celebrated coup d'état that took place a decade later in Cuban politics. Seeking a cure for his blindness, Arsenio Rodríguez immigrated to New York City in 1950 and turned over the reins of his celebrated *conjunto* to his lead trumpeter Félix Chappottín. As Chappottín y sus Estrellas, the updated group was one of the most important ensembles in the history of Afro-Cuban music. Although the Arsenio Rodríguez *conjunto* was the progenitor, Chappottín's version quickly developed its own musical character.

A major reason for the great success the band enjoyed for over three decades is that two other eminent musicians from the Rodríguez group maintained a long-term relationship with the Chappottín-led version. Luis "Lili" Martínez was the pianist as well as chief composer/arranger for Arsenio Rodríguez. He retained a similar role in the new band and created many of the songs in the repertoire of the Estrellas. As a pianist Martínez influenced generations of pianists and many salsa-era pianists have cited him as a major influence.

Singer Miguelito Cuní was another indispensable member of the Estrellas. One of the preeminent Afro-Cuban singers, Cuní was as important to the group as the leader Chappottín. The trumpeter and the singer shared a similar sense of intricate phrasing and lyricism. Chappottín once stated, "Chappottín was Cuní and vice versa, because we really formed a unit. We met through music and music still unites us. When I joined Arsenio's group, Cuní was there, and he handed over the position of director to me, because his personality wasn't the most suited for that, as he told me" (Fernández 1995).

Martínez, Cuní, and Chappottín remained long-term members of the Estrellas and together created a recorded body of work that is a cornerstone of the Afro-Cuban genre. Many of the songs they recorded in the 1950s, 1960s, and later became standards and were reproduced by many bands in the salsa era.

Even though Félix Chappottín died in 1983, Conjunto Chappottín y sus Estrellas has continued to perform and record. The legacy version of the band has included the family members of Chappottín and other original group members. The trumpeter's son and nephew have been in charge of the group since 1983. His son, Angel Chappottín Valdéz (d. 2001), played *bongó* with the group, and nephew Angel Chappottín Coto has been director and trumpeter, assuming the role that Félix Chappottín occupied for thirty-three years. Miguelito Cuní Jr. (Miguel Arcáye Conill Hernandez) has been a singer in the modern Estrellas, thereby fanning the flame of his famous father. Conjunto Chappottín y sus Estrellas has made recent recordings that include the latest generation of Chappottíns, including a young trumpet player who sounds remarkably like his famous ancestor.

Due to the longevity of the group, Chappottín y sus Estrellas had a large repertory of songs. While standard *son*-based pieces and slow *boleros* made up most of the songs they recorded, the Estrellas also did a certain number of pieces in different styles such as *merengue*, *conga*, and even novelty songs. One of their biggest hits was a song called "Guarapachanga," which reflected the *pachanga* craze of the 1960s and had an unusual upbeat groove. However, because the song form that is most representative of the Estrellas and the *son* tradition is the standard *son montuno,* the three pieces analyzed in this chapter are from this genre. Two of these, "Quítate el chaquetón" and "No tiene telaraña," will be described briefly. The third, "Camina y prende el fogón," will be analyzed in more detail.

"QUÍTATE EL CHAQUETÓN"

"Quítate el chaquetón," like the other pieces analyzed in this chapter, is a *son montuno*. In the parlance of jazz, the *son montuno* was the "meat and potatoes" of bands like Chappottín y sus Estrellas. Even though the *bolero* was a big favorite of the mainstream *conjunto* and the *merengue* and other exotic forms made up a substantial portion of the repertoire of the Estrellas, the *son montuno* was the genre that personified the band. The Estrellas performed their *son montunos* in the tradition of Arsenio Rodríguez. However, there were slight stylistic differences between the two groups. For instance, the Rodríguez ensemble tended to have a harder, edgier drive than the Estrellas. Because of Rodríguez's strong identification with his African roots, there were more folk music and tribal elements in his approach than in the music of the more mainstream Estrellas. On the other hand, the Estrellas had an elegance and sophistication that was sometimes lacking in the Rodríguez group.

Starting in two-three *clave,* the first eleven bars of "Quítate el chaquetón" contain a slick and upbeat horn section arrangement. With a pickup in m. 11, the entrance of the *coro* switches the *clave* to three-two in m. 12. Harmonically, the trumpet introduction is the most sophisticated part of the song. Except for this introduction and the first two *soneos,* the entire piece is built around a two-measure dominant-tonic *montuno* pattern. This progression is repeated twice in the four-measure *coro.* Following the first and second *coro* an eight-measure melody is sung by the *sonero.* After the second *soneo,* the trumpet section performs the harmonized *coro* melody. This is followed by a series of call-and-response sections with the *coro,* the solo trumpet trading off the first two times before being replaced by the *sonero.* A piano solo follows the last of these *coros.*

In his two solo sections, Chappottín plays with a rhythmic sophistication that demonstrates why he was considered to be among the best soloists in the history of this music. This subtle command of time shifting is also used by Miguelito Cuní in his *soneos* and shows why these two masters are so at home in each other's company. The third member of triumvirate, Luis "Lili" Martínez, plays a twelve-measure piano solo following the final *coro.* His solo perfectly balances virtuoso flourishes and intricate syncopations. A piano version of the *coro* figure follows the pianist's improvisation.

After the piano cue, a new shorter (one-measure) *coro* enters with a response from the trumpet section on the second measure of the two-bar progression. The solo trumpet fills in the holes of this intricate musical texture. After four repetitions, the horn section drops out, leaving more space for Chappottín's musings. After two solos, the trumpet figures return and the piece ends with a rhythmic break figure.

"NO TIENE TELARAÑA"

Like "Quítate el chaquetón," "No tiene telaraña" is a *son montuno* that was a popular Estrellas recording. Starting with a two-note cowbell pickup, the rhythm section enters with a two-three two-measure *montuno* pattern that permeates the song. In the first four measures of the nine-measure introduction, the trumpet section shakes a note on the upbeat of three in the second and fourth bars before changing to an eighth-note figure in the next two *montuno* patterns. In the ninth measure there is a break figure that theoretically should turn the *clave* around. However, the initial pattern resumes in the tenth measure. While this is unorthodox, switching back to the original *clave* after a break of an odd number of measures does occur on occasion in Afro-Cuban music.

A four-measure *coro* over the *montuno* begins the *largo* section. This *coro* is followed by a two-measure instrumental break that introduces the eight-measure *soneo*. This *coro*-break-*soneo* is then repeated. It is only during these breaks and *soneos* that the *montuno* pattern is abandoned for a more elaborate chord progression.

Following the second *soneo*, the *montuno* section begins in earnest with a shortened *coro* that contains the first half of the original *coro* phrase. In the usual fashion, this two-measure *coro* alternates first with Chappottín's trumpet and then with vocalist Miguelito Cuní. These are evenly divided with the trumpeter playing the first three solos followed by three by the *sonero*. Both musicians again demonstrate their mastery of the elasticity of time.

A twenty-measure *tres* solo follows the final *soneo*. A four-measure instrumental break then brings in the two-measure version of the *coro* and then a busy trumpet section figuration. The *coro* is then shortened again with only the title ("No tiene telaraña") being annunciated within the brass figure. After four repetitions, the *coro* continues with Chappottín's soloing replacing the trumpet section. After a few repetitions in this configuration, the entire nine-measure introduction is performed to end the piece.

"CAMINA Y PRENDE EL FOGÓN"

In addition to being one of the most popular songs recorded by the Estrellas, "Camina y prende el fogón" exemplifies the typical *conjunto* performance in the 1950s. This *son-montuno*, with its four-measure minor key *montuno* pattern, presents a concept that was emulated over and over by New York *salsa* bands. A good comparison would be Eddie Palmieri's *salsa*-era recording of "Bilongo" (see chapter 6). It is almost certain that Palmieri and his trumpeter Alfredo "Chocolate" Armenteros were familiar with this recording. In addition to the piano introduction of "Bilongo" being almost identical (albeit in G minor instead of B♭ minor), the initial Chappottín solo in "Camina y prende el fogón" is played almost verbatim in the first half of Armenteros' trumpet introduction on "Bilongo." "Camina y prende el fogón" was given further homage when the Puerto Rican band Sonora Poncena made a popular remake of the song.

Because this Chappottín recording is so prototypical of the mainstream *son-montuno*, an analysis of the entire arrangement in addition to the trumpet solos will be provided. Table 4.1 contains a time line of the composition.

Table 4.1. Time Line of "Camina y prende el fogon"

Time-(min./sec.)	Section	Description
	Part A	
0:00	1. mm. 1–4	First part of introduction.
0:07	2. mm. 5–9	Second part of introduction with Chappottín trumpet solo.
0:16	3. mm. 10–20	Third part of introduction with syncopated horn section parts.
0:32	4. mm. 21–30	*Largo*-section A.
0:48	5. mm. 31–39	*Largo*-section B.
1:02	6. mm. 40–44	Brass interlude.
1:09	7. mm. 45–54	Repeat of *Largo*-section B.
1:24	8. mm. 55–56	Brass section transition to *montuno* section.
	Part B	
1:27	1. mm. 58–59	1st *coro*.
1:29	2. mm. 59–62	1st trumpet solo.
1:33	3. mm. 62–63	2nd *coro*.
1:36	4. mm. 63–66	2nd trumpet solo.
1:39	5. mm. 66–67	3rd *coro*.
1:42	6. mm. 67–70	3rd trumpet solo.
1:45	7. mm. 70–71	4th *coro*.
1:48	8. mm. 72–73	1st *sonero*
1:51	9. mm. 74–75	5th *coro*.
1:54	10. mm. 76–77	2nd *sonero*.
1:57	11. mm. 78–79	6th *coro*.
2:00	12. mm. 80–98	*Tres* solo.
2:30	13. mm. 99–102	Piano break.
2:36	14. mm. 103–112	Truncated *coro* and trumpet section figures.
2:51	15. mm. 113–120	Original *coro*. and solo trumpet figures.
3:04	16. mm. 121–123	Coda.

"Camina y prende el fogón" opens with a highly syncopated one-measure piano vamp (figure 4.1) outlining the B♭ minor tonic harmony. The rest of the rhythm section enters in the second bar. This vamp is repeated continuously for the first nine measures of the piece. Again Eddie Palmieri, in the piano vamp at the start of his recording "Bilongo," echoes this opening, albeit in a more freewheeling manner.

Figure 4.1. "Camina y prende el fogon": Piano opening vamp

Chappottín begins his famous opening solo (figure 4.2) on the upbeat of four in the fourth measure. Beginning on F4, the solo arpeggiates through the B♭ minor triad using upbeat quarter notes. At first ascending to F5, the arpeggio reverses direction to B♭4 before returning for three repetitions of the F5. The last two of these while still syncopated are lengthened slightly. Starting on beat four of m. 7, the final note of this solo is a sustained D♭5. This final note and an eighth-note F5 on beat three of m. 5 are the only nonsyncopated notes in the entire solo. Although notated here as straight eighth notes, in reality the syncopations stretch in the direction of quarter-note triplets.

Figure 4.2. "Camina y prende el fogon": Trumpet solo and ensemble introduction

The second half of the introduction features the trumpet section (see figure 4.2). Beginning in m. 10 they play a six-note harmonized module that is sequenced twice, descending each time by a diatonic third. Each module contains two three-note cells consisting of a note and its repetition followed by another note a perfect fourth higher. The first three-note figure in the module contains syncopated eighth notes on the upbeats of two and three followed by the ascending note on beat four. The second half of the module contains down-beats on the first three beats of the following measure. After the third sequence, a similar module is started a step higher. In this case, an additional note is added to each half of the module. In m. 16 an additional syncopated eighth note is added on the upbeat of one and the ascending fourth occurs immediately on the next upbeat and is repeated twice. An extra quarter note is added to the second half of the module. In this case, the melody descends linearly instead of moving up a fourth. This descending four-quarter-note figure is a characteristic motive of the piece and reoccurs at various times.

In the final three measures of the introduction, the trumpets perform an eighth note–based unison melodic line. This line starts on an F4 on the upbeat of one and contains seven consecutive eighth notes in m. 18. The initial F4 leaps to a B♭4 and then con-tinues ascending stepwise to E♭5. The line then returns via a C5 and D♭5 escape sequence to a B♭4 on the first beat of m. 19. A rep-etition of the last five eighth notes of m. 18 then leads again to B♭4 on the first beat of m. 20. In this case, the B♭ is the first of two as-cending eighth notes leading to a quarter note D♭5 on beat two. The introduction is brought to a close with a single note (F5) piano bell tone on beat three of m. 20, which introduces the three eighth-note solo vocal pickup to the *largo* A section sung by Miguelito Cuní (figure 4.3).

Cuní sings the first four measures solo before the *coro* comes in to finish off this eight-measure section. Following the pickup, the first module of the A section moves down the B♭ minor chord from the fifth to the tonic and leaps back to a sustained E♭ start-ing on the upbeat of four in m. 21 that reflects the harmonic change to the subdominant. A similar three eighth-note pickup leads in m. 23 to the four-note figure that was first introduced by the brass section in m. 17 and is the main recurring motive throughout the piece. A series of harmonized note pairs (mostly syncopated) descends the scale from F to a sustained C that introduces the dominant harmony. The phrase is brought to a close in m. 28 with F repeated three times. The third F is sustained for six beats, extending the A section to ten measures.

Figure 4.3. "Camina y prende el fogon": The *largo* A section—vocal and trumpet section

A sophisticated approach to horn section arranging is used in "Camina y prende el fogón." More akin to methods used by American jazz arrangers than the tradition as represented by the Arsenio Rodríguez *conjunto*, the vocal parts are backed by syncopated trumpet harmonies, which are replaced by unison brass lines during sustained notes or respites in the vocal melody. For example, in m. 21 the horns play sustained chords supporting the syncopations of Cuní's vocal melody. When the vocal rests in m. 24 the trumpet section plays an ascending unison figure. In m. 25, syncopated brass chords return, supporting the entrance of the *coro*. When the *coro* drops out in m. 27, the trumpeters again play an eighth-note dominated unison line, which in this case is divided into octaves. As the *coro* sustains their last chord in the next module to finish the phrase, the brass section performs an ascending syncopated line in mm. 28–30.

Miguelito Cuní sings the entire B section (figure 4.4) over the dominant harmony before the trumpet section enters on the resolution to tonic in m. 40 with an extended repetition of their figure from mm. 18–20 in the introduction. The first eight measures of the B section vocal melody contain four repetitions of a two-measure module that is varied slightly on each repetition. Rhythmically each module begins with a three eighth-note pickup. Except for in the initial module these pickups are repeated E♭s. The first module begins with an ascending pickup that is similar to the beginning of the A section. In this case the figure leads to an E♭ on beat one of m. 31. Each of the repeated modules then continues with an eighth note on the following beat and three syncopated notes the last of which is sustained into the next measure. Melodically, the E♭ on the first beat moves linearly to C before jumping up to an E♭ and back to the C. The next three modules are identical except for the switch in the pickup figure to three E♭s and a jump to G♭ and F in mm. 37–38. A three-note syncopated pickup in the sec-

Figure 4.4. "Camina y prende el fogon": The *largo* B section—vocal and trumpet section

ond half of m. 38 leads to the four quarter-note hook that was introduced earlier in m. 17 and m. 23, in this case leading to the trumpet line in m. 40.

While the first two and a half measures of this horn line are identical to the one starting in m. 18, the figure continues to ascend in m. 42 before landing on a harmonized variation of the quarter-note hook, which in this case finishes on the dominant harmony instead of the tonic. After syncopated brass on the upbeats in the first half of m. 44, Cuní comes in with the pickups to the repetition of the B section (figure 4.5). Instead of unison figures, the horns end the second B section with a short, harmonized syncopated figure that introduces the *montuno* section (mm. 54–56).

While the vocal in the second B section (see figure 4.5) is almost the same as in the first, the horn section figures that alternate with the vocal modules are different. Rhythmically these trumpet parts are the same both times. However, in the first case the horns perform three unison four eighth-note figures (m. 32, 34, and 36) each

Figure 4.5. **"Camina y prende el fogon": Repetition of *largo* B section**

of which starts a diatonic third lower than the previous version. In the second B section the four eight notes are harmonized (m. 46, 48, and 50), with the first three notes repeated and the fourth one ascending a third. The third figure is slightly different in that the first two chords are repeated and the third and fourth chords each ascend a third.

Following the fourth repetition of the vocal module in B2 (which this time is exactly the same as the previous ones), the horns play a harmonized upbeat hit on the end of beat two in m. 52 before joining the vocalists on the four quarter-note hook figure in m. 53. Finally the *largo* ends in m. 54 and the *montuno* section begins in m. 55 with a two-measure harmonized horn figure. In m. 54 the melody of the figure begins with a Bb4 on the second half of beat one and a Db5 on the upbeat of two, leading to a trio of F5 quarter-note triplets in the second half of the measure. The second bar of the horn figure coincides with the beginning of the first four-measure *montuno* pattern. Here the trumpet melody contains upbeats on one and two (Db5 and Bb4) and quarter notes (Gb5 and F5) on beats three and four. The horn figure ends with an Eb5 at the beginning of m. 56, which sets up the first of the repeating *coros* in the *montuno* section.

The *montuno* pattern that prevails for most of the rest of the recording is a typical four-measure minor key I-V-V-I chord progression. This *coro* (figure 4.6) is two bars in length and is unusual in that it occupies the middle two measures (dominant harmony) of the four-measure pattern. The remaining two measures are occupied either by Chappottín's solo trumpet or Cuní's vocal *soneos*. At this point in the song there are six *coros*. The first three *coros* trade with the trumpet. *Coros* five and six are followed by the solo vocal and the final *coro* leads to an extended *tres* solo. Starting on the upbeat of two in the second bar of the pattern, the *coro* sings the title phrase over a seven-note melodic module. The first five notes of the *coro* melody are F4s. After two syncopated notes, the remaining three Fs are all quarter-note downbeats with two additional quarter notes (E♭4 and D♭4) finishing out the module on beats three and four in the third measure of the four-bar chord progression. Although different melodically, the final four notes of the *coro* module again reinforce the aforementioned hook motive, especially in terms of harmonic and rhythmic placement.

Figure 4.6. "Camina y prende el fogon":The *montuno* and *coro* pattern

Félix Chappottín in his short solos in "Camina y prende el fogón" demonstrates a mastery of rhythmic manipulation that is unsurpassed in the annals of Afro-Cuban music. Although an attempt has been made here to render these solos in music notation, these are useful only as guides and cannot pretend to be rhythmically accurate in more than a general way. In certain cases, rhythmic deviations from the notated examples will be described discursively. As mentioned, the trumpet solos at the beginning of the *montuno* occur in the spaces between the *coros*. There is overlapping in most cases. In other words, Chappottín usually starts his solo section during the final part of the *coro* and ends it during the beginning of the following *coro*. All three of the trumpet solos from the beginning of the *montuno* section are shown in figure 4.7.

Figure 4.7. "Camina y prende el fogon":Trumpet solos

As Chappottín comes in at m. 59, the beginning of his first solo overlaps with the end of the *coro*. Although most of the figures in his solos are notated as quarter-note triplets, they are actually in the gray area between that rhythm and straight syncopated quarter notes. In the first solo, he enters after the second beat in m. 59 on a D♭5 and ascends linearly to F5 a beat later. Chappottín remains on or around F5 for most of this solo before descending to B♭4 in m. 62. His phrasing in this solo is primarily behind the underlying pulse. Even the quarter notes in m. 60 are slightly behind the beat.

Coming in on the last half beat of the next *coro* (m. 63), Chappottín jumps up to an impressive D♭6 and begins a long twisting descent that finally reaches the D♭ an octave lower, ten beats later, before leaping back to a G♭5 and F5 to end the solo over the start of the next *coro*. His third solo starts the same way the previous one ended, although in this case it descends all the way to B♭4 before it leaps to the G♭5. In m. 69, the solo uses an eighth-note F major triad arpeggiation to lead up to the first of two triplet groupings, each of which descends. The first grouping moves from E♭5 to C5 and second from F5 to C5. The last two notes in the second grouping are performed in front of the beat and lead to a final, muffled B♭4-A4-B♭4 trio of notes.

As the fourth *coro* section comes to an end, Cuní enters with the first of two solo vocal sections. Unlike the trumpet, Cuní does not overlap with the *coros* but confines his singing to his allotted two-measure sections. Otherwise he demonstrates the same sophisticated rhythmic give and take that characterizes the playing of his colleague Chappottín.

After the sixth and final *coro* in this section, the *tres* performs an extended solo (mm. 80–98). This solo is followed by a three-measure piano break and a one-measure brass pickup figure to the ending section of the piece. At this point the *montuno* pattern is truncated to a two-measure length with a shortened one-measure *coro* (figure 4.8). For the next eight measures the horn section trades one-measure sections with the *coro*. In this case, the *coro* sings the second half of their previous *coro* phrase (the four-note hook).

Figure 4.8. **"Camina y prende el fogon": Short *coro* in ending section**

The trumpet section figure in this part (figure 4.9) is a harmonized arpeggio of an Eb minor sixth chord.

Figure 4.9. **"Camina y prende el fogon": Trumpet figure from ending section**

In the first two beats, the arpeggio ascends in eighth notes with the lead part moving from C5 to Bb5. The second half of the measure descends back down the chord with an eighth-note Gb5 on the upbeat of three and an Eb5 on the fourth beat. Additionally the horn section plays chords in support of the last two *coro* quarter notes. After the four repetitions in this two-measure configuration, the solo Chappottín replaces the trumpet section and the original *coro* is resumed. However, the revised two-measure *montuno* chord pattern is retained. This setup is repeated once before the brass section returns during the final four *coro* notes and ends the piece with a shortened paraphrase of the initial brass figure from the introduction and a final three-note punch figure by the entire group (figure 4.10).

"Camina y prende el fogón" is a masterpiece in the Afro-Cuban *son/conjunto* tradition and demonstrates the typical way in which much of the music from the golden age of Afro-Cuban music and *salsa* is put together.

Figure 4.10. **"Camina y prende el fogon": Trumpet section ending**

5

SALSA

The term *salsa* was coined in the late 1960s or early 1970s and is generally attributed to the publicity efforts of various Latin music industry executives (Manuel 1995). Regardless of its origins, *salsa* has come to represent to many the whole of Afro-Cuban music.

For the purposes of this study, *salsa* will be defined in two different ways. In addition to the more general meaning described above, the term *salsa* also refers more specifically to music from the New York Latin scene that developed during the 1960s and 1970s (Manuel 1995). This narrower usage refers to the music of artists like Eddie Palmieri, Willie Colón, Johnny Pacheco, and others who recorded for labels such as Alegre, Tico, and Fania starting in the early 1960s. In this chapter, the more limited definition will be assumed.

A number of influences factored into the development of *salsa*. The most important influence was the Cuban *son* and *conjunto* tradition as represented by groups such as Sexteto Habanero and the *conjunto* of Arsenio Rodríguez. It can be convincingly argued that *salsa* is simply a renaming and updating of the *son/conjunto* genre. While this assertion is in many ways valid, several other factors

(both musical and nonmusical) contributed to the particular manner in which *salsa* music evolved. In addition to the *son/conjunto*
(and to an important extent the traditional *charanga*), the primary
musical influences on *salsa* were the Latin jazz bands of New York
from the 1940s (such as those led by Dizzy Gillespie and Machito),
the large Cuban bands of the 1950s (like the one led by singing star
Beny Moré), and the *mambo* movement centering around New
York clubs (most notably the Palladium), which reached its zenith
in the 1950s via the bands led by the big three: Tito Puente, Tito
Rodríguez, and Machito (Roberts 1979). Yet another significant influence on *salsa* was the *descarga*, or Cuban jam session, which
originated in Cuba in the mid-1950s and is most closely associated
with the bassist Israel "Cachao" Lopez.

As important as all of these musical sources were in the development of *salsa*, political and social issues were equally influential
in the development of *salsa* during the 1960s and 1970s. By far the
most important political event to impact on the future of Afro-
Cuban music was the communist revolution of Cuba, which took
place in 1959 under the leadership of Fidel Castro (MacGaffey
and Barnett 1962).

Another social event also impacted the evolution of *salsa* music.
However, this revolution did not, like the Castro takeover, occur
overnight but evolved over several decades: the large-scale immi-
gration of Puerto Ricans to New York and other North American
cities in the middle decades of the twentieth century. Because of
its cultural similarity to Cuba, Puerto Rico, while having its own indigenous music styles, swung for the most part to the Cuban beat
(Boggs 1992). Although the Puerto Rican *bomba* and *plena* styles
are vital, the famous Puerto Rican New York Palladium bandleaders Tito Puente and Tito Rodríguez both performed music that was
derived almost entirely from the Cuban *son* (Boggs 1992).

Another important social influence on the *salsa* scene was
purely North American in origin and was dictated by economics.
As the American music industry evolved from the jazz-oriented

music of the 1930s and 1940s to the rock era that started in the 1950s, the trend toward small groups (as opposed to the earlier big bands) had a similar effect on Latin music. In the same way that the jazz big bands of bandleaders like Benny Goodman and Tommy Dorsey were being replaced in the North American commercial music industry by the smaller guitar-driven bands backing popular artists like Chuck Berry and Elvis Presley, the mambo-era big bands of Machito, Tito Puente, and Tito Rodríguez were replaced in the 1960s by smaller *conjuntos* (and *charangas*) led by a newer generation of primarily Puerto Rican musicians.

Although the new North American model did have other stylistic effects on some forms of *salsa* (most notably the *búgalu*), its main influence showed in the economically induced reduction in ensemble size. Ironically, the trend toward smaller groups in the Latin field actually created a renaissance of traditional Cuban forms in most of the early *salsa* bands, as the reduction in size created ensembles that resembled the instrumentation of the earlier Cuban *conjuntos* and *charangas* rather than the New York Latin big band. One of the first events to involve the new generation of New York *salsa* musicians was the *charanga* craze of the early 1960s. Duboney, the *charanga* group led by pianist Charlie Palmieri (and featuring flutist Johnny Pacheco), is generally credited with being the initial force in creating the new musical fashion. "[Duboney] became so popular during 1960 that the band was working several dances each night" (Roberts 1979). The band that Charlie Palmieri formed, with its four violins and flute, was a distinct departure from the large brass- and saxophone-dominated New York Latin music of the previous two decades.

In addition to the flute/violin front line, there were other instrumental changes that resulted from the *charanga* vogue of the early 1960s. The percussion instrument most closely associated with the traditional *danzón* and *charanga* was the *timbales*. This instrument reasserted its dominance in the rhythm section during this *charanga* revival and continued to be included as well in most of the

New York *conjuntos* that took over the *salsa* scene following the brief *charanga* craze. Additionally, there was a new duet-based singing style and "a classicism of sound and form that gave the *charangas* a grace and tension quite new to the New York scene" (Roberts 1979). Many of the great Cuban flutists who had immigrated previous to or during the Castro revolution (including Pupi Legaretta, José Fajardo, and veteran Alberto Socarras, who had been performing in New York since the 1920s) suddenly found themselves extremely busy on the new *charanga* scene that was fueled by a dance fad called the *pachanga*.

Two artists who later became *salsa* stars fronting horn-oriented bands made their start in this *charanga* fad. Puerto Rican Ray Baretto and Cuban Mongo Santamaria both play *conga*, and both achieved their early success fronting *charanga* groups. Baretto had a number of hits in this format, including "El Watusi." Santamaria, with fellow percussionist Willie Bobo, formed a group called La Sabrosa, which preserved the traditional flute/violin front line and also fused jazz and other non-Latin music into the sound. The most famous recording by La Sabrosa is "Afro-Blue," which also became a jazz standard recorded by (among others) jazz saxophonist John Coltrane (Roberts 1979).

Even though the *charanga* craze instigated by Charlie Palmieri ran its course in about three years, a few of the *charanga* groups that were started at the time proved to have staying power. Orquesta Típica Novel and Orquesta Broadway (started by Cuban singer Roberto Torres) have continued to perform with various degrees of regularity for the past three and a half decades and are still popular today.

By the mid-1960s, the popularity of the *charanga* waned, and the instrumentation of most of the mainstream *salsa* bands switched from the *charanga* instrumentation to that of the *conjunto*. Perhaps the most famous example is Johnny Pacheco, who switched to the *conjunto* format when he started Fania Records in 1964 (Manuel 1995). A musical conservative, Pacheco emulated the traditional *conjunto* to the point of recording several covers (remakes) of Arsenio Rodríguez compositions.

While the *conjunto* became the most dominant format, most of these bands retained some aspects of the *charanga* instrumentation. Although the classic *conjunto* of the 1940s did not use the *timbales*, the new *salsa conjuntos* added this instrument to create, along with the *congas* and *bongós*, a three-man drum battery. Because Pacheco played the flute, he included this *charanga* horn in his otherwise traditional trumpet-oriented *conjunto*.

Another band that included both the flute and *timbales* in a *conjunto* format was the innovative La Perfecta, led by Eddie Palmieri (the younger brother of Charlie). Eddie Palmieri's band was considered by many to be the "seminal" group of the early *salsa* era (Roberts 1979). One major innovation of this group was the use of trombones in place of trumpets. This change came about through the collaboration of Palmieri and trombonist Barry Rogers. Because of the band's use of trombones alongside the *charanga*-associated flute and *timbales*, Palmieri's brother Charlie coined the term *trombanga* to describe La Perfecta. (Following this overview, the music of Eddie Palmieri, as it pertains to the playing of Armenteros, will be analyzed in greater detail.) The use of trombones instead of trumpets as the horn section was an innovation by La Perfecta that had a major influence on other *salsa* bands in the mid-1960s and later, such as the one led by *salsa* legend Willie Colón.

Among the next generation of groups to use trombone-only horn sections were those associated with the *bugalú* (or boogaloo). The *bugalú* music of leaders such as Joe Cuba and Johnny Colón was one of the most successful (if short-lived) crossover successes in the early *salsa* era. The *bugalú* was the first major fusion of *salsa* and North American rhythm and blues. While it retained its *salsa* context, the *bugalú* added blues-based elements and English lyrics to the mix. There was a reciprocity of influence, however; many North American pop groups of the time were impacted by the boogaloo.

One of the most important proponents of the *bugalú* was trombonist/bandleader Willie Colón, who recorded his first hit record when he was seventeen years old and "was to be among the most creative and innovative bandleaders of the 1970s" (Roberts 1979). Among his contributions to *salsa* was the use of a "high proportion of instrumentals and solos" (Roberts 1979). Colón was also instrumental in giving *salsa* more of a New York Puerto Rican identity. Two of the most important singers in *salsa*—superstars Hector Lavoe and Ruben Blades—achieved their initial fame with Willie Colón.

As the 1970s began, however, there was a return by some to the more traditional Cuban forms of music. Even musicians like Ray Barretto, who had with great success ridden the various waves of change throughout the 1960s, reverted to a more conservative *son*-influenced format. Both he and Mongo Santamaria had had great success adapting both jazz and rock elements to their music in the late 1960s. Barretto returned to Cuban roots by the start of the new decade; Santamaria, meanwhile, continued to work in the Latin jazz fusion arena.

A new instrumentation change took place in the early 1970s: an increase in the size of the horn section. Although many groups still utilized the all-trumpet or all-trombone horn formation, many *salsa* bands began to use a larger brass configuration: combining two trumpets with two trombones and creating a powerful and versatile horn section, made even more formidable by the addition of a baritone saxophone on the bottom. Many of the groups associated with Fania Records used this extended horn section format. Variations of this particular five-piece horn combination are still commonplace on the present-day *salsa* scene.

THE DESCARGA

A major influence on Cuban-derived music's evolution in the *salsa* era was the *descarga*. Most closely associated with the bassist Israel

"Cachao" Lopez, the *descarga* is a Cuban jam session. Because the *descarga* started in Cuba, it is relatively free of jazz influences. Whereas the Latin jazz that evolved in the 1940s and 1950s around musicians like Machito and Dizzy Gillespie was highly influenced by the language of modern jazz, the *descarga* was purely Cuban in origin. Instead of applying the exotic harmonies and virtuosic lines of modern jazz to the *clave* context (in the manner of Machito or Gillespie), the *descarga* that Cachao began recording in the late 1950s was firmly anchored in the *son* tradition.

Although *descargas* sometimes included vocals, in most cases they were instrumental pieces based on simple *montuno* patterns. However, instead of being limited to the call-and-response role prescribed in the *septetos* and *conjuntos*, the horn players in a *descarga* could stretch out and perform longer solos. Often, one horn player would play a continuous figure while another performer improvised. This practice of riffing behind a soloist had a strong influence on *salsa* bands such as those led by Eddie Palmieri and Willie Colón. This riff figure was referred to as a *moña*.[1] Cachao's *descarga* group, like the *salsa conjunto*, also utilized the three-piece percussion combo of *bongó*, *conga*, and *timbales*. This addition of *timbales* to the *conjunto* battery possibly reflected Cachao's tenure with Arcaño's *charanga*. In the traditional *charanga* (dating from the late nineteenth century), the *timbal* was the primary (and often only) percussion instrument.

The *descarga* format was borrowed and given a New York flavor when Charlie Palmieri led a series of recorded jam sessions in the mid-1960s for Al Santiago's record company, Alegre (Boggs 1992). Alegre (along with Tico Records) was one of the most prominent early *salsa* labels. The "label band," Alegre All-Stars, recorded several albums structured along the same lines as the earlier Cuban *descarga*. Although there were more jazz elements present in this new *descarga* than in its Cuban cousin, the standard forms of the *son* and *conjunto* were utilized in much the same way that artists like Cachao borrowed the traditional Cuban genres in their mid-1950s *descarga*. The Alegre All-Stars existed for a short period of time and produced only a handful of recordings, yet their influence was extensive; there were numerous copycat studio bands, including the Tico All-Stars and the Fania All-Stars, that represented the other major record labels of the *salsa* era (Roberts 1979).

In the early 1990s, there was a renaissance of the *descarga*, and in 1995 Cachao formed a new group that recorded two popular and award-winning CDs entitled *Master Sessions* I and II. Cuban actor Andy Garcia produced both albums as well as a critically acclaimed movie (*Como Su Ritmo No Hay Dos*) featuring the Cachao group. The group included both younger musicians (trombonist Jimmy Bosch and saxophonist Paquito D'Rivera) and veterans (Armenteros and pianist Alfredo Valdez, Jr.). Cachao also revived the traditional *danzón* and the *charanga* with this group. In fact, this ensemble was two bands in one. When a *danzón* was performed, the ensemble included a string section and the flutist Nestor Torres. A horn section replaced these players when a *descarga* was performed. These recordings amply demonstrate that Armenteros had lost little, if any, of his trumpet playing acumen in the years immediately preceding his seventieth birthday.

EDDIE PALMIERI

Eddie Palmieri has been one of the innovators in the history of *salsa* and Cuban music (Roberts 1979). Although his heritage is Puerto Rican, his musical idiom is firmly Cuban. He took the musical styles invented by musicians like Arsenio Rodríguez and Israel "Cachao" Lopez and created his own unique interpretation.

Palmieri, the quintessential *salsa* "New Yorican," was born in the Bronx in 1936. He began playing piano at eight years of age and started his first band when he was fourteen (Larkin 1995). In 1955, he turned professional and performed with various groups before joining the big band of legendary singer Tito Rodríguez in 1958. He played with Rodríguez for two years before starting his own band, La Perfecta, in 1961.

A brief overview of La Perfecta's work will help to establish the context for Palmieri's later work with Armenteros. La Perfecta, with its unique instrumentation of two trombones, flute, piano, bass, *bongós, congas,* and *timbales,* is one of the landmark groups in the history of modern Latin music. Starting in 1962, La Perfecta made a series of recordings on the Alegre and Tico record labels (Roberts 1979). Palmieri made his first three recordings with La Perfecta between 1962 and 1964 on Al Santiago's Alegre label. Most of the core members of the band were present on the 1962 debut album, *Eddie Palmieri and His Conjunto La Perfecta:* trombonist Barry Rogers, *timbalero* and *bongosero* Manny Oquendo, flute player George Castro, and vocalist Ismael Quintana. The second LP, *El Molestoso,* vol. II, was released in 1963, followed a year later by *Lo Que Traigo Es Sabroso.* With the addition of trombonist Jose Rodrigues in 1963, the core group had been finalized.

In 1964, Palmieri switched to Tico Records, and his initial recording on the label was *Echando Pa'lante (Straight Ahead).* In the following three years, La Perfecta recorded four additional albums for Tico: *Azucar Pa' Ti (Sugar for You), Mozambique, Molasses,* and *Bamboleate,* which was a collaboration with jazz vibraharpist Cal Tjader. The group also made an additional recording with Tjader for the Verve jazz label.

For a number of reasons (primarily economic), La Perfecta disbanded in 1968. However, the legacy of this "brilliant, ferociously swinging outfit" (Larkin 1995) has had a strong impact on *salsa* music in general and directly on the recordings that Palmieri made in the following years, many of which featured the playing of Armenteros.

It is in the decade following the breakup of La Perfecta that Palmieri's career is of paramount importance to the study of Armenteros; between 1968 and 1978, Armenteros played on almost half of the recordings made by Eddie Palmieri (Larkin 1995). Armenteros was in his forties at the time, at the peak of his performing prowess. The trumpeter's prodigious talent, combined with the innovative music of Palmieri, produced some of the finest trumpet soloing in the history of the Cuban genre. For this reason, it is important to analyze the recordings from this period of Eddie Palmieri's career in detail, with an emphasis on the playing of Armenteros.

Because Palmieri changed formats and added trumpet to the three Tico record albums that immediately followed the breakup of La Perfecta, and Armenteros was featured often and significantly on two of these Tico recordings, *Justicia* and *Superimposition,* they will be examined in greater detail than later Palmieri/Armenteros collaborations. After a brief general description of the two volumes, individual selections on which Armenteros is featured prominently will be discussed in greater depth. The recording of "Bilongo" from *Superimposition* will be given a full musical analysis, especially as it pertains to Armenteros and brass playing. The later Palmieri/Armenteros affiliations also will be cited, albeit in lesser detail; certain selections with significant contributions by Armenteros will be discussed.

A SELECTIVE SURVEY OF BRASS PERFORMANCE WITH PALMIERI

Champagne

The first Palmieri recording on which the trumpet participates is *Champagne,* on the Tico label. This is also the first recording by Palmieri following the breakup of La Perfecta, and a number of former La Perfecta members are included, most prominently the trombone tandem of Barry Rogers and Jose Rodrigues. In addition to Roy Román on trumpet, Palmieri uses the legendary Cuban bassist Israel "Cachao" Lopez on this recording. Coming on the heels of the *bugalú* craze, *Champagne* includes a number of crossover rhythm and blues elements. However, while there are a couple of pieces on the recording that are in the *bugalú* style (most notably "The African Twist"), the numbers which feature trumpet solos are firmly in the Afro-Cuban tradition.

"Cintura" contains rhythm and blues elements, especially in some of the horn parts, but in essence the composition is resolutely ensconced in the *son/conjunto* tradition. Built on a G minor *montuno* pattern, "Cintura" for the most part follows the standard form of a typical La Perfecta piece. However, in this piece, the influence of the *descarga* is stronger than in most of the La Perfecta recordings. Even though the early Palmieri works innovatively apply *descarga* elements, such as *moñas* and extended solos, to the *conjunto* sound, these elements are never used as extensively as they are on "Cintura" and other recordings of the post–La Perfecta period. Rogers and Rodrigues creatively use the improvisatory *moña* in an extended fashion in "Cintura," especially behind Román's lengthy trumpet solo.

"Cintura" opens with a rhythm section introduction that features a *bugalú*-like piano/bass line and a similarly rhythm and blues–influenced percussion battery, complete with tambourine and back beat. In the ninth measure, the brass section enters, and the song changes to an Afro-Cuban feel. The initial vocal *largo* section is unusual in that it starts out with two iterations of the *coro* pattern from the *montuno* section before it goes into a more *largo*-like eight-measure pattern. Following a repeat of the entire structure, the initial *coro* with responding *sonero* continues as the *montuno* section begins. After several *coros*, the *montuno* continues with a reiteration of the opening piano/bass figure. This vamp continues with a number of overlaying brass figures. This section returns to the regular *montuno* with a shortened *coro* and a continuous *sonero*.

Following this short vocal section, the *moña* style of the La Perfecta trombone section combines for the first time on record with trumpet playing. The technique exhibited by Román in his solo is considerable, and the trombone *moña* is the epitome of *salsa* swing. However, compared to Palmieri's later collaborations with Armenteros, both the solo and *moña* are relatively conservative.

In his solo, Román plays with a virtuosic linear style but does not utilize the upper range of the instrument in the way Armenteros does on the Palmieri recordings that soon followed. Most of the trumpet solos on the Armenteros pieces are noted for their prodigious use of the instrument's upper register. The trombone *moña* behind the solo is less adventurous than the *moñas* that followed on later albums. Indeed, many of the *moñas* on the classic La Perfecta recordings were more spontaneous and improvisatory (if shorter) than this unvarying harmonized effort in "Cintura." One of the most significant aspects of the classic La Perfecta recordings are the freewheeling trombone *moñas*, which change constantly and often feature independent interweaving lines by the two trombonists. The credits on many of the La Perfecta recordings uniquely refer to Rogers as lead trombone and Rodrigues as "contrapuntal" trombone.

Another selection on *Champagne* featuring the soloing of Roy Román is the Arsenio Rodríguez composition "Si las nenas me dejan, que" ("Si las nenas"). This is one of the few compositions on the volume that does not exhibit any *bugalú* influences. Instead, Palmieri emulates the Rodríguez style, even including a *tres* on the recording that is played impressively by none other than trombonist Barry Rogers. The opening *tres* vamp starts out like a typical Rodríguez piece but expands slightly, with syncopated brass notes and a more freewheeling *tres* part than was customary on a Rodríguez recording. Following a break, the piece progresses like a typical *montuno*: four-measure *coros* in call-and-response patterns with horn parts, *soneros*, and two trumpet solos. Both solos are firmly in the Cuban *conjunto* tradition, albeit in a higher trumpet register than that used by the young Armenteros and other trumpet masters of the 1940s. The second of these solos ends with a trumpet shake that contains elements of both Chappottín and a modern jazz lead-trumpet players like Maynard Ferguson. Following a piano solo, there is a *salsa mambo*.

One of the first uses of the word *mambo* referred to the innovative way that the traditional *charanga danzón* was adapted and extended in the late 1930s by the Arcaño band and its creative musical director, Israel "Cachao" Lopez. The name *mambo* reached its greatest prominence in referring to the New York City music associated with the Palladium nightclub in the 1950s (Roberts 1979). Because the Arcaño *charanga* had very little in common with the Palladium big bands of Machito, Puente, and Tito Rodríguez, the *mambo* had a different meaning to 1950s New Yorkers than it did to Cuban *charanga* fans of the 1940s. *Mambo* was again redefined in the *salsa* era. While there is undoubtedly a musical connection between these various *mambos*, establishing this connection constitutes the subject of an entire research endeavor and lays beyond the purview of this book. However, the *salsa* version of the *mambo* will be described below because of its pertinence both to Palmieri's music and to later *salsa* recordings featuring Armenteros.

To the *salsa* musician of the past thirty years, the *mambo* is a musical interlude that is introduced into the *montuno* of a composition following an initial *coro/sonero* section and/or an instrumental solo. The *mambo* can either be a simple variation of the prevailing *montuno* or an elaborately arranged departure from the *montuno* that often includes major changes in the music harmonically and rhythmically. The changes are achieved through various techniques.

One common strategy is to reverse the prevailing *clave* by shifting the measure and using a break figure of an odd number of measures. Because the *clave* is sacrosanct in Cuban music, the only legitimate way to change from a two-three *clave* to a three-two *clave* (or vice versa) is to reemphasize the structure through a transitional phrase of an odd number of measures. When the *mambo* section ends, there are two possible ways to continue the composition: either with the altered *clave* or with a return to the original *clave*. If there is a change in the *clave* in the *mambo*, and the original *montuno* returns, there must be another transition section of an odd number of measures to reestablish the original *clave*.

Another common ploy in a modern *mambo* section is the use of elaborate formal and harmonic strategies. Many *salsa* arrangers use the *mambo* as an excuse to show off their writing prowess and often create ornate extended musical interludes. After a *mambo* section, the music returns to the *montuno* pattern. In many cases, this is the same *montuno* pattern that preceded the *mambo*. However, often there is a completely different *montuno* figure that might or might not prevail until the end of the piece.

Yet another common feature of *salsa mambos* is the use of rhythmic breaks. Usually located at the beginning and/or end of the *mambo* section, these breaks represent a departure from the ongoing *montuno tumbao*. As an element of the predetermined arrangement, the break figure can be performed by either the entire ensemble or a portion of the group (typically the rhythm section). These types of breaks can occur anywhere in a piece. However, they are almost always part of a *mambo* section (or a setup to this section).

Finally, another common element in a *mambo* arrangement is the melodic treatment of the piano and bass parts. In a departure from their usual rhythm section roles, the two instruments often perform a repeating melodic line over which the horn section melody enters. The two instruments either play an identical line, or the bass provides a supporting figure to the piano melody.

In "Si las nenas," the *mambo* section is preceded by a four-measure break, which features an ascending piano–and-*tres* unison line. The break figure ends with the rhythm section playing a series of eighth-note hits. Following a repeating *tres* melody that is accompanied by a pedal-like bass counterpoint, the horn section plays a four-measure melody that is repeated once. Following the repetition of the phrase, the brass players repeat the final three notes of the phrase three times, leading to a reprise of the break that initiated the *mambo*. Unfortunately, the extension to the four-measure horn melody is an odd number of measures because the break figure enters on the wrong side of the *clave*. This crossing of the *clave* is usually considered unforgivable and only the skill of the musicians involved prevents this *faux pas* from being more noticeable. Despite these irregularities, when the *sonero* and *coro* reenter following the *mambo*, the music is firmly in two-three *clave*. In the *conjunto* tradition, the *coro* in the final part of the piece is shortened and occurs in two- instead of four-measure patterns. After several occurrences of call and response between *sonero* and *coro*, there is a sixteen-measure trumpet solo over the prevailing *coro*. There are several more *sonero/coro* patterns before the piece ends with the horn line from the *mambo* section.

Justicia

Like *Champagne*, *Justicia* (Palmieri) contains both traditional Cuban and American crossover elements. The pieces on *Justicia* run the gamut from a 1930s Septeto Nacional update to a jazz waltz complete with electric guitar and jazz drum set. At over eleven minutes, "Verdict on Judge Street" is the longest work on the volume. This piece, a typical jazz waltz, features long instrumental solos and contains few Latin elements. Another piece that has strong North American influences, "Everything Is Everything," uses English lyrics and is based on a typical blues form. The rhythm section parts are performed in a style reminiscent of funky jazz groups from the 1960s such as those led by Ramsey Lewis, Lee Morgan, and Herbie Hancock.

Armenteros is featured on four compositions. He plays a subdued muted trumpet behind the singer on "Amor ciego" and a short solo at the end of the folkloric-sounding "My Spiritual Indian." However, the title tune "Justicia" and the Ignacio Piñeiro standard "Lindo yambu" contain classic solos by the trumpeter and will be discussed in more detail than the other selections.

Written by Eddie Palmieri, "Justicia" epitomizes the *salsa* style. Based firmly in the Afro-Cuban tradition, "Justicia" reverberates with a rhythmic drive that reflects its New York City genesis. One of the driving forces behind this version of the Palmieri ensemble is the *timbalero* Nicky Marrero. He and the other percussionists keep a relentless pace that is reinforced by ever-changing trombone *moñas* and some of the best soloing by Armenteros on record.

Although "Justicia" reflects the basic *largo/montuno* formal structure of the Afro-Cuban *son*, there are several ways in which this piece also denotes the *salsa* spin on the Cuban model. One element that reflects late-1960s *salsa* is the elaborate and lengthy horn-driven introduction. The *largo* section, with its carefully orchestrated horn parts and numerous rhythm section break figures, also distinguishes the *salsa* style of Eddie Palmieri from the simpler 1940s *conjunto* music of his forebear Arsenio Rodríguez. These elements and the Palmieri ensemble's patented rhythmic drive create a music that both respects its roots and reflects the hyperactivity of 1960s and 1970s New York City.

While the arrangement of "Justicia" may be more elaborate than earlier pieces in the Afro-Cuban genre, the basic formal characteristics remain the same; most of these formal elements have been described elsewhere in this book. The following section will describe the *montuno*, the trombone *moñas*, and Armenteros' solo.

The *montuno* section of "Justicia" is based on a two-measure, two-three *clave*, C minor chord progression. In the *salsa* jargon, a *montuno* based on both this type of chord progression and its major key equivalent is referred to as a one-four-five (figure 5.1).

Figure 5.1. "One-four-five" progressions in C minor

An example in a major key is the famous "Peanut Vendor" (Manisero). The name of the progression is based on the harmonic movement of the pattern. This movement consists of a tonic harmony for two beats followed by the subdominant on the last half of the first measure. In the second half of the two-measure phrase, the dominant harmony of the first two beats returns to the subdominant for the final two beats. Although the three chords in the progression represent all of the primary harmonies of the tonal system, the shortness in duration of the pattern and of each harmonic element creates the impression of a harmonic ground. This paradoxical combination of harmonic verticality and horizontalization is a common strategy in Cuban music.

The *coro* is also two measures in length, and the *montuno* section begins with the usual call-and-response tradeoff between the *coro* and *sonero*. A short Palmieri piano solo and a much longer *conga* solo over a driving *tumbao* follow. The *conga* solo ends with the singers intoning the second half of the *coro* pattern ("La Justicia"), repeating every two measures. After several iterations, a harmonized trombone *moña* figure enters and continues as the rhythm section plays a lengthy rhythmic lead-in break to the trumpet solo. As the solo begins, the harmonized trombone line continues briefly before the two players divide into contrapuntal parts that evolve behind Armenteros in a semi-improvisational fashion for his entire solo.

This type of *moña* playing is much looser in concept than the strict trombone accompaniment to the trumpet solo in "Cintura," and while the "Justicia" trumpet solo shares many characteristics with Román's work on "Cintura," Armenteros turns up the heat in this solo, playing with more technical dexterity and greater range than Román does on the earlier recording. On his "Justicia" solo, Armenteros amply demonstrates the high-note virtuosity that made him famous. As the solo section ends, the trumpet solo and trombone *moñas* are replaced by the shortened "La Justicia" *coro* and the *sonero,* which continues as the piece is electronically faded.

The re-recording of a piece from the Cuban tradition was a common practice on the La Perfecta recordings and continued on the three volumes discussed in this chapter. Palmieri's ensemble and other groups from the *salsa* era (such as the band led by pianist Larry Harlow) often paid tribute to landmark Cuban groups, including the early *son* bands Sexteto Habanero and Septeto Nacional and the great 1940s *conjunto* of Arsenio Rodríguez (and the group's successor Chappottín y sus Estrellas), by recording new versions of works by these seminal groups. Arsenio Rodríguez was by far the favorite for the young *salsa* bandleaders. Palmieri, Harlow, and others produced several Rodríguez remakes on recordings. The three albums examined here contain two recordings of Rodríguez songs as well as a Septeto Nacional piece written by Ignacio Piñeiro. In addition to "Si las nenas" on *Champagne*, Rodríguez is represented on *Superimposition* by a remake of the classic "Dame un cachito pa'huele."

On *Justicia*, the *son* tradition is represented by a rendering of the Pineiro *son* "Lindo yambu," which was originally recorded in 1930 by the Septeto Nacional. Although the basic elements of the original "Lindo yambu" are present in the Palmieri version, this material is presented in an updated format. Reminiscent of an Arsenio Rodríguez approach, the piece starts with a one-measure vamp (in this case piano instead of a Rodríguez *tres*), with the rest of the rhythm section entering in the second measure. Continuing with the horn section, the introduction concludes with a break figure that neither Rodríguez nor Septeto Nacional would have produced but is typical to the New York *salsa* style of Palmieri.

In most aspects, the Palmieri version of "Lindo yambu" differs completely from the one recorded by Nacional. The *largo* section of Palmieri's version contains the most similarity to the original, yet the two sections differ in both music and text. Perhaps the most important common denominator in the *largo* is the harmonic movement between relatively long tonic and dominant areas. Even here, the Palmieri version moves briefly to the relative minor key.

The newer recording is much slower than the original, which, in the fashion of the *son* era, accelerates at the *montuno* section. While a comparison of these two recordings merits extended academic analysis, the following discussion will be confined to the Palmieri version.

There are two different *montuno* patterns in the *montuno* section. After the *largo* section, the initial pattern is a four-measure chord progression in C major. This progression consists of the tonic harmony in measure one, the subdominant in the second measure, and the dominant harmony in the final two bars. In the classic *conjunto* fashion, the four-measure *montuno* is initially divided between a two-measure *coro* part in the first half of the pattern and trumpet soloing in the second half. Again, the Rodríguez model is observed when the *sonero* replaces the trumpet after two Armenteros solos. Armenteros' playing in these two solos combines the nuance of the Chappottín tradition with the athleticism of primetime Armenteros. Although both solos utilize the trumpeter's impressive high range, the second also demonstrates a linear dexterity that surpasses the trumpet technique used (by even the young Armenteros) in the golden age of *conjunto* trumpet playing.

After three complete *coro/sonero* iterations, Palmieri plays a piano solo that begins after the final unanswered *coro*. A break leading to the *mambo* section follows the piano solo. In addition to changing the three-two *clave* to a two-three, the break introduces a change from the four-measure harmonic progression to a *montuno* pattern based solely on the dominant harmony. The *mambo* starts with a four-measure *tumbao* that then supports four iterations of a four-measure horn section figure. Following the *mambo*, the *montuno* pattern is two measures in length, with the *coro* occupying the first measure and interacting with a trumpet solo for the first three patterns. Although the solo begins on the second measure of the first pattern, the pattern performs continuously until the solo's completion. When the *sonero* replaces the trumpet, it also overlaps the *coro* to some degree but for the most part retains its "response" role to the *coro*'s "call." After several repetitions of the *coro/sonero*, the trumpet replaces the solo singer for six iterations of the two-measure *montuno* pattern, this time accompanied by both the continuing *coro* and a trombone section *moña*. In this solo, Armenteros plays primarily broken rhythmic figures alternating with double-time lines in a high tessitura. The *sonero* then replaces the horns for several repetitions before the four-measure *mambo* horn figure is performed twice, with a one-bar extension that returns to both the three-two *clave* and the original four-measure *montuno/coro* pattern. After one repetition of the *coro*, the piece ends with a reprise of the introduction.

Superimposition

According to many sources and to its listing in the Tico catalog, *Superimposition* followed *Champagne* and *Justicia* in chronological order. However, Palmieri, in referring to *Superimposition* in a recent interview, states that following this album "one goes into *Justicia* and *Vámonos Pal Monte*" (Carp 1998), indicating that the true chronology is *Champagne*, *Superimposition*, and then *Justicia*. For the purposes of this examination, the temporal order of *Superimposition* and *Justicia* is not essential in that both albums were recorded in such close proximity that the musical elements involved are very similar.

As with *Justicia*, the musical material on *Superimposition* can be split into two major divisions. Like "Lindo yambu" and the title tune on *Justicia*, the first three numbers on *Superimposition* are in the mainstream Afro-Cuban influenced *salsa* style. Similarly, the final three selections on *Superimposition* (all instrumentals) are more experimental and/or include elements borrowed from North American genres. As in the discussion of *Justicia*, the focus here will be on the more traditional material featuring Armenteros. The first of the instrumentals, "Que lindo eso, Eh!/Isn't It Pretty," is an innovative tour-de-force example of the Palmieri piano style; however, the horn players (including Armenteros) are not present. The instrumentals "Chocolate Ice Cream" and "17.1" belong in the *descarga* realm, although North American elements are present.

Even though Palmieri and Armenteros share writing credits on "Chocolate Ice Cream," it sounds like a studio jam session. The song opens with a funky piano vamp and bass line over a two-three *clave*. After the initial vamp, Palmieri plays a simple funky melody that is gradually embellished until a full-blown piano solo is under way. Throughout his lengthy solo, Palmieri borrows liberally from the blues and pentatonic vocabulary of jazz pianists like Ramsey Lewis, Les McAnn, and Horace Silver. On occasion, he plays a figure more in the Afro-Cuban vein, but for the most part, he stays within the funk-jazz framework.

Armenteros in his solo also borrows from the American model in his use of pentatonic scales and blues licks. He is less convincing than Palmieri in the handling of these elements. This solo is unusual in the length of time he plays with only a rhythm section accompaniment. Normally there would be continuous *coro* or horn section *moña* material supporting a solo.

Eddie Palmieri came up with the name "17.1" by calculating the average age of his three young percussionists: Nicky Marrero, Eladio Perez, and Chuckie Lopez (Carp and Polin 1998). Firmly in the *descarga* mold, "17.1" is built entirely around a C7 dominant harmony. Like "Chocolate Ice Cream," "17.1" is, for the most part, a spontaneous jam session in the studio. This instrumental, more than the two previous examples, is ensconced in the Cuban style with few overt North American influences (although in his soloing, Palmieri borrows many voicings and advanced tonal and melodic elements from his jazz peers). A *timbale* solo by Marrero follows the piano, and the rhythmic heat quotient is gradually increased throughout the solo until, by the time Armenteros starts his solo, the band is performing at a frantic pace. As in "Chocolate Ice Cream," the solo trumpet performs for a considerable amount of time with only the rhythm section before the solo trombone *moña* begins. In this (again) lengthy solo, Armenteros displays his considerable bag of tricks, emphasizing a dramatically rhythmic use of staccato tonguing in various places. After the trumpet solo, "17.1" ends with a solo by the *bongosero* that is faded electronically.

The three vocal selections on *Superimposition* are all firmly within the Afro-Cuban/*salsa* tradition and feature some of the best solo performing by Armenteros on record. Two distinct types of *salsa* music are represented respectively by "Se acabo la malanga" ("Se acabo") and "Pa' huele." Like "Cintura" and "Justicia," "Se acabo" is a piece that was composed specifically for the band. Conversely, "Pa' huele" is a remake of a classic Arsenio Rodríguez recording (originally "Dame un cachito pa' huele") in the tradition of Palmieri's previous covers of "Si las nenas" (with Rodríguez) and "Lindo yambu" (with Septeto Nacional). Aside from the question of origin, there are certain musical characteristics that differentiate the original compositions from the remakes.

"Se acabo" and the other two originals are up-tempo tunes featuring driving rhythm section parts and extended solos. Conversely, the re-recordings of the classics are slower in tempo; in the case of "Lindo yambu," the tempo is significantly slower on the Palmieri version than on the original Septeto Nacional recording. The remakes follow many of the traditional formal structural elements (e.g., call and response) of their predecessors. Despite this adherence to traditional formal structures, the remakes all use the newer *salsa*-style *mambo* sections that the originals do not have. Although the *mambos* in the three remakes are on the simple side as *salsa mambos* go, they are nevertheless innovations that are nonexistent in the early prototypes. The reason that the original compositions (especially "Justicia" and "Se acabo") don't contain *mambos* is, perhaps, the highly improvisational nature of these songs, which contain numerous and lengthy solos and *montunos*. Once the *largo* section has made its transition into the *montuno* section in these pieces, the music jumps into a higher gear in terms of rhythmic drive, and a diversion into a *mambo* section would only impede the flow. In this case, the comparatively intense *moña* is more appropriate than the *mambo* for incorporating horn parts into the texture of the music.

Although "Bilongo," the third vocal piece on *Superimposition*, is a classic which had been recorded previously by a number of groups (most notably that of Tito Rodríguez), Palmieri's treatment of "Bilongo" is more characteristic of how he performs his own original compositions than how he covers other artists' material (e.g., that of Arsenio Rodríguez, etc.). "Bilongo" will be given an extensive analytical treatment in the next chapter.

Eddie Palmieri did not write "Se acabo" (unlike "Cintura" and "Justicia"); however, it was composed specifically for the group by one of the percussionists, Rudy Callzado. Of all the pieces examined here, "Se acabo" is one of the most dynamic. At the beginning, the two-three *clave* is applied with a high degree of rhythmic thrust by a piano/bass line and cowbells. This is followed, four measures later, by syncopated piano chords that lead to the *largo* section. The *largo* consists of a repeated eight-bar *coro* melody alternating with an eight-measure solo vocal that also repeats. The chorus part is over a cowbell-driven *tumbao* with carefully orchestrated horn parts. Dropping the cowbell, the solo singer performs over steady percussion with horn and *timbale* break figures. These breaks and the solo singing sections occur over an extended dominant harmony that resolves in the last two bars of the eight-measure section. The eighty-measure *largo*, which begins and ends with the chorus section, is followed by a four-measure break leading to the *montuno* section.

Built on a two-measure I-IV-V-I progression, the *montuno* pattern contains the *coro*-intoned "La malanga" in its second measure, alternating with the *sonero*. A brass *moña* and break introduce a brief *conga* solo by Eladio Perez. A trombone *moña* begins at the end of the *conga* solo and serves as a four-measure introduction to a trumpet solo by Armenteros. The entire eighty-measure solo is supported by a continuously evolving trombone *moña*. At first, the *moña* is performed by a single trombonist (Jose Rodrigues), who is later joined by another player (Lewis Kahn). The second trombonist plays a countermelody to the first, with both parts continuously changing until the end of the trumpet solo. A variety of *timbale* break patterns also supports Armenteros. His solo features a rich mix of virtuoso lines, syncopated rhythmic figures, and bravura high notes. The analysis in the next chapter of Armenteros' solo on "Bilongo" will examine his general approach to these elements in his solo style in more detail. In the final eight measures of the solo, the *coro* returns, followed shortly by the conclusion of the solo and the entry of the *sonero*. The *coro* and *sonero* continue until interrupted by a four-measure brass section coda.

Palmieri's "Pa' huele" is very similar to the Arsenio Rodríguez original. Written by Rodríguez, "Pa' huele" is a *son/montuno* with the emphasis on *montuno*. The entire composition is based on a two-measure IV-I-IV-V *montuno* pattern. A solo piano figure, very similar in nature to the type of *tres* introduction favored by Rodríguez, begins the recording. After four measures, the rest of the rhythm section joins the solo piano. After four more measures that conclude with a very modern-sounding, two-measure, lead-in figure, a four-measure *coro* enters and in effect announces that this piece will consist of a *montuno* section from beginning to end. In this case, brass figures alternate with the first few *coros* instead of the solo trumpet of the Rodríguez version. Both the Palmieri and the Rodríguez recordings eventually replace the horn responses with *soneros*.

A Palmieri piano solo follows the final *coro*. The solo ends with a rhythm section break that introduces the *mambo*. This break technique is the same as that used in "Lindo yambu" and "Si las nenas" to initiate their *mambos*. Although the singers don't usually take part in a *mambo* section, in this case, the *coro* comes in at the end of the break on the words "Pa' huele." This *coro* continues on the second bar of the two-measure *montuno* pattern. A unison horn section alternates with the short *coro* before the *mambo* gives way to a short trumpet solo over the continuing *coro*. The *sonero* replaces the trumpet solo and continues until a harmonized two-trombone *moña* enters and provides support for an Armenteros solo that is significantly longer than the earlier one. After several repeats of their harmonized *moña*, the trombonists divide into separate contrapuntal lines for the remainder of the solo. Armenteros provides a stellar performance on his solo and demonstrates why *Superimpostion* is one of the outstanding recordings in the trumpeter's catalog of solo performances.

With the short *coro* continuing, the *sonero* replaces the horns as the piece comes to its conclusion. The coda consists of two repetitions of the *mambo* horn part alternating with the short *coro*, followed by one final recitation of the original four-measure *coro* and a reprise of the rhythm section break from the beginning of the *mambo*. A final "Pa' huele" *coro* and an ensemble figure of two eighth notes conclude the piece.

NOTES

1. *Moña*—a short repetitive horn line (either written or improvised).

6

"BILONGO"

Although Eddie Palmieri's version of "Bilongo" was not the first or last recording of the standard song, it is one of the most renowned. The eight-measure introductory solo by Armenteros has become a classic in the New York *salsa* scene of the last two decades. Since this classic introduction was recorded, trumpet players frequently have played these eight measures when performing "Bilongo" live. The entire introduction in this recording is twelve measures in length; Armenteros' eight-measure solo comes in following a four-bar rhythm section vamp. When the *largo* starts in measure thirteen, Armenteros' role changes from soloist to accompanist. Behind the *sonero's* melody line, Armenteros performs embellishments in a virtuoso mellismatic style. Before discussing the brass playing in the first part of the recording, the *largo* structure of "Bilongo" will be described in detail, and an overview of the entire piece will be provided.

For the purposes of the *largo* melody analysis, the version of "Bilongo" printed in *The Latin Real Book*, published by Sher Music Company, will be the primary music source material. (See table 6.1. for timeline.)

Table 6.1. Time Line of "Bilongo"

Time-(min./sec.)	Section	Description
	Part A	
0:00	1. mm. 1–4	Rhythm section introduction.
0:05	2. mm. 5–12	Introductory trumpet solo.
0:15	3. mm. 13–28	*Largo*-section A.
0:35	4. mm. 29–33	Interlude with pickup measure.
0:45	5. mm. 34–40	*Largo*-section B. 3-2 *clave*.
0:52	6. mm. 41–48	*Largo*-section C. 2-3 *clave* with trombone background.
1:02	7. mm. 49–56	Repeat of section C with trumpet background.
1:12	8. mm. 57–61	Interlude with pickup measure.
1:22	9. mm. 62–68	*Largo*-section B. 3-2 *clave*.
	Part B	
1:29	1. mm. 69–72	1st *coro* with pickup.
1:34	2. mm. 73–76	1st *sonero*.
1:38	3. mm. 77–80	2nd *coro*.
1:43	4. mm. 81–84	2nd *sonero*.
1:48	5. mm. 85–88	3rd *coro*.
1:53	6. mm. 89–92	3rd *sonero*.
1:59	7. mm. 93–96	4th *coro*.
2:03	8. mm. 97–100	4th *sonero*.
2:09	9. mm. 101–104	5th *coro*.
2:14	10. mm. 105—108	5th *sonero*.
2:19	11. mm. 109–112	6th *coro*.
2:24	12. mm. 113–148	Piano solo.
3:08	13. mm. 149–152	Break.
	Part C	
3:13	M1. mm. 153–164	1st *moña* section.
3:29	M2. mm. 165–180	2nd *moña* section.
3:49	M3. mm. 181–200	3rd *moña* section.
4:14	M4. mm. 201–230	4th *moña* section.
4:50	M5. mm. 231–236	5th *moña* section.
	Part D	
4:58	1. mm. 237–240	*Sonero*.
5:03	2. mm. 241–244	*Coro*.
5:08	3. mm. 245–248	*Sonero*.
5:13	4. mm. 249–252	*Coro*.
5:18	5. mm. 253–268	Horns.

As presented in the Sher Music edition, "Bilongo" was written by Guillermo Rodríguez Fiffé and originally published in 1957 by the Peer International Corporation. In the nomenclature of the Sher version, the *largo* corresponds to the section from letter A to letter E in the published manuscript. The Sher Music imprint indicates that the arrangement as published represents the Tito Rodríguez version of "Bilongo."

The version of "Bilongo" on the Palmieri recording differs considerably from the Sher Music lead sheet in terms of musical arrangement. While the *largo* sections of the two versions directly correspond in length, the improvisatory aspects of the Quintana vocal create significant variations between the written and recorded melodies.

In this chapter, only the examples that refer to the melody of the "Bilongo" *largo* (see figures 6.1, 6.2, 6.4, and 6.5) will be notated exactly as they appear in the published manuscript. The chord symbols accompanying the melody in the notation examples represent the basic underlying harmony on the recording and have been stripped of the numerous embellishing chords present in the arrangement published by Sher Music.

While the melodic aspects of the *largo* section will be discussed using the published version as a reference, elements of Palmieri's recorded arrangement of the *largo* have been transcribed and will be introduced as they apply, especially in the discourse on the interlude section.

The fifty-six measure *largo* section consists of four vocal sections and two interludes (figure 6.1).

The first vocal section (A) is eight bars in length and is immediately repeated. A five-bar interlude section follows and introduces the second vocal section (B), which is seven measures in length and proceeds directly into another vocal section (C). Section C is a variation in B♭ major (the relative major) of section A. A reprise of the initial interlude and section B ends the *largo* section.

Bilongo—Largo

Figure 6.1. "Bilongo": The *largo* section

The somewhat unusual form of the *largo* section of "Bilongo" is one of the reasons for its popularity. The "Bilongo" *largo* is a case study in *clave* shifting. The practice of switching from one form of *clave* to another (e.g., from two-three to three-two or vice versa) usually occurs during a *mambo* section or in the introduction or coda. However, as relatively rarely as *clave* shifting occurs in a *largo* section, "Bilongo" manages to shift *clave* four times before the *montuno* section begins. Each of the four uneven measured sections switches the *clave* to its counterpart. The prevailing *clave* of "Bilongo" is two-three, and the *largo* A section reflects that configuration. It is the first five-measure interlude that creates the first shift to three-two. While the B section has a strong three-two feeling, its seven-measure length returns the *clave* back to two-three for the C section. This sixteen-measure section in the relative major key is followed by another five-measure *clave* changing interlude. Three-two is presented for the final time in a reprise of section B, which, due to its seven-measure length, returns the *clave* to the two-three that prevails for the duration of the recording.

Following the introduction, the vocal part starts the *largo* with an eighth-note pickup on the last half beat of m. 12. This first section (A) is a repeated eight-measure vocal melody over a basic G minor chord progression (figure 6.2).

Figure 6.2.   "Bilongo": The *largo* A section

In this case, the progression begins with three measures of tonic harmony. In the fourth measure, the dominant harmony takes over for four measures before returning to G minor in the final measure of this section. Each four-measure phrase consists of two melody modules. The second phrase is a repetition of the first phrase but a diatonic step higher in pitch.

Motion in thirds is the main melodic characteristic of the first module. Following an initial ascent from the pickup B♭4, the tonic chord is outlined in descending movement from D5 to G4. A quarter-note and two eighth-note repetitions of the D5 fill the first two beats of the module. The motive, consisting of the eighth-note pickup leap to a quarter- and two eighth-note repeated figures on the first two beats of the phrase, is the most important feature of the "Bilongo" melody. In the fifty-six measure *largo*, this figure occurs eight times. Six of those times, the four-note figure is followed by a descent to the third below the repeated notes. Even the phrase openings in "Bilongo" that do not exactly reflect this motive are very similar. Two B♭4s follow, including a quarter note on beat three and an eighth note on beat four, which leads to a syncopated tonic note on the second half of the same beat, which sustains into the following measure.

The second module in the first phrase starts out like the first, with an ascending movement from B♭4 to D5 (in this case with a passing note C5). However, the characteristic movement in this module is stepwise instead of by thirds. After two quarter notes (D5 and C5) on the first two beats and an eighth-note B♭4 on beat three, the line reverses to an upbeat quarter-note C5 before descending a minor third to A4, which introduces the dominant harmony and ends the phrase. Although the second phrase is melodically a sequence of the first transposed a diatonic step higher, the first module arpeggiates down on the upper chord extensions of the dominant harmony starting on the minor ninth and going through the seventh and fifth. Aside from its harmonic implications and step-size adjustments to conform to the diatonic implications of the key center (and one or two embellishment notes), the second half of the section is identical to the first, half albeit a step higher.

The first interlude section is introduced in the final measure of the repeated A section. The transcription of Palmieri's recorded version will be used in the analysis of the interlude (figure 6.3).

Figure 6.3. "Bilongo": The *largo* interlude

In m. 28, the final vocal note (Bb4) on the first beat is followed by a series of one-measure break figures that strongly emphasizes the fourth beat of each measure. The final break measure is followed by a measure-long pickup vocal figure to section B in m. 33. In m. 28, the entire break figure is performed by the horns, piano, and bass, with the percussion joining in on the fourth beat. Starting on the second half of the first beat, an eighth-note G minor triad ascends to a quarter-note G on beat three and an F quarter note on beat four, which introduces the F dominant seventh harmony of m. 29.

This same pattern is sequenced in the following four measures. In these measures, however, the first part of the figure is performed by solo piano, with the rest of the ensemble entering on the fourth beat. In mm. 28–30, this fourth beat is a quarter note. An Eb major harmony is introduced in m. 30 and the dominant D harmony in m. 31. In mm. 31 and 32, the ensemble's answer to the initial piano arpeggio is a three-note figure repetition of the D harmony, consisting of two eighth notes on the fourth beat followed by a quarter note on the first beat of the following measure. The last hit on the first beat of m. 33 is followed by the pickup vocal figure of the B section.

Although still in G minor, the progression in section B is different than the one in section A (figure 6.4). Here, the progression starts with two measures of the dominant harmony (continued from the interlude) before resolving to G minor in the second half of the phrase. The second phrase in the B section starts out the same as the first, but because the section is seven bars in length, the resolution part of the phrase is truncated to one measure. In

Figure 6.4.   "Bilongo":The *largo* B section

the first case (m. 40), the G minor harmonic rhythm is shortened even further by the insertion of an F dominant harmony in the last two beats of the measure, which facilitates the transposition to the key of B♭ major in the C section.

Each phrase in section B consists of two melodic modules. Including the anacrusis measure, the first module is two measures in length, while the second module is five beats in length, followed by three beats of rest. Both modules in the first phrase begin with two upbeat A4s, the first starting on the second half of beat one. Likewise, both lines continue with a minor third ascent to C5 on the third beat. In the first case, the C5 is repeated a half beat later and followed by two upbeats on D5; the second, an eighth note returning to C5 on the second beat of m. 34. After a brief descent to A4 on the second half of this beat, the module ends with a halfnote C5. In the second module, the C5 that follows the initial two As is a quarter note and helps to emphasize the two-side of the *clave*. A B♭4-D5-B♭4 movement resumes the syncopation and ends the module on the second half of the first beat concurrent with the resolution to tonic in m. 36.

With the exception of the pickup bar and the truncated ending, the second phrase of section B is identical to the first. The pickup figure in the second phrase is a step higher because it takes place over the tonic harmony rather than the dominant, as in the initial phrase.

Following the half-note F dominant harmony at the end of the seven-measure B section, "Bilongo" again reverses *clave* to twothree and modulates to B♭ major for the C section (figure 6.5).

Figure 6.5. "Bilongo": The *largo* C section

Harmonically, the C section corresponds directly to the G minor A section. Adjusting for tonal and modal differences, both sections have many melodic similarities. The initial four-note motivic figure that begins both phrases in section A is also used to initiate both phrases in section C. In the first phrase, this four-note figure is followed by melodic material that differs significantly from its counterpart in section A.

In reality, these differences have little bearing on the Palmieri recording, since the Ismael Quintana vocal interpretation is highly improvisatory. On his rendition, the initial phrase of section C more closely follows the melodic contour of phrase one in section A rather than the section C published equivalent. Because of the strong oral component in Afro-Cuban music, any melodic analysis will be completely relevant only to a particular performance or written version. However, as jazz researchers have shown (Baker 1969; Coker 1986), it is always useful to examine the original source material when analyzing an interpretation.

Instead of dropping a third after the initial four-note figure, as in all other instances, the line in the first phrase of section C ascends from F5 to a G5 quarter note on beat three of m. 41. On the fourth beat, the line returns to F5, which becomes the focal point for the remainder of the phrase. In m. 42, the suspended F5 initiates a quarter-note triplet figure that skips down a perfect fourth to C5 and ascends a step to D5, the final member of the triplet. The D5 then skips to G5 on beat three and F5 on beat four, imitating the previous measure. In m. 43, the quarter-note triplet motif is repeated, with the D5-E♭5-D5 triplet returning to the prevailing F5 one last time for a beat and a half before a final C5 in the last half beat of the measure.

Melodically, the second phrase of section C is almost identical to the second phrase of A. In this case, the melody has not joined the harmony in the minor-third leap from G minor to B♭ major; the one significant melodic difference between the two phrases is the two-beat-long F4 that starts on the upbeat of two in m. 46. This F in the melody helps emphasize the dominant harmony of B♭ major.

After a repetition of the C section, the original five-measure interlude (see figure 6.3) returns, complete with break figures between piano and ensembles. As before, the interlude's odd number of measures changes the *clave* around for the final B section (see figure 6.4). Likewise, this three-two-powered section ends the *largo* by using its seven-measure form to introduce the *montuno* section and to return (for the last time in the piece) to the two-three *clave*.

Before addressing the trumpet playing in the introduction and *largo* in detail, a perfunctory description of the remaining overall formal structure of the recorded performance will be presented. Some portions of the *montuno* section (most notably the trumpet solo and trombone *moñas*) also will be analyzed in greater depth following this overview.

The *montuno* pattern of "Bilongo" is based on one of the most common chord progressions in *salsa*: the only harmonic movement in this progression is the time-honored dominant-tonic shift. In "Bilongo," the four-measure pattern begins with a tonic G minor chord in the first measure. The dominant harmony is performed for the middle two measures of the pattern before returning to G minor for the final measure. At times, a subdominant or supertonic harmony is inserted in the second measure of the progression.

The *montuno* section begins immediately following the *largo*, with a four-measure *coro* that starts initially with a three-note pickup figure in the final measure of the seven-measure B section (figure 6.6).

Figure 6.6. "Bilongo": The *montuno* and *coro* pattern

The initial *coro* figure (which includes the three pickup notes and the note on the first beat of the following measure) is common to both the published and recorded versions. However, the two versions of the *coro* vary after that point. The recorded version will be used in this portion of the analysis.

The Palmieri *coro* is a harmonized vocal line consisting of two repetitions of a seven-note rhythm cell on the text "Quiquibu mandinga." On the repetition, the notes of the cell change to reflect the change of harmony. In the first instance, the three pickup notes of the lead voice, all D4, are rhythmically situated on the upbeats of two and three and the downbeat of four in the fourth measure of the *montuno* progression. The quarter note on the first beat of the *montuno* is also a D4 and completes the initial figure in the cell. The three notes of the second half of the cell are on the upbeats of three and four in the first measure of the pattern and the upbeat of one in the second measure. Reflecting the change to dominant, the lead melody performs C4, E♭4, and C4 on these upbeats.

The cell begins anew one beat later. This time the first four-note figure is on C4 in the lead voice, which is the seventh of the dominant D harmony. As the harmony resolves back to G minor, the final three notes of this cell are B♭4, D4, and B♭4. In the universal *son* tradition, the *coro* trades *montuno* patterns with the solo singer. For the first forty-four measures of the *montuno* section, the call and response between *coro* and *sonero* continues until the piano solo begins in m. 113. In all, there are six *coros* and five *soneros* in this section.

As often happens in Afro-Cuban music, the boundary between the *coro/sonero* sections is blurred by a constant overlapping of the parts. This overlapping is the result of two factors: the relatively long pickup figure of the *coro* blurs the beginning of the *montuno*; and the *soneros*, as sung by Quintana, always start during the last half of the *coro* section. Thus, the sections cannot be divided evenly along *montuno* boundaries; in one case, the *sonero* starts immediately following the beginning of the *coro*.

Beginning in m. 113, Palmieri plays a short piano solo that is simple but elegant in its conception. This piano solo section is thirty-six measures in length and can be divided into two distinct parts. The first twenty-bar section of the solo is notable for its use of repetition. The final sixteen measures of the solo consist of four repetitions of a four-measure figure that is very *moña*-like. Although the figure that Palmieri performs in the first phrase of the solo is complex rhythmically and melodically, it is sequenced in the following two phrases. In the second four-bar phrase, the figure is played a step lower. The third phrase is an exact repetition of the first. The final two *montuno* phrases of the first twenty-measure part of the solo provide contrasting material and also present some of the modern jazz–influenced chord voicings and scales that Eddie Palmieri is noted for introducing into the *salsa* lexicon.

Similar in concept to the *coro*, the repeated four-measure piano figure in the final sixteen measures also is made up of two repetitions of a two-measure rhythm cell (figure 6.7).

Figure 6.7. **"Bilongo": Piano figure**

In this case, the cell consists of eight notes. As in the *coro*, the pitch of the notes are altered to reflect the changing harmonic progression. Also as in the *coro*, the melody line is harmonized a third lower. The harmony line here is doubled by the left hand an octave lower. Due to the length of the pickup figure (almost one full measure), the phrase structure is opposite to the *montuno* pattern. The first cell begins on the fourth measure of the progression with upbeats on all four beats. In the lead voice, the notes are B♭4 on the second part of beat one and D5s on all the other upbeats. The second half of the cell consists of two dotted quarter- and eighth-note patterns. In the lead melody, the first two notes are C5s, and the second two are B♭4s. The cell repeats in the second measure of the *montuno*. In this instance, the melody is transposed a step higher. During the final part of the piano solo, the continuous repetition of the two-measure cell gradually increases the rhythmic intensity.

In the final bar of the solo (m. 48), two Ds are performed on the upbeat of three and the downbeat of four and lead to a four-measure break consisting of non-stop eighth notes. The bass and piano perform D unisons for the entire four measures. The *bongosero* drops his *bongós* and picks up the cowbell, and he and the other percussionists all perform the continuous eighth-note break. When the break finishes and the trombone *moña* begins the trumpet solo section, the *timbalero* has also abandoned the polite *cascara* figure that accompanied the piano solo and switches to his fixed bell. This creates the familiar two-cowbell *montuno* that is typical of New York *salsa* and effects a high-energy drive when combined with the syncopated *moñas* and the trumpet solo.

This *moña*/solo part is eighty-four measures in length and contains a continuously shifting *moña* under an improvised solo by Armenteros. Like the brass playing in the beginning and *largo*, this section will be deferred for analysis until this overview of the entire piece is completed. The *sonero* reenters in the final *montuno* pattern of the trumpet solo and initiates two alternations of *sonero/coro* patterns starting on m. 237. Following the second *coro*, the brass section enters playing the *coro* line, which it performs four times. The last note of the figure is left off the final time, and the piece ends in the next measure with the entire group playing a two-note figure (melodically, these two notes are D and G) on the upbeat of two and the downbeat of four.

INTRODUCTION

When Armenteros (starting in m. 5) performs one of the most famous eight-measure trumpet moments in Afro-Cuban music history, he provides a simple and elegant exercise in playing over *clave* on a G minor harmony (figure 6.8).

Figure 6.8.   "Bilongo": Trumpet introduction

In the first four measures of the solo, the rhythmic and melodic material performed by Armenteros is contained almost totally in the first two measures of the phrase. The second half of the phrase (mm. 7–8) consists solely of a sustained B♭4. In mm. 5–6, a note is played on the second half of every beat in the two measures. The B♭4 on beat two of m. 5 is the only nonsyncopation performed in the entire four-measure phrase.

Melodically, the phrase contains only the chord tones of the G minor triad between G4 and D5. Starting on the upbeat of one, G4 initiates the triadic ascension to the D5 on the second half of the beat using the aforementioned B♭4 as a go-between. These three notes are the first instance of a rhythmic cell consisting of three eighth notes starting on an upbeat. This cell is repeated throughout the second half of the trumpet introduction and the vocal background. The six upbeats following this cell contain a repeated D5, a descent to B♭4 and G4, a reprise of the repeated D5s, and the final extended B♭4. Rhythmically, the phrase is begun slightly behind the prevailing tempo, before moving to the front of the beat by the second half of beat three in m. 5. This rhythmic placement continues until the final two notes, which are slightly delayed.

The prolonged G minor harmony continues in the second phrase of the introductory trumpet solo (mm. 9–12). However, the solo part in this phrase is quite different from the initial solo. In addition to having twice as many notes, the musical activity is extensive throughout the first three measures of this phrase and only subsides on the final D4, which sustains through most of m. 12. This phrase covers a much wider pitch range than the first phrase; instead of the narrow perfect fifth bandwidth of the first phrase, this part of the solo encompasses an impressive range of an octave and a minor sixth from D4 to B♭5. Harmonic and melodic elements are also much more complicated in this phrase than in the earlier one. Although all of the notes in the first four measures of the solo are contained within the G minor triad, the second phrase contains several nonharmonic tones. Not only is this melody linear rather than arpeggiated, like the first part; there are a number of chromatically altered notes as well. Despite the increased complexities, the unity of the phrase is provided by the continued repetition of the three-note rhythmic cell that opened the solo. In the first two beats of m. 9, the first of these cells consists of two D5s on the second half of beats one and two surrounding a chromatically altered lower-neighbor C♯5 on beat two. The following three notes start a linear ascent of E5, F♯5, and G5. Because the first two notes are chromatically altered from the natural minor scale and harmonically represent the major sixth and major seventh of the underlying G minor tonality, there is an increase in harmonic dissonance. In the following cell, on the first two beats of m. 10, the intensity of the music is enhanced in different ways. Only one of the three notes is a chordal tone (the B♭5 on beat two). The A5 on the upbeat of one is the ninth of the harmony, and the major seventh again sounds with the F♯5 on the upbeat of two. Another factor that intensifies the music is the movement into the high range of the trumpet, which climaxes with the B♭5 on beat two.

The final two repetitions of the three-note rhythmic figure quickly lowers the range to G4 on the second half of beat two in

m. 11. A support of this abatement in the intensity that was created in the first part of this phrase is the return to a more consonant environment, in which the major ninth is the only nonchord tone present in the final part of the phrase. Although the ninth (A5) on the upbeat of three in m. 10 initiates this rapid descent, the notes G5, D5, and B♭4 that follow it outline the underlying harmony. On beat two of m. 11, an A4 and G4 complete the final repetition of the three-note rhythmic cell in the introduction. The two eighth notes (A4 and G4) are immediately repeated on beat three before the descent to the final sustained D4 that starts on the second half of beat four in m. 12. Although the first three-note figure is slightly behind the tempo, most of the phrase is firmly in front of the beat. The only exceptions are the final three notes of the phrase, in which the time is subtly delayed.

VOCAL ACCOMPANIMENT

Following the entrance of the vocal in m. 13, Armenteros switches roles from soloist to accompanist. Before addressing Armenteros' work in detail, it will be useful to briefly describe the entire section in general terms.

The repeated sixteen-measure A section (mm. 13–36) is notable for the gradual increase in complexity of the trumpet solo material. While tonal dissonance was an important factor in the development of the introductory solo, range and rhythmic density are the intensifying factors in the trumpet solo work in the A section. Neither interlude contains trumpet improvisation. However, the solo material in both B sections is very similar in terms of linear movement. For the first eight measures of the C section, Armenteros relinquishes solo control to the trombone of José Rodrigues. The second half of this section is an Armenteros interpretation of the "Mexican Hat Dance." The final B section (and its virtuoso trumpet figures) ends the *largo* and introduces the *montuno*.

In m. 14, a measure after the entrance of the lead vocalist, Armenteros echoes the initial figure of his own solo introduction (figure 6.9).

Figure 6.9.   "Bilongo":Trumpet background section AI

Aside from their displacement to the other side of the *clave* and the substitution of E♭5 for D5 on the second half of beat two, the first three beats of m. 14 are identical to those of m. 5. Because the D5 that initiates on the second half of beat three in m. 14 is held into the next measure, the only note that originates in m. 15 is the eighth-note B4 on the last half beat of the measure. Like the first measure of this phrase, a maximum amount of space is allocated in m. 15 for the *sonero* without interference from the trumpet solo. Even though little of the remaining background trumpet solo material is as sparse as in this first phrase, Armenteros' playing is always complementary to the *sonero*.

The final part of the first phrase starts with the prevailing three-note cell, this time starting on a B4 on the upbeat of four in m. 15. This altered tone leads to the beat-one C5-seventh interval of the newly arrived dominant harmony (in m. 16) and then completes the cell with a major ninth E5 on the upbeat, followed by the minor ninth E♭5 on beat two. The harmonic ambiguity is continued with an escape tone–like figure on the last one and a half beats of m. 16. Two G4s on the upbeats of three and four surround a B♭4 on beat four. The second G4 moves through a G♯4 on the last quarter beat of the measure to resolve on an A4 half note in m. 17. This four-note figure can be interpreted as a rhythmic alteration of the main cell.

Yet another example of the three-note cell is the descending arpeggio in the last two beats of m. 17 on the seventh (C5), fifth (A4), and the third (F♯4); the line continues to descend to C4 on the first beat of m. 19. This descent is not straightforward. Before the D4 quarter note on beat four of m. 18 is reached, there is a sixteenth-note embellishment on the third beat. In addition to adding melodic variation, this sixteenth-note figure increases the rhythmic complexity of the music. Beginning with the two eighth notes (C4 and D4) on beat one of m. 19, the rhythmic intensification continues on beat two as the line ascends rapidly in sixteenth notes to the B♭4 eighth note on beat three. Briefly descending to G4 (embellished with A4 on beat four), the phrase ends in m.20 with an eighth-note B♭4 on beat one and an extended D5 a half beat later. These notes represent a return to the G minor tonic harmony.

The repeat of the A section starts with yet another example of the three-note cell (figure 6.10).

Figure 6.10.   "Bilongo": Trumpet background section A2

In this case, Armenteros treats the C♯5 on the upbeat of one in m. 21 as a chromatically altered embellishing glissando to the D5 on the second beat, ascending a perfect fourth to G5 a half beat later. A repetition of this interval occurs on the upbeats of three and four. A descending version of the cell takes place in a return to D5 on the upbeat of one in m. 22 that continues downward with a B♭4 and A4 on beat two. On the third beat, the G returns, although in this case an octave lower. The G4 is repeated on the upbeat of four, following F♯4 and A4 embellishing neighbor tones. The G-D fourth relationship is reestablished when D4 is sounded on beat one in m. 23 and

G4 a beat and a half later. The F♯4 and A4 that surround the fourth-beat G4 set up the change to the dominant structure in m. 24. A final confirmation of the prominence of the D note in the melodic structure of this phrase is its final appearance as a sustained D5 starting on the second half of beat two in m. 24. It is directly preceded by B♭4 and E♭5 eighth notes. These two notes also reprise the perfect fourth motif from the first part of the phrase.

A feature of the final phrase in the A section is an increase in the rhythmic density of the solo trumpet part. Much of this increased activity occurs in the first and third measures of the phrase and overlaps the singer's line, in direct contrast to the first half of the A section, where the singer was avoided. It is a tribute to the musicality of Armenteros and Quintana that their complex lines fit together so smoothly. The trumpet solo in this final part of the A section is similar in melodic shape to the previous phrase. However, instead of rhythmically and intervalically separated syncopated notes, the final phrase contains a stepwise linear approach with quick, continuous rhythmic groupings. Following the initial D5 in m. 25, there is a sixteenth-note descending scale between F5 on the upbeat of two to A4 on beat four.

In the written example, the six-note figure starting on beat four in m. 25 is notated using dotted eight and sixteenth notes; it could just as easily have been written out in eighth notes. Neither notational version is a completely accurate representation of what is really going on in the solo. In all of the musical examples, the true rhythmic subtleties can be understood and appreciated only through a thorough listening to the recorded versions. A4 is the anchoring melodic factor in this six-note module. Although the line moves first to C5 and then to G4 and F♯4, it always returns to the A4. The three-note rhythmic cell returns with C4-E♭4-D4, starting on the upbeat of four in m. 26. Starting on the second beat of m. 27, an ascending version of the sixteenth-note line from m. 25 connects C4 to B♭4 on the second half of beat three. In addition to being inverted, the line starts a half beat earlier in the measure than the earlier version. Two sixteenth notes (F♯4 and A4) and an eighth note (G4) on the fourth beat of m. 27 make this measure the densest rhythmically up to this point. In the final measure of the A section, Armenteros stops his improvisation and joins with the trombone and the rhythm section in starting the interlude section. In the first two beats of m. 28, the brass section and the pianist play an ascending arpeggio using the prevailing cell. In the trumpet part, these notes are G4, B♭4, and D5. These three notes are followed by quarter notes G5 on beat three and F5 on beat four. In the following four measures, only the pianist performs the arpeggio figure on the first three beats of each measure. In these measures, the horn players enter on the fourth beat. An isolated quarter note is performed on beat four in m. 29 (E♭5) and m. 30 (D5). In mm. 31–33, the brass section performs a three-note figure on D5 consisting of two eighth notes on beat four and a quarter note on beat one of the following measure.

As mentioned earlier, both seven-measure, B-section background trumpet solos are similar in their general linear shape. Both solos start on D4 and rise linearly, using the ascending version of the G melodic minor scale (with E and F♯) to B♭5, and then descend almost two octaves before eventually returning to B♭4 and the middle range. However, the manner in which these two solo sections go about achieving these results is completely different.

Most of the variations between the two B-section solos are created through rhythmic means. Remarkably, the two solos are melodically identical for the first fifteen notes. Although both solos ascend from D4 to B♭5 and return linearly to G5 in exactly the same way, there is a significant difference in how the notes are realized rhythmically. The second B section (see figure 6.14) is denser rhythmically than the first one. Because the first B section starts with mostly syncopated quarter notes instead of the continuous eighth notes of the second one, the progression of the melodic line occurs earlier in the second B version. In the second B section, the melodic progression from the initial D4 to the high note B♭5 is completed by the upbeat of one in the third measure of the phrase (m. 64). In the first B section solo, the B♭5 is not reached until the first beat of the fourth measure (m. 37). A detailed analysis of each B section will appear as those sections occur.

Emphasizing the change to three-two *clave*, Armenteros starts the initial B section with a D4 on the upbeat of two and E4 on the fourth beat (figure 6.11).

Figure 6.11. "Bilongo": Trumpet background section B1

Following this most characteristic of three-side rhythms, the ascending line continues in m. 35 with four consecutive upbeat quarter notes. The fourth of these is a B♭4 on the upbeat of four. After briefly announcing the change to the G minor tonic harmony, the B♭4 yields to a continuation of the ascending scale. Starting on the upbeat of two in m. 36, C5, D5, and E5 are performed as three eighth notes (the opening cell). A series of quarter-note triplets is initiated in the second half of m. 36 with the final three-note ascent (F♯5-G5-A5) to the B♭5 on the first beat of m. 37. The triplets then reverse direction and descend with A5, G5, D5, and B♭4 before leaping up to F5 on the final quarter-note triplet in m. 37.

Beginning in m. 38 with the E5 on the upbeat of one and an eighth-note triplet (E♭5-F5-E♭5) on beat two, a bebop-like line starts the final descent to the D4 on the second half of beat three in m. 39. All of the notes between the triplet and the D4 are eighth notes starting with D5, C5, B♭4, and A4 on the third and fourth beats of m. 38. In m. 39, the scalar movement ends on an F♯4, on the upbeat of one, that is prolonged by being repeated after a brief return to the higher A4. Following the final two eighth notes (E♭4 and D4), this part of the solo trumpet ends with a minor sixth leap to the quarter-note Bb4 on beat four and the final G4 on beat one of m. 40, as the harmony returns to the tonic in the last measure of the truncated three-measure phrase.

Trombonist Jose Rodrigues takes over the role of soloist from Armenteros for the first eight measures of the C section (figure 6.12).

Figure 6.12.   "Bilongo":Trombone section C1

The trombone solo begins in the last measure of the B section with a Bb arpeggio (Bb4-D4-F4) that heralds the change to the relative major key. Interestingly, the arpeggio that starts on the upbeat of one in m. 40 uses the same rhythmic cell that played such an important part in the trumpet introduction and the beginning half of Armenteros' accompaniment. Even though the note on the upbeat of three in the pickup bar is a G4 that extends into m. 41, most of the trombone melody throughout this solo consists of arpeggiated chord tones. In the first seven measures, the only non-chord tone is G4, and although it is a significant melodic presence, its harmonic importance is innocuous in Bb major; it is the root of G minor, but it can be absorbed into the relative major key as the ninth of the dominant and the major sixth of the tonic. After the G4 in m. 41, a chordal melody of five eighth notes starts on an upbeat of two F4. A downward leap to D4 returns to F4 before another D4 on the fourth beat descends to Bb3.

On beat two of m. 42, the D4 starts an ascending eighth-note figure through the Bb triad to Bb4 on beat three and a downward step to the major seventh A4 a half beat later. The harmonically static G4 dominates the next six beats, becoming a ninth of the F dominant in m. 44 before the arpeggio motif returns with three sequences of a two-beat module that includes an ascending third melodic movement and an eighth-note/dotted quarter-note rhythmic cell. Starting on beat two of m. 44, the first module consists of the fifth (C4) and seventh (E♭4) of the dominant seventh harmony. On beat four, the second version of the module consists of A3 and C4 (the third and fifth). On beat two of m. 45, the final module consists of the F3 root and the A3 third.

As the dominant harmony continues in mm. 46–47, Rodrigues continues his swinging chordal style of soloing. Starting on the second half of beat two, the original three-note cell is performed using the root (F3), third (A3), and fifth (C4), continuing upward to the seventh (E♭4) on the upbeat of four. The D4 on the upbeat of three in m. 47 anticipates the return to the B♭ tonic harmony in m. 48. Rodrigues finishes his solo in m. 48 with his only blatantly nonharmonic tone. This beat-one leading-tone C♯4 quickly resolves to the tonic chord third (D4) a half beat later. The trombone solo finishes with the second beat eighth notes G4 and D4 and quarter notes F4 and E♭4 on beats three and four.

Overlapping the last two trombone notes in m. 48 is the reentry of Armenteros (figure 6.13).

Figure 6.13. "Bilongo":Trumpet background section C2

Starting on F4 with a three eighth-note, second-inversion, ascending-B♭-triad pickup on the last beat and a half of the measure, Armenteros launches into a version the "Mexican Hat Dance." In this case, the triple meter of the original melody is changed into a series of eighth notes accented every third note.

In m. 49, the melody consists of a descending root position B♭ chord (F5, D5, and B♭4), with each chord tone moving to a lower-neighbor tone and back before moving to the next chord tone. In the first two cases, the E5 and the C♯5 are chromatic alterations; in the last half beat of four, the A4 is the major seventh of the underlying harmony. This A4 returns to a quarter-note B♭4 on beat one of m. 50 that drops to F4 on beat two. Instead of straight triplets, the ascending line of the "Mexican Hat Dance" melody is realized with three repetitions of a cell consisting of two eighth notes and a quarter note. The first instance of the cell starts with eighth notes D4 and E♭4 on the fourth beat of m. 50 followed by a quarter-note F4 on beat one of m. 51. On beats two and three, the cell contains G4, A4, and B♭4. The final repetition of the cell contains C5 and D5 eighth notes on the fourth beat and the quarter-note E♭5 on beat one of m. 52. A C5 on beat two follows the final repetition of the cell.

The first part of the second half of the "Mexican Hat Dance" melody is a sequence, a diatonic step lower, of its counterpart in the first half. In this case, the descending arpeggio is the seventh, fifth, and third of the dominant harmony. As opposed to in the opening line, here the initial lower-neighbor note is diatonic, while the following two are chromatically altered. This entire melody section is rhythmically displaced by one beat. In the first phrase (m. 49), the "Mexican Hat Dance" melody begins on the first beat of the measure. Its sequence begins on beat four of m. 52 a beat earlier in the phrase structure. In this case, the final note of the melody is F4 on the first beat of m. 54.

It is the final segment of the "Mexican Hat Dance" melody that receives the highest level of embellishment. After three successive F5 eighth notes starting on the second half of beat three in m. 54, there is a descending diminution of the ascending cell figure from mm. 50–52. Instead of two eighth notes and a quarter note, this version of the cell consists of two sixteenth notes and an eighth note.

Following the last note of the melody on a beat-one B♭4, the interlude is reintroduced the same way as before, with the exception
of an F4 on the upbeat of one in m. 56 substituting for the G4 in
m. 28. This subtle difference reflects the underlying harmony. In
m. 28, the G4 signifies the minor tonic, while in m. 56 the F4 is the
fifth of the relative major. Aside from the first note, this interlude
is exactly the same as the initial version.

Starting on the third beat of m. 62 in the last B section (figure 6.14), the ascending G melodic minor scale proceeds from D4
to B♭5 as it did in the first B section.

Figure 6.14.   "Bilongo":Trumpet background section B2

Here, the rhythmic motion is denser than before. A quarter-note
triplet initiates the line with D4, E4, and F♯4. Beginning on G4 and
ending on G5, the complete ascending melodic minor scale is realized in eighth notes in m. 63. This stream of eighth notes continues
throughout mm. 64–65. A5 is the dominant note of m. 64. In the
underlying G minor harmony, this note is the ninth of the chord. A5
on the first beat moves to B♭5 (the highest note in this B section) before returning to A5 on the second beat. The line descends to F♯5
on beat three before returning to A5 for the final time on the upbeat of three. On beat four, a descending fourth effects a register
shift, and the first four notes of m. 65 are a repetition (an octave
lower) of the four notes starting on the upbeat of one in m. 64. The
eighth notes in the last two beats of m. 65 are buried in the ensemble and difficult to hear. However, D4 on the first beat of m. 66 reflects the change to the dominant harmony. Beat two contains two
eighth notes; the first is an ascent to the minor ninth E♭4 and the

second a return to D4. The following six eighth notes outline the minor ninth dominant chord, starting with the seventh on beat three. This arpeggiation contrasts with the stepwise linearity of most of the trumpet solo work in this section. A dotted-quarter-note D5 on beat two of m. 67 follows the sixth eighth note (the minor ninth). The entire *largo* ends with a final version of the three-note rhythm cell that opened the trumpet introduction. In this case, the notes are B♭4, C5, and A4, resolving to a final B♭4 and the last tonic harmony of the *largo* section. Throughout the second half of the C section and the final B section, the trombonist supports the trumpet solo with rhythmic pedal-like figures.

PART C—THE SOLO/MOÑA

After the final sixteen measures of the piano solo section (four repetitions of a four-measure piano vamp—figure 6.7) and a four-measure break, Rodrigues starts a *moña* figure in m. 153. Following the *montuno* pattern, this *moña* is four measures in length. For the first two and a half repetitions of this *moña*, Armenteros performs a counter-*moña* before starting his improvisation. Rodrigues plays throughout this eighty-three-measure solo/*moña* section, and there are five distinctive trombone *moñas*. For the purposes of this analysis, the solo/*moña* part will use each change in *moña* to delineate a section. While this method of division is artificial, in that the only real underlying formal structure in the *montuno* of "Bilongo" is the four-measure *montuno*, it is helpful to establish formal signposts at larger structural intervals than the four-bar phrase when analyzing the solo. In this case, the use of the trombone *moña* change as a structuring device is supported in that Armenteros' solo part seems also to change gears at each new *moña* section boundary.

Multi-*montuno moña* sections create a framework over which the foreground trumpet material can be examined with a widened field of perception. While most of this analysis will be at the cell, module, and phrase level, in music analysis it has always been considered useful to step back and examine a work at the middle and background levels. These arbitrary divisions by trombone *moña* will help to provide an overview perspective.

Before analyzing the trumpet solo, the five *moñas* will be discussed. After describing the *moña*-derived structure, each *moña* will be described in detail.

The M1 section is twelve measures in length and starts in m. 153. In m. 165, the second *moña* section (M2) begins and lasts for sixteen measures. Twenty measures in length, the third *moña* (M3) begins in m. 181. Measure 201 is the start of M4, which at thirty measures is the longest section. The final *moña* (M5) starts in m. 229 and finishes out the solo section seven measures later.

When describing these *moña* sections, foreground details are ignored. In reality, the transition between *moña* sections is not as clear-cut as indicated here; overlappings of one or more measures are the rule. Nevertheless, the sections will be determined using *montuno* boundaries. While ignored as structural elements, these transitional discrepancies will be described in more detail as the individual *moñas* are analyzed.

Section M1 (mm. 153–164) contains three repetitions of the first trombone *moña* (figure 6.15).

Figure 6.15. **"Bilongo": Section M1—trombone and trumpet** *moñas*

Against this, Armenteros performs a contrasting trumpet *moña* for the first eleven measures of the section before starting his improvisation in the twelfth bar. Rodrigues' opening *moña* contains every member of the *clave* except for the first rhythm on the three-side. The *moña* consists of a two-measure module and its repetition, which is altered to reflect the *montuno* chord progression. Although in some cases preceded by an eighth-note D3, the module otherwise begins with four ascending eighth notes starting on the second beat of the first *montuno* measure. This configuration emphasizes the second and third beats of the measure (the two-side of the *clave*). In both of the modules, these four notes move from G3 to E♭4. Although the first, third, and fourth notes (G3, C4, and E♭4) are identical in both modules, the second note reflects the change in harmony. In the first module, this note is the B♭3 third of the tonic harmony; in the module repetition, the A3 is the fifth of the dominant. Of the final five notes in the module, the first four are on the upbeat; the final D4 is on the fourth beat in the second measure of the module. Along with this final D4, the initial D4 on the upbeat of four in the first measure of the module and the E♭4 on the upbeat immediately preceding the final note of the module are identical in both modules. The upbeats of one and two in the second-module measure reflect the harmonic changes. The first version of the module is over the dominant chord and contains the pitches A3 (the fifth) and C4 (the seventh). A B♭3 is sounded twice on the two upbeats in the module's repetition and represents the third of the G minor tonic chord. Although the analysis of the trumpet improvisation will occur after this discussion of the *moñas*, the initial trumpet *moña* will be described here.

Like the other *moñas* in this recording, the trumpet counterpoint consists of repeated two-measure modules. As part of its contrapuntal nature, this module begins on the second and fourth measures of the *montuno* pattern and ends with two quarter notes (E♭5 and D5) on the first two beats of the first and third bars. The module is identical in both versions, with the exception of the first note. When performed over the dominant harmony, the module begins with an A4 on the upbeat of one. Over the tonic chord, the note is B♭4, which is the third of a G minor chord. Whether over tonic or dominant, the initial note is followed by the eighth notes C5 and D5 on beat two and quarter notes E♭5 and D5 on beats three and four, the quarter notes being repeated on the first and second beats of the next measure to end the module. The initial part of the trumpet *moña* is omitted at the beginning of the entire section, and the pickup to the trumpet improvisation replaces the final *moña*.

As Armenteros starts his solo, the trombone *moña* changes in m. 165, and the second section of part C begins (see figure 6.16).

Section M2 is sixteen measures in length and consists of four repetitions of the second trombone *moña* (figure 6.16).

Figure 6.16. **"Bilongo": Section M2—trombone** *moña*

This *moña* is a variation of the first one. The first measure of each module is exactly the same in both *moñas*. However, the second measure of the module in the M2 *moña* is a simplified version of its counterpart in the first *moña*. Instead of the three upbeats and quarter note of the first *moña*, the second measure of this *moña* consists of two notes; over the dominant chord, these notes are an A3 on the second half of beat one and a dotted-half-note C4. On the tonic harmony, these notes are G3 and B♭3. The first iteration of the second *moña* varies slightly from the other repetitions.

As the new trombone *moña* starts to evolve in the previous measure, section M3 begins in m. 181.

Except for the final coda-like six-measure *moña*, each successive *moña* section is longer than the previous one. In the case of M3, the section is twenty measures in length and consists of five repetitions of *moña* three (figure 6.17).

Figure 6.17. **"Bilongo": Section M3—trombone** *moña*

Unlike the first two trombone *moñas*, which are very similar to each other, *moña* three represents a departure. One difference in this *moña* is that the repetition of this two-measure module contains completely different melodic material than the initial one. While the first two *moñas* contain several tones that are common to both versions of their modules, in the third *moña* every single note changes when the module is repeated. One reason for this is that every single note in the *moña* is a member of its respective harmonic underpinning. In the opening G minor chord, the *moña* starts with a B♭3 on the upbeat of two and moves to the quarter-note D4 on beat three. This D4 emphasizes the two-side of the *clave*. The eighth-note B♭3 on beat four is the third of the G minor harmony, and the A3 on the upbeat anticipates the dominant harmony of the second and third bars of the phrase. This fifth of the dominant chord is repeated one beat later on the upbeat of one, followed by the seventh (C4) on the next upbeat. The module ends with quarter notes on beats three and four. These quarter notes make this third *moña* more similar to the opening trumpet *moña* than to either of the first two trombone *moñas*; however, in this case, the notes descend by a skip (third) rather than the stepwise motion of the trumpet version.

In order to facilitate the harmonic movement, the first three notes in the repeated module are a diatonic step higher than their counterpart in the first module. Because the *montuno* returns to tonic in the fourth bar of the phrase, the last part of the module is also transposed, in this case a step lower. Transposing each part of the module in different directions to accommodate the harmony creates greater melodic variety than a simple unidirectional transposition would. At thirty measures in length (mm. 201–230), the fourth *moña* section (M4) is the longest section of the solo/*moña* part. This *moña* evolves from *moña* three, and although there are similarities between the two *moñas*, there are also significant differences (figure 6.18).

Figure 6.18. "Bilongo": Section M4—trombone *moña*

Like the other *moñas* in this piece, *moña* four consists of two versions of a two-measure melodic module. While *moñas* three and four both begin with a three-note eighth-note figure starting on an upbeat, *moña* three starts on the second half of two, and *moña* four begins on the upbeat of three. After that, both *moñas* are exactly the same for the next four notes in the module. Instead of the last note of the melody occurring on beat four as in the previous version, *moña* four prolongs the note on beat three (with a lower-neighbor note) for an extra beat before bringing the module to completion on beat one. A displacement occurs in that *moña* four both begins and ends one beat later in the *montuno* pattern than *moña* three does.

Section M5 consists of the last two four-bar phrases of part three, although in reality the *moña* figure itself doesn't change until midway through the penultimate *montuno* pattern. In this coda-like *moña,* the ending of the solo/*moña* part is signaled by a shorter but rhythmically dense melodic module (figure 6.19).

Figure 6.19. **"Bilongo": Section M5—trombone *moña***

While the module occupies the usual two measures, the rhythmic cell is only four beats in length. The four beats containing musical movement are the final two beats in the first measure of the module and the first two beats of the second measure. Each of these two-beat areas consists of an eighth rest and three eighth notes, the last eighth note of the second area extending for an additional two beats. In module one, the first three notes are the third and fifth of the G minor tonic harmony (B♭3 and D4) and a half-beat anticipation of the dominant chord (A3). This A3 and its repetition a beat later are artifacts from the previous two *moñas.* This second A4 then proceeds up the dominant chord structure with the seventh (C4) and the minor ninth (E♭4), which is held. The second module is a diatonic step lower and reflects the cadential resolution back to tonic.

THE SOLO

It is in the M2 section, with its pickup bar, that the trumpet solo begins in earnest (figure 6.20).

Figure 6.20.   "Bilongo": Section M2—trumpet solo mm. 164–166

As discussed earlier, Armenteros performs a contrapuntal *moña* for
most of M1. In m. 164, he plays a quarter-note triplet D5-E5-F♯5
starting on the third beat, with the initial D actually beginning a
half beat earlier. Although figure 6.20 shows an eighth note tied to
the first triplet quarter note, each note in the entire triplet is ahead
of the underlying tempo by a gradually lessening degree. By the
time the quarter-note triplet (G5, A5, B♭5) continues the ascent in
m. 165, the line is back to the middle part of the rhythmic time
continuum. The final notes of the first three-bar melodic figure re-
tard against the time. On beats three and four of m. 165, there are
four eighth notes that descend linearly from A5 through G5 to F♯5
and back to G5. As these notes progress, they gradually stretch in
time until they acquire the qualities of quarter-note triplets. The
true rhythmic value of most of these notes is in the gray area between the eighth-note and the quarter-note triplets. By the time
the final return to A5 enters in m. 166, it is at the position of the
second note of a quarter-note triplet rather than on the upbeat of
one.

Shifting between eighth-note and quarter-note triplet values is a
characteristic feature of the Afro-Cuban trumpet solo performance style. Armenteros uses this transitional technique and other
methods to subtly affect the rhythmic flow of his solo. Notation is
inadequate when a line is stretched in the manner described
above. For this reason, the notation examples can only approxi-
mate the rhythm values, and rhythmic nuances must be described
discursively. In order to understand this music, it is important that
the recorded examples are continuously consulted. Because these
tempo variation techniques are used continuously throughout the
solo, this discursive analysis will be limited to the most significant
examples of this type of rhythmic variation.

The trumpet phrase that extends from m. 167 to m. 171 overlaps two *montuno* patterns (figure 6.21).

Figure 6.21. "Bilongo": Section M2—trumpet solo mm. 167–171

Two characteristics of the entire solo are amply demonstrated in this phrase. One is the impressive use of trumpet technique. Armenteros had arguably the best technical skills of the golden age Afro-Cuban trumpet masters. This phrase demonstrates extensive skills in high-range playing and linear dexterity. The other characteristic is the wide pitch range utilized in the solo. This has both melodic and technical ramifications on the music.

In m. 167, a quarter-note triplet A5, B♭5, and C6 ascends to a D6 eighth note on beat three. This is the highest note in the range of the solo and is only played once more in m. 196. Following this D6, two sixteenth notes (C6, B♭5) start the gradual descent that reaches its lowest point on F♯4 on beat two in m. 169. Beat three and four in m. 167 and beats one and two in m. 168 contain a descending movement that features a two sixteenth-note/one eighth-note embellishment of the main notes in this line. On the fourth beat of m. 167, the C6 sixteenth note moves to B♭5 a quarter beat later and to A5 on the last half of beat four. This lower-neighbor note returns to B♭5 on the first beat of m. 168. This same pattern continues until a series of eight eighth notes begins on A5 on beat three of m. 168. Here, a descending arpeggio movement through the first inversion G minor chord lands on A4 on beat one in m. 169, accelerating the downward melodic progression. After the A4, the eighth-note line finishes with a further descent through G4 to F♯4 and a return to G4. On the upbeat of three, the line leaps a minor seventh to F5 and sustains an additional one and a half beats. After a passing eighth-note E5 on the upbeat of one, the descending melodic scale outlines the downward movement to the C5 quarter note on beat one in m. 171. On beat two of m. 170, an eighth-note triplet, consisting of two E♭5s surrounding an upper neighbor F5, moves to the D5 tonic note of the underlying dominant harmony. An upper neighbor E♭5 on the upbeat of three returns to D5 on four, which escapes to A4 before ending on the C5 quarter note in m. 171.

With the exception of the E5 and F♯5, the first nine notes of mm. 164–165 are repeated in mm. 172–173 (figure 6.22).

Figure 6.22. "Bilongo": Section M2—trumpet solo mm. 172–173

In this case, the D5 on the upbeat of one and the second-beat eighth notes G5 and A5 reach the high note B♭5 on beat three, almost a measure earlier than the line that starts in m. 164. This B♭ begins a series of nine quarter-note triplets that continues through m. 173. Starting on the third beat of m. 172, the high note B♭5 descends through A5 and G5 to the second triplet that begins on the F♯5 on beat one of m. 173. This F♯ returns to B♭5 through the second and third triplets of the first two beats (G5 and A5). The triplet starting on the B♭5 is completed with A5 and C6 and the progression to the dominant harmony.

The F♯5 to B♭5 linear movement continues with the melodic module that starts on the second half of the third beat in m. 174 and ends on the third beat with an A5 in m. 175 (figure 6.23).

Figure 6.23. "Bilongo": Section M2—trumpet solo mm. 174–177

Again, the high range is featured in this module and over the following four measures. The initial F♯ ascends through a fourth beat passing tone G5 to a chord tone A5 on the upbeat. Sixteenth notes on the upbeat on one in m. 175 include an upper neighbor B♭5 and another A5. A passing note G5 on the second beat returns to the third (F♯5) of the harmony, which returns directly to A5 on the third beat.

A two-measure melodic module is set up with an eighth-note D5 on the last half beat of m. 175. Again, the F♯5-to-B♭5 linear movement is the primary melodic material used in this module. Initially, the movement is descending from the B♭ on beat one to the F♯ on beat two. This descent is accomplished using a sixteenth-note triplet with a B5 embellishment note. Starting on a beat-two F♯5 in m. 176, eighth-note triplet figures move continuously between the F♯ and B♭. The connecting notes are G5 and A5 as the line ascends and descends until the final B♭5 is reached on beat three in m. 177. A sixteenth note, this final B♭ is followed by three other sixteenth notes (A5, G♯5, and A5) before moving to a quarter-note C6 on beat four.

This entire module is a classic example of the time-stretching technique discussed earlier. In this case, the repeating triplets that start on beat two gradually increase in speed from being extremely behind the beat on the first triplet to becoming sixteenth notes by the last two notes of beat two in m. 177. This transition is so gradual that true eighth-note triplets exist for only a short portion of the entire line.

Measure 178 starts out the same as m. 174, albeit a beat earlier (figure 6.24).

Figure 6.24. "Bilongo": Section M2—trumpet solo mm. 178–180

The initial four notes spell out the final F♯5-to-B♭5 motif. On the last half beat of four, a C6 initiates a descending line full of embellishing figures. After the C6, a four sixteenth-note figure (A5, G5, F♯5, and A5) begins the downward movement that ends a measure later with the same figure an octave lower and a final G♯4. Beat two of m. 179 is the densest beat rhythmically in the entire M2 section and consists of two sixteenth notes (F♯5 and E♭5) and three sixteenth-note triplets that add a chromatic element with a D♭5 inserted between a D5 and a C5. The descent is temporarily diverted on beat three by a leap back to E♭5 before continuing in a downward direction with a C5-and-B♭5 sixteenth-note pair on the upbeat. After landing on A4 on beat four, the line is again interrupted with a C5 on the upbeat of four, which continues the octave-lower repetition of the first beat in m. 179.

The argument that the trumpet solo also changes when the trombone *moña* does is most clearly supported at the beginning of section M3 (figure 6.25).

Figure 6.25.   "Bilongo": Section M3—trumpet solo mm. 181–184

In this section, the entire character of the solo changes from the virtuoso linearity of M2 to a syncopated and simplified melodic style. With the exception of the final phrase, this entire section consists of melodic units reminiscent of the *septeto* trumpet tradition. Beat one in m. 181 contains a two eighth-note octave leap from D4 to D5. On the second half of beat two, a five eighth-note line begins again with a B♭-to-F♯ movement, this time an octave lower than before. After ascending to G4 on the last half beat of four, the melody leaps a minor seventh to an F5 on the first beat of m. 182 and is followed by two other quarter notes in the opposite direction (E♭5 and A4). Fourth-beat eighth notes (A4 and C5) lead to a repetition of the of the F5-E♭5-A4 motive, this time as two eighth notes and a quarter note on the first two beats of m. 183.

The use in this motive of an F and an E♭ over the D7 harmony is a standard way, in Afro-Cuban music, of performing over the dominant harmony in a minor key. Derived from the descending melodic minor scale, this note (F) is also often used as the root of a substitute chord for the dominant harmony in minor and also hints at the relative major key. Continuing the prevalence of arpeggio figuration in this section, an ascending G4-Bb4-Eb5 on the last one and a half beats of m. 183 is countered in the following measure by a descent through the root position G minor triad in the first two beats, which brings the phrase to a close.

A pickup C#5 at the end of m. 184 begins the second phrase in section M3 (figure 6.26).

Figure 6.26. **"Bilongo": Section M3—trumpet solo mm. 184–188**

Armenteros uses this C# as a gliding embellishment to the eighth-note D5 on beat one of m. 185, which leaps immediately to a sustained G5. Returning to D5 on the upbeat of four, the melody pivots downward with Bb4 on the second half of beat one in m. 186 and A4 a half beat later. When the ascending fourth movement is sequenced (C5-F5) during the last beat and a half of the measure, an implied three-four meter has been established. This implication is abandoned by the eighth-note figure that begins with Eb5 on the upbeat of one in m. 187. Returning to the modal F5 and back again on beat two, the eighth-note line ends during beat three with the seventh (C5) and the fifth (A4) of the dominant chord. The configuration of syncopated notes Bb4 and A4 and second beat G4 is similar to the three-note figure starting on the upbeat of four in m. 185. The final note of this module is a return to the D5 that opened the phrase.

Two modules comprise the third phrase of M3 (figure 6.27).

Figure 6.27. **"Bilongo": Section M3—trumpet solo mm. 189–192**

Again, arpeggiated movement dominates, with the opening five eighth notes ascending through the tonic triad from G4 to G5 and back to the D5 fifth of the chord. This movement is initiated on the upbeat of one in m. 189. An isolated syncopated F5 ends the measure before another five eighth-note cell starts on the upbeat of one in m. 190. Except for the first note (C5), the rest of this cell is a roughly inverted and transposed version of the movement in the five-note cell of m. 189. Here, the last four notes descend from E♭5 to D5 to A4 before skipping back to C5.

The second module begins with a repetition of the initial part of the first module, transposed a step higher. In this case, the arpeggio moves between the octave fifths (A4-A5) of the dominant harmony using the seventh (C5) and the minor ninth (E♭5). The A5 then moves down a third to F♯5, which is the first use of the seventh degree of the G minor scale in its leading tone version in the M3 section. In this version, the upbeat following the initial five-note cell (A5) is not isolated but leads directly to the phrase-ending G5 on the first beat of m. 192.

Phrase four in M3 starts in m. 193 and is preceded by an eighth-note D5 (figure 6.28).

Figure 6.28.   "Bilongo": Section M3—trumpet solo mm. 192–196

Each of the two-measure modules is built around a simple melodic fragment of four eighth notes. The primary configuration of the fragment consists of three repetitions of a tone followed by an ascending leap of a third. In both modules, the first measure contains a version of the fragment and an immediate repetition. Over the tonic harmony in the first module, the fragment consists of three G5s (the root) and a B♭5 (the third). After its repetition, this figure moves up a step, but instead of a third, the three A5s are followed by a B♭5, which ascends to the final quarter-note C6 on the third beat of m. 194. In m. 195, the fragment again starts on A5, this time ascending a third to C6. Following its repetition in the second half of the measure, the fragment is submitted to extensive alteration in the first half of m. 196, when, in addition to ascending linearly to a final quarter note (D6) as in m. 194, a lower-neighbor A5 replaces the second of what would have been three Bb4s.

Section M3 ends with a long descending series of eighth-note triplet figures (figure 6.29).

Figure 6.29.   "Bilongo": Section M3—trumpet solo mm. 197–201

Two eighth notes (A5 and Bb5) on beat one of m. 197 provide the lead-in to the triplet line that starts on C6. Descending through the G minor scale, each triplet moves down two steps of the scale before ascending back one step. In this manner, the first note of each triplet is preceded two notes earlier by the same pitch; the intervening pitch acts as a lower-neighbor tone. In m. 197, the first note of each of the triplets starts the descending version of the G minor melodic scale with the fourth (C6), third (Bb5), and second (A5). Measures 198–199 contain the entire descending melodic version of the scale on each of the downbeats from G5 on beat one of m. 198 to G4 on beat four in m. 199. On occasion, the major sixths and sevenths are borrowed from the ascending version of the melodic minor scale when the note is used as a lower neighbor. E and F♯ only occur in the third position of a triplet figure. Because of this, the F♯ occurs twice in the phrase, each time as a lower neighbor to a pair of Gs. There is one E, which plays a similar lower-neighbor role for the two Fs in the first half of m. 198.

The triplet line ends with a pair of eighth notes (F4 and Eb4) on the first beat of m. 200, which is the final measure of the M3 section. A final triplet (D4, E♭4, and D4) on beat two leads to a lower-neighbor C♯4, which is the lowest note in the phrase. The return to D4 is followed by an ascending eighth-note arpeggiation of a root position E♭ major triad, which starts on E♭4 on beat four and ends with E♭5 on the upbeat of one in m. 201 (the first measure in section M4). D5 on the second beat finishes the elongated final phrase of section M3.

The long, elaborated, unidirectional descending line of the final phrase is an extended recapitulation of the line in mm. 167–168. As he did in signaling the transition to M3, Armenteros uses this extended linear descent to announce the change to section M4.

Because of the prolongation of the previous section and the measure-long pickup to the following phrase, the primary musical material in this phrase is truncated into a two-measure module (mm. 202–203) over the dominant area of the *montuno* pattern (figure 6.30).

Figure 6.30.   "Bilongo": Section M4—trumpet solo mm. 202–203

Again, a change in the trumpet solo style coincides with the introduction of a new trombone *moña*. Starting with this module, the first two phrases of section M4 replace the eighth note and eighth-note triplet rhythmic texture of the previous section with a predominantly quarter-note triplet texture. In m. 202, the subdominant A minor is arpeggiated, with three eighth notes starting on the upbeat of one and representing the root, third, and flatted fifth of the A minor triad. The seventh of the chord, G5, finishes the ascending arpeggio on beat three and begins the first of two quarter-note triplet groupings. Beginning on beat three, the first grouping consists of the G5, a lower-neighbor F♯5, and another G5. In the following triplet, F♯5 and G5 are repeated. In this case, the F♯ is the chord tone (the third of the dominant harmony) and the G is a passing tone to A5, the fifth of the chord, and the final note of the triplet.

One of the most rhythmically interesting phrases in the entire solo begins in m. 204 (figure 6.31).

Figure 6.31. "Bilongo": Section M4—trumpet solo mm. 204–208

Based around quarter-note triplets, the main organizing process used here is the alternating of notes and rests. Following an eighth-note D5 on the upbeat of one and a G5 quarter note on beat two, the first quarter-note triplet appears as an A5 on the third beat. A rest in the second part of the triplet grouping and a B♭5 in the final part follow. Beats one and two of m. 205 contain a quarter-note triplet grouping consisting of two rests surrounding another A5. A G5, a rest, and an F♯5 comprise the triplet in the second half of the measure. In m. 206, the pattern is altered in that a note (F5), instead of a rest, begins the measure. However, the pattern of rest-note alternation continues, with a rest and an E5 completing the first triplet in the measure. This pattern ends (following a rest and an E♭5) in the last half of m. 206, when the final member of the triplet is divided into two eighth notes instead of a rest. M. 207 contains six uninterrupted quarter-note triplets. Starting off the measure are C♯5, C5, and E♭5; and B♭4, A4, and C5 occur in the last two beats before a final B♭4 on the second half of one in m. 208 finishes the phrase.

Armenteros shifts gear in the phrase that starts on m. 209 (figure 6.32).

Figure 6.32. "Bilongo": Section M4—trumpet solo mm. 209–211

Each of the two modules in the phrase is built around a series of repeating D5s and a leap to a final note: A5 in the first case and B♭5 in the second. Starting out behind the beat in m. 209, the first module contains ten repeated D5s over five beats before the A5 on the second beat of m. 210. The rhythmic configuration of the ten notes consists of a quarter note, two eighth notes, three eighth-note triplets, and four eighth notes. Nine D5s are performed in the second module before the final B♭5 on the upbeat of four in m. 211. In this case, the rhythmic density of the repeating D5s is greater than in the first module. Two eighth notes, six eighth-note triplets, and a single eighth note bring on the final note a beat and a half earlier than in the first module. Armenteros starts the second module with a short glissando lead-in and ends with a quick drop from the final B♭5.

In m. 212, there is a three eighth-note pickup (A5, B♭5, and C6) to the next phrase, which is similar to the final phrase of section M3 (figure 6.33).

Figure 6.33. "Bilongo": Section M4—trumpet solo mm. 212–215

Although this phrase is more varied rhythmically than the earlier triplet line, the same pattern of descending scale tones with lower-neighbor notes predominates. Aside from the two opening eighth notes, the first measure is made up of eighth-note triplets (or triplet notes combined with rests). Measures 214–215 contain regular eighth notes with the exception of the final beat, which is an extension of the D5 begun a half beat earlier. The chromaticism of the upcoming first phrase in section M5 is hinted at in m. 214. In m. 215, an eighth-note B♭4 is followed by a final trio (chord tone G4, lower-neighbor F♯4, and chord tone G4) and a leap to E♭5 and the final D5.

The melody from the pickup and first measures (mm. 216–217) of the next phrase is one that has occurred previously, in one form or another, several times in the solo (figure 6.34).

Figure 6.34. **"Bilongo": Section M4—trumpet solo mm. 216–220**

The opening phrase of section M2, this motive also shows up in mm. 172–173, mm. 174–175, and in mm. 204–205. While the initial D5 is notated on the upbeat of two in m. 216, it can be viewed as an anticipation of the first note of the quarter-note triplet that continues with G5 and A5. M. 217 contains six quarter-note triplets moving from B♭5 to F♯5 on the third beat. As described earlier, the B♭-to-F♯ line is also an important organizing factor in the solo. G5 and D5 complete the second triplet. Another descending fourth (F5 to C5) starts a quarter-note triplet in m. 218. In skipping to E♭5 from the C5, a series of eight ascending skips of either a third or a fourth is continued from the previous D5 and F5. Except for the first two, all of the skips are between eighth notes starting on a downbeat. The first note of each skip gradually descends to an F♯4 on the third beat of m. 219, with the F♯ repeating a beat later and resolving to G4 on beat one of m. 220. After the G4 skips to B♭4, another ascending skip, of a third to a half-note D5, concludes the phrase.

The phrase starting in m. 221 (figure 6.35) extends a rhythmic idea (three against four) that was briefly introduced by Armenteros in m. 185.

Figure 6.35. **"Bilongo": Section M4—trumpet solo mm. 220–224**

In this case, a three-note melodic cell starts on the upbeat of four in m. 220 and is repeated, with variation, four more times. Because the cell is three beats in length and is repeated immediately following its predecessor, the entire phrase is an example of the trumpet playing in three-four time over the underlying four-four-time continuum. There are two versions of this short melodic cell. Initially, the eighth-note pickup to m. 221 is an E♭5 and is immediately followed by two quarter notes on the first two beats of the new phrase. While all five versions of the cell contain both the E♭5 pickup and the following quarter-note D5, the second quarter note is varied to allow for changes in the harmonic progression. In the first and fifth versions of the short module, the second quarter note drops to G4, which is the root of the tonic chord. An A4 is the second note of choice in the middle three versions and represents the fifth of the dominant harmony. A quarter-note rest on beat three in m. 224 adds the extra beat needed to complete the sixteen beats of the four-bar phrase.

The final phrase of M4 is again an example of three against four, and again Armenteros performs exclusively in three-four meter (figure 6.36).

Figure 6.36. "Bilongo": Section M4—trumpet solo mm. 224–228

In this case, he is much subtler with his technique. Instead of continuous, nearly exact repetitions of a single cell, as in the previous phrase, Armenteros combines increased syncopation with contrast to create a more complex realization of three-four groupings. Although a similar three-note cell is the main melodic material used in this phrase, the second and third notes of the cell are eighth notes instead of quarter notes, as in the previous phrase. This new configuration increases the intensity of the music in that the third note of each cell is (along with the first note) syncopated. Another complication is added to the musical texture in the addition of contrasting material. Instead of five repetitions, this phrase contains only three versions of the three-note cell. As in the previous phrase, the first cell is immediately followed by a varied repetition. However, instead of continuing the repetitions, this phrase provides contrasting material where repetitions three and four were situated in the previous phrase. Following this brief diversion, the original cell is reinstated, creating a three-four A-A-B-A form in miniature.

Melodically, the first two notes (E♭5 and D5) in each three-note cell are the same here as in the previous phrase. As in the previous cell, the third note is altered to reflect the harmonic underpinning. The musical tension is increased by this third note because, in addition to being a syncopation, it is inverted and ascends by a leap into the upper range of the trumpet instead of skipping downward, as in the previous phrase. In the first and second instances of the cell, the third note is an octave higher than its equivalent in the previous phrase. Following the contrasting material, the final version of the cell, starting on the upbeat of four in m. 227, has a B♭5 as its third note instead of the octave transposition of the G4 in the prior phrase.

The contrasting portion of the phrase contains elements of the three-note cell. Although the first two notes of the cell are replaced in m. 226 by a single G5 on the upbeat of three, the A5 on beat four matches up exactly with its octave-lower counterpart in the preceding phrase. Pitch-wise, the first three notes in m. 227 are the same as in the corresponding measure in the previous phrase (m. 223). Like all of the cell figures in the last two phrases of M4, the first two notes in m. 227 are E♭5 and D5. Unlike in the other examples, these two notes are played here as eighth notes on the first beat. This reverses the rhythmic roles of the notes, with the E♭ becoming a downbeat and the D a syncopated note. Like the cell figures in this phrase, the A5 on beat two is an octave transposition of its equivalent in the prior phrase. However, in this case, it is performed a beat earlier than its A4 predecessor.

An A5 eighth note on the second half of beat three in m. 228 and a fourth-beat quarter-note B♭4 introduce the final M5 section (figure 6.37).

Figure 6.37.   "Bilongo": Section M5—trumpet solo mm. 228–233

This section is two phrases in length and acts as the finale of the solo/*moña* section. Starting as it does in the last measure of the previous phrase, and prolonging for an entire measure into the final *montuno* pattern of the solo, the first phrase in M5 (figure 6.37) is one of the longest in this entire part of the recording. It is also the last example of the recurring long descending line. In this case, the line extends downward from B♭5 on beat one in m. 228 to D4 on the last beat of m. 233. In m. 229, the B♭5 is the first member of an eighth-note triplet and is joined by A5 and G5. On the second beat, another G5 is played as an eighth note with an eighth-note F♯5 coming in a half beat later. The repeated Gs are the first of seventeen pairs of repeated notes. An isolated G5 (on the upbeat of three) precedes the second pair (F5s) on beat four. After a half-beat rest on beat one of m. 330, the repeated note pairs continue back to back as eighth notes until the end of the phrase. The first of these pairs is an E5, with the first note on the upbeat of one and the second note on two. Likewise, throughout the rest of the phrase the syncopated nature of the music is supported in that the first note of a new pair is always on the upbeat, and the second note is on the following downbeat. Each pair is delineated by a change in pitch, and the melodic tension is increased by the chromaticism of the line. Starting with the initial E5 in m. 330, each succeeding note pair is one half step lower until a pair of D4s is reached in the last half of m. 233. After the final D4 on beat four, the prolonged phrase ends on A4 a half beat later.

In the final three measures of the solo (figure 6.38), Armenteros returns to the three-against-four pattern from the two phrases that start in m. 221.

Figure 6.38.   "Bilongo": Section M5—trumpet solo mm. 234–236

In this case, he utilizes only the first two notes (E♭5 and D5) of the recurring cell, starting on the upbeat of two in m. 234. As Armenteros repeats these two notes three more times to finish up his solo, Quintana returns with the solo vocal in preparation for the final part of the piece.

7

ALFREDO "CHOCOLATE" ARMENTEROS

One of the most legendary debuts in the history of recorded music occurred when twenty-one-year-old Alfredo "Chocolate" Armenteros played his first recorded trumpet solos on "Para las niñas y para las señoras" with Cuban bandleader René Alvarez in 1949. In Chocolate's case, this auspicious start was completely fulfilled in a career that is unmatched in the annals of Cuban brass playing. When Armenteros performed these aggressive solo spots on the Alvarez recording, he convincingly assumed his role as heir to the *septeto* trumpet tradition propagated by older masters such as Félix Chappottín and Enrique "Florecita" Velazco.

From his very first recordings, Armenteros has demonstrated a mature grasp of the Cuban style and a commanding technical prowess. In the five decades between "Para las niñas y para las señoras" and his still-active New York City career, the septuagenarian has taken part in many of the landmark musical events in the historical development of the modern Afro-Cuban and *salsa* music styles. From the *conjunto* of Arsenio Rodríguez in the late 1940s, to the *salsa* of Eddie Palmieri and Larry Harlow in its 1960s heyday, to the recent 1990s renaissance of *descarga* and other traditional

Cuban styles instigated by Israel "Cachao" Lopez and others, Armenteros has been the most celebrated trumpet player in the history of modern Afro-Cuban/*salsa* music.

Alfredo "Chocolate" Armenteros was born on April 4, 1928 in Ranchuelo, Santa Clara, in the Cuban province of Las Villas. His mother was Angelina Abreu; his father, Lazaro Alfredo Armenteros, played trombone in his youth. Because of his early death, however, the elder Armenteros had little musical influence on the young Alfredo. In tribute, Armenteros displays his father's horn on his East Harlem apartment wall.

Among Armenteros' earliest listening experiences on the radio were recordings by the seminal *son* bands Sexteto Habanero and Septeto Nacional.[1] His first music teacher was Eduardo Egües (father of Richard Egües, the flute player for Orquesta Aragon). Eduardo Egües was a tenant of the Armenteros family, and in the process of creating a local children's musical group, he recruited Armenteros at the local public school. In the children's group, the training started with lessons in solfège and music theory. Only after a certain amount of proficiency was achieved in these areas would the student start the study of an instrument. As fellow music students, Armenteros and Richard Egües were friends; Armenteros would often help Richard clean his father's "Academy," and they spent a good deal of the time practicing. As a result, Armenteros soon became a regular member of the children's band, where he improved his reading skills and was exposed to the brass literature. Armenteros' considerable performance skills are a testament to the highly regarded Cuban system of music education, which has produced generations of virtuoso musicians.

After moving to Havana in 1949, Armenteros began his professional career with the legendary Sexteto Habanero, led by Gerardo Martínez, who was one of the original members. Habanero (along with Ignacio Piñeiro's Septeto Nacional) was the most important early large *son* ensemble. Historically, Habanero traces its origins to the very earliest years of the twentieth century. Originally called the Trio Oriental, the group relocated from the eastern Oriente province (the cradle of the *son*) to Havana in 1910, and over the following decade gradually evolved into the Sexteto Habanero (Robbins 1990). When Habanero and other early *son* groups added trumpet to increase the size of the group to seven pieces, the basic instrumentation (with some important later additions) and prototypical formal structures of the modern Afro-Cuban/*salsa* ensemble were set. The early *septeto* trumpet players (including the great Félix Chappottín) created the tradition that formed the core of the performance style of Armenteros and other mainstream, modern-era, Afro-Cuban/*salsa* brass players. Even though Armenteros' tenure with the past-its-heyday late-1940s version of Habanero was short-lived, a historical validation seems to have occurred when one of the most *típico* of modern Afro-Cuban trumpet players began his Havana career by working with the most tradition-laden Cuban *son* band.

Shortly afterward, Armenteros played on his first recordings with bandleader René Alvarez and his group Los Astros. Among these recordings was the aforementioned "Para las niñas y para las señoras," which contains some of the most important early solo work by Armenteros. Even though he was just shy of his twenty-first birthday, Armenteros' solo style was fully developed. Andy González, noted New York bass player and *salsa* historian, considers the short trumpet solo sections on "Para las niñas y para las señoras" a textbook on Afro-Cuban-style soloing: he claims that, if music students "study that solo, they will know what the 'swing' of *son* is" (González 1997). Although the recording is difficult to find, its importance to Armenteros is signified by the position of a framed copy of the original 78 on the wall of his apartment just below his father's trombone.

In addition to recording with Alvarez and Los Astros, Armenteros performed live with the group. It was during a Los Astros performance at the Polar Brewery in Havana that Arsenio Rodríguez, the most famous bandleader of the era, first heard the young trumpet player and offered him a job. Armenteros jumped at the chance of playing with Rodríguez and alongside the legendary trumpet maestro Félix Chappottín. For Armenteros, "working with Arsenio back then was the best; I felt like Amalia up in the seventh heaven didn't have it any better than me" (Armenteros 1998). While his tenure with Rodríguez and his *conjunto* was not lengthy, Armenteros is represented on a number of the group's recordings.[2] The Rodríguez *conjunto* was the most celebrated ensemble of its type in the 1940s and was both a consolidation of the *son* tradition and a precursor to the New York City *salsa* movement that took place two decades later. Chapter 3 contains additional material about the Rodríguez group and an analysis of his recording of "No puedo comer vistagacha," which features the playing of Armenteros.

THE 1950s

In the early 1950s, Armenteros played with various groups, including the famous Sonora Mantancera. While on tour in Mexico with the group in 1951, Armenteros met Machito, singer and bandleader of one of the most famous Latin groups on the New York scene in the 1940s and 1950s. Machito offered Armenteros a job in his New York–based orchestra. However, Armenteros was planning a musical collaboration with his cousin Beny Moré, and the collaboration was in the planning stages. While flattered by the job offer from Machito, Armenteros decided to remain in Cuba and participate in the inception of his cousin's band. Moré was not only Armenteros' cousin and the godfather of Armenteros' first daughter; he is considered by many to be the greatest singer in Afro-Cuban music history. His large band became the toast of Havana in the mid-1950s in much the same way that Machito (along with Tito Puente and Tito Rodríguez) ruled the New York *mambo* scene. Many of the Beny Moré recordings on which Armenteros performed in the mid-1950s have been reissued on CD, including the release *Yo Hoy Como Ayer* by Beny Moré y su Orquesta Gigante de Estrellas Cubana, which is on the RCA label. Unfortunately, much of this material consists of big band instrumentation with set arrangements, and very little spontaneous instrumental (e.g., Armenteros) soloing is contained on these studio recordings.

Armenteros played with Moré's band from 1953 to 1956. In addition, throughout the 1950s, he was a busy Havana studio musician and a staff member of the studio orchestra of the Cuban radio and television station CMQ (Larkin 1995). Besides working with Moré, Armenteros performed and/or recorded with numerous other musicians and groups in Cuba in the 1950s before his relocation to New York (Clarke 1998). During this time period, he recorded with the famed Latin jazz bandleader/composer Chico O'Farrill, who was closely associated with Dizzy Gillespie. Another well-known musician Armenteros recorded with in the late 1950s was pianist Bebo Valdés, who is now best known as the father of piano virtuoso Chucho Valdés. One of the trumpeter's most renowned Havana record dates in the 1950s was *Cole Español*, featuring the American pop singer Nat "King" Cole. Other Cuban artists Armenteros performed with before his move north were singers Cheo Marquetti and Joseito Fernández. The latter composed the Cuban standard "Guantanamera," which was recorded by Armenteros over two decades later on *Chocolate y Amigos*.

Armenteros made his initial foray to New York City in the late 1950s on tour with flute player José Fajardo. In 1960, he relocated permanently to New York and finally joined the Machito band, starting a long on-and-off relationship with the orchestra, which has survived to this day, with Machito's son taking the reins as bandleader following his father's death. Armenteros insists that the politics of Castro's revolution had very little to do with his decision to immigrate to New York. Armenteros asserts that "I have never been involved in politics. I've been a musician all my life and that's it" (Armenteros 1999). His reason for relocating was a renewal of the longstanding offer by Machito and Mario Bauza of a job with the Machito orchestra. Because Armenteros had recently left his cousin Beny Moré's group, the trumpeter readily accepted this new offer of employment.

Besides working with Fajardo and Machito in New York, Armenteros quickly became busy as a freelance trumpet player, recording with almost every up-and-coming New York *salsa* bandleader. In the 1960s and 1970s, Armenteros worked with (among others) Eddie Palmieri, Charlie Palmieri, Larry Harlow, Johnny Pacheco, Mongo Santamaría, Ismael Rivera, and Roberto Torres. One early (1964) *salsa* record album he played on was Orlando Marin's *Que Chevere*, volume 2. Armenteros also performed on many recordings released by the major Latin labels and performed by their studio "All-Star" groups, such as the Tico All-Stars, Alegre All-Stars, and Fania All-Stars (Larkin 1995). His recording work with pianist/bandleader Eddie Palmieri is of particular importance and is examined in more detail in chapters 5 and 6.

SALSA

The New York *salsa* scene of the 1960s and 1970s is of paramount importance to the examination of the Armenteros solo performance style. When he made his landmark recordings with Eddie Palmieri (e.g., *Justicia* and *Superimposition*), Armenteros was in his early forties and at the peak of his instrumental prowess. In his extended solos on these recordings, he was able to push the envelope of the *típico* Cuban solo trumpet style well beyond its conservative role in the earlier (1940s) mainstream *conjunto*. His work with Palmieri and on other recordings of the 1970s, such as the two volumes released by the Grupo Folklórico y Experimental Nuevayorquino (Grupo Folklórico), represents one of the high-water marks of Armenteros' career and comprises some of the most notable recorded trumpet solo playing in the Afro-Cuban/*salsa* historical continuum.

One of the first *salsa* groups to record using a four-piece horn section with two trumpets and two trombones was Orchestra Harlow, led by pianist Larry Harlow. In the years immediately preceding his first work with Eddie Palmieri, Armenteros recorded a number of albums with Orchestra Harlow on the Fania label. Two of these albums were *Gettin' Off* (*Bajandote*), released in 1967, and *Heavy Smokin'*, which followed a year later. Although Armenteros was featured sporadically on all of these albums, his soloing skills are prominently demonstrated on *Heavy Smokin'*. His solo playing on *Heavy Smokin'* holds added significance in that it precedes his classic work with Eddie Palmieri on recordings such as *Justicia* and *Superimposition*. Armenteros' extended *septeto*-style soloing on these innovative Palmieri sides is presaged (albeit in a more limited fashion) on *Heavy Smokin'*.

On "La juventud," he performs a solo in a setting that recalls the mainstream 1940s *conjunto* style. While the solo is relatively short in length and is placed over the ongoing *coro*, its facile technical maturity and highly charged rhythmic drive anticipate the classic 1970s Armenteros performances with Palmieri and Grupo Folklórico. On "Chez Jose," in response to a four-bar *coro* over a minor key *montuno*, he plays a series of solo spots that are pensive, yet show off his impressive technical skills. Armenteros' work here demonstrates his finely tuned Cuban-style rhythmic sensibilities.

On "Rica combinación," Armenteros' soloing over the two-cowbell-driven *salsa* swing is a miniature version of his playing on future Palmieri classics like "Justicia," "Se acabó," and "Bilongo." His Cuban roots shine through in a couple of short solo spots on the dance-hall *rumba* "Mi guaguancó." In the early *son/septeto* tradition, "Maria La O" starts with an introductory horn section statement of the solo vocalists' *largo* melody. After the *largo*, the trombonists perform the instrumental version of the *coro* figure, with Armenteros providing improvised trumpet responses. Before the vocal *coro* and *sonero* take over, there are four iterations of the trombone section/trumpet solo version (the final one overlapping with the singers). Following a *bongó* solo and a horn section riff-figure, Armenteros plays an extended solo over the *coro*. The brief return of the *sonero* and a final brass break bring the piece to a conclusion.

GRUPO FOLKLÓRICO Y EXPERIMENTAL NUEVAYORQUINO

In 1975, two events played an important role in Armenteros' career. One was the release of a two-volume recording by a workshop group of musicians, organized by musicologist René Lopez, with the daunting name Grupo Folklórico y Experimental Nueva-yorquino (Grupo Folklórico). The other significant event for Armenteros was the start of his career as a leader, with the recording *Chocolate Aquí.*

Grupo Folklórico was a renaissance movement featuring some of the best young New York musicians of the mid-1970s as well as Cuban veterans like Armenteros. Most of the musicians involved in the project were mainstream, New York City–based *salsa* musicians. However, the organizing element behind the recording was the return to Afro-Cuban (and Afro–Puerto Rican) fundamentals. By reconsidering fundamental Cuban elements like the *rumba* and the *son*, the music was revitalized. The group was a mixture of young (mostly Puerto Rican) musicians like the González brothers (Jerry and Andy), who were dogged in their pursuit of historical knowledge about the Cuban style, and older musicians like Armenteros, who were a product of that tradition. Armenteros is prominently featured in several selections on the two volumes. His trumpet playing was an essential element in this tribute to traditional Afro-Cuban music in its myriad manifestations.

While both volumes of the recording contain important pieces, the first volume will be examined in more detail. "Cuba Linda" begins with a lengthy *conga* solo, which evolves into a series of drum section breaks and finally into a traditional dance-hall *guaguancó*. Armenteros plays a brief introductory solo over the initial tonic pedal before a sixteen-measure chant melody and chord progression are performed twice in the *rumba* tradition of substituting syllabic sounds for words. A short trumpet solo interlude leads to the solo singer and the extended main portion of the *largo* form. Armenteros supports the *sonero* through much of this section with background soloing. When the *coro* and *montuno* section finally arrive after an extensive prolongation of the *largo*, the three-two *rumba clave* and the usual call and response between *coro* and *sonero* are established. After several repetitions, Armenteros replaces the solo singer and plays his longest solo on the piece over the ongoing *coro*. Following piano, flute, and percussion solos, the *coro* and overlapping horn *moñas* bring the piece to its final coda section.

Armenteros is credited as the composer of "Choco's guajira," which is a typical, slow tempo, minor key *guajira*. The *guajira* is a musical form that Armenteros has returned to continually throughout his career. His initial soloing, both in the introduction and in the following call-and-response section, is moody and less technical than his playing on the earlier Palmieri sides. After a lengthy *sonero* and solos by the *tres* and flute, a fairly lengthy speaking dialogue ensues between the singer and Armenteros over the ongoing *coro*. Trombone and flute enter with contrapuntal *moñas* at the end of the dialogue section and introduce an overriding trumpet solo. Although the trumpet playing is more complex and virtuosic at this point than at the beginning of the piece, it is still very conservative and *típico*.

"Anabacoa" is a *guaguancó* based on a two-measure *montuno* pattern that is unchanging throughout the entire piece. The trombone, trumpet, and flute alternate improvised solos with the *coro* for two sequences. These two four-bar solo spots are the total extent of Armenteros' improvised work on this selection. "Adelaida" and "Luz Delia" are both examples of traditional folk styles associated primarily with Puerto Rico. While extremely interesting in their own right, neither selection contains soloing by Armenteros. On "Carmen la ronca," the trumpeter begins the piece *son* style by playing the first part of the vocal melody. When the solo singer enters with the same melody, Armenteros plays background figures throughout the vocal *largo*. After the recapitulation of the *largo* (with trumpet introduction), Armenteros trades *montunos* with the *coro*. After four solos, the trumpet is replaced by the *sonero*. These four solos are examples of the mature Armenteros in complete command of his medium. The *coro/sonero* section leads to a *tres* solo followed by a *conga* solo. Armenteros then plays a lengthy solo, which is similar in style to his playing on the earlier Palmieri recordings. The solo begins and ends with the trumpeter intoning the *coro* melody. After a few *coro* and *sonero* trades, the piece ends with a single horn section performance of the *coro* melody.

After two *santería*-influenced and *bata*-driven pieces, which consist almost entirely of percussion and vocals (although the second one contains fine playing by bassist Andy González), Armenteros is featured again on "A papá y mamá." "A papá y mamá" is a freewheeling dance-hall *rumba* featuring an abundance of traditional chants and some of the most exciting playing by Armenteros on the entire volume. His opening phrases over the initial tonic pedal are somewhat reminiscent of his famous introduction on Eddie Palmieri's "Bilongo" a few years earlier. Armenteros provides sporadic fill figures throughout the lengthy *largo* section, which consists of numerous exchanges between wordless vocal chants and lyric-based sections. The numerous exchanges between *coro* and trumpet solo at the beginning of the *montuno* section demonstrate Armenteros' mastery of the primordial, *son*-based, call-and-response trumpet solo style.

Volume 2 of the Grupo Folklórico recording features another diverse set of compositions. In addition to the mixture of traditional Cuban and Puerto Rican forms, there is a Brazilian number, "Ao meu lugar voltar," which features a Brazilian singer. Armenteros is featured on four numbers. The album opens with "Cinco en uno cal-letero," which features the trumpet player at various places through-out. The *guaguancó* "Trompeta en cueros" is a tour-de-force for Armenteros and was reprised a decade later on the Armenteros recording *Chocolate en Sexteto*. This selection contains some of his best soloing on the entire two-album recording. "La mama" is an old *guaguancó* which in this case contains a *santería* element in the use of a battery of traditional *bata* drums. Armenteros and trombonist Jose Rodrigues both provide notable solos on this piece. "Dime la verdad" is a *bolero-son* in the old *septeto* style. The trumpeter's *típico* soloing is compared to the master Florecita (one of Armenteros' mentors) in the notes accompanying the recording.

CHOCOLATE: THE LEADER

An impressive body of work is represented on the numerous recordings Armenteros produced as a leader during the 1970s and 1980s, a time period that represents his peak years as a trumpet soloist. Except for Armenteros' very first recording as a leader, *Chocolate Aquí* (released in 1975 by the Carib Musica label), these recordings can be divided into three basic groupings, each of which can be identified by the particular label he was signed with at the time. Each grouping will be identified by the label name. Chronologically, the three labels are Salsoul, SAR, and Caiman.

Three of Armenteros' albums from the mid-1970s were eventually consolidated on the Salsoul label and can be considered as one grouping. *Chocolate Caliente* and *Juntos* (a collaboration with Roberto Torres) were originally released on the Mericana label and later reissued on Salsoul. *Chocolate en el Rincón* was released in 1976 directly on Salsoul. The second grouping of recordings includes the three albums *Prefiero el Son, Y Sigo Con Mi Son,* and *Chocolate Dice*, all of which were released on the SAR label in the early 1980s. The first two have been re-released in CD form as *Lo Mejor de Chocolate,* volumes 1 and 2. These three SAR recordings were the most *típico* that he had recorded up to this time. The Caiman albums, the last of the three groupings, were recorded in the mid-1980s and contain Armenteros' most *descarga* and Latin jazz–oriented recordings as a leader. Using an all-instrumental format with Mario Rivera sharing the front line on baritone saxophone, Armenteros exhibits his most extended soloing as a leader on the Caiman recordings: *Chocolate en Sexteto, ¡Rompiendo de Hielo!,* and *Chocolate y Amigos.*

Chocolate Aquí

Coinciding chronologically with the Grupo Folkórico recordings was the release of the first recording to feature Armenteros as a leader: *Chocolate Aquí.* This album, released in 1975 on the Carib Musica label and featuring rhythm section, singers, and the solo horn of Armenteros, is more reflective of the "back to the roots" values that surfaced in the Grupo Folklórico recordings than of the modernistic *salsa* associated with the post–La Perfecta recordings by Eddie Palmieri that featured extended solos by Armenteros. Most of the ten selections on the album are firmly in the Afro-Cuban tradition, but without the primal energy of the Grupo Folklórico recordings. One area in which *Chocolate Aquí* differs from a typical *conjunto* recording is the extended role of the trumpet soloist. While there are vocals on the album, they are mostly in the form of *coros.* There are a number of examples of solo singing, but they are primarily limited in use to *largo* sections and an occasional *sonero* in a *montuno* section. In most of the tunes, the trumpet replaces the solo singer in call-and-response exchanges with the *coro.*

Salsoul

In 1975 Armenteros released the first of his three albums on the Salsoul label. Entitled *Chocolate Caliente,* the album features a larger and more dynamic instrumentation than *Chocolate Aquí*. Although considered by many to be superior to the earlier recording because of its higher production values and energy level, *Chocolate Caliente* nevertheless lacks some of the lyrical intimacy of Armenteros' playing on *Chocolate Aquí*. In January of 1977, Salsoul released *Chocolate en el Rincón*, which features Manny Oquendo and Andy González (both of whom later turned the Grupo Folklórico project into the internationally acclaimed Conjunto Libre). The final Salsoul release is a collaboration between Armenteros and producer Roberto Torres entitled *Juntos*. All three Salsoul albums are similar in concept and in personnel.

Armenteros shares leader billing with Roberto Torres on *Juntos*. This collaboration is important in that Torres later on produced the Armenteros recordings on the SAR label, which was headed by Torres. Although released later, *Juntos* was actually recorded in 1974 and predates *Chocolate Aquí* (the trumpeter's first recording as a full-fledged leader). Containing ten selections, *Juntos* is a slicker production than the other two Salsoul recordings and contains intricate arrangements, short song lengths, and catchy hook-oriented melodies. Although there are classic examples of soloing by Armenteros on the album, they are less numerous than on the other two Salsoul records. There are ten selections on *Juntos*. Armenteros does not solo on "Yamismo" and the *chachachá* "La tierra de sabor." Most of his soloing on the uptempo *salsa* songs is confined to the end of each piece. One example is "Castigador," the first selection on the album. This is a remake of a minor hit previously recorded by Roberto Torres. Here Armenteros plays over the *moña* and *coro* sections at the end of the piece. His solo on the end of "Déjeme tranquilo" is a dynamic showcase of trumpet performance virtuosity. He also plays solos at the end of "Mulato" and "Barco sin rumbo." Both of these songs are in a minor key, a trend that pervades all of the Salsoul sides. Armenteros' solo work on "Barco sin rumbo" is some of the best on the album. Another highlight is "Para que aprendas," which is a *guajira*. Armenteros is famous for his *guajira* playing; almost every recording and public performance by the trumpet player includes at least one *guajira*. He plays long solos both at the beginning and ending parts of "Para que aprendas." "El gordito de oro" features an extended *largo* and a laid-back trumpet solo, while "Un caminante con salsa" features a lengthy solo over *moñas* and *coros* in the Eddie Palmieri mode.

Chocolate Caliente was recorded approximately a year later than *Juntos* and contains many similarities. Except for the American rhythm and blues–influenced "Hot Chocolate," the songs are a mixture of medium-tempo *son-montunos*, *boleros*, and the requisite *guajira* ("Guajira inspiracíon"). "Estoy enamorado" and "Comprensión" are both *boleros* and contain a minimal amount of improvised solo playing, although there is some fine lead and solo melody playing by Armenteros. Four of the medium-tempo *salsa/son-montuno* numbers ("Retozón," "Sigan la clave," "Nicolaso," and "Que sepa") are in a minor key; Armenteros plays outstanding solos on "Sigan la clave" and "Nicolaso." Another example of the mature Armenteros at his best is his soloing on the opening "La Mula," which is based on a continuous dominant seventh harmony and a two-three *clave*. Although there are many similarities between *Juntos* and *Chocolate Caliente*, the latter lacks some of the production values of *Juntos* and sounds less commercial. At times there are severe intonation problems within the horn section, and the neo-*búgalu* "Hot Chocolate" suffers in the test of time, with its mid-1970s American pop music associations. However, the songs on *Juntos* tend to be more commercially oriented than the selections on *Chocolate Caliente*; at times *Juntos* suffers from an overly cute sentimentality.

Armenteros' final Salsoul album, *Chocolate en el Rincón*, was released in 1976 and contains two distinct components. The first five selections are similar in concept and personnel to *Juntos* and *Chocolate Caliente*. However, the final four pieces are in the *descarga* mode and feature a different group of musicians.

These musicians include all-star *salseros* Andy González on bass and percussionist Manny Oquendo. The first part of *Chocolate en el Rincón* contains a typical *salsa/conjunto* format with *sonero* Willie Garcia and a four-piece horn section. Following a trend on the two earlier albums, the first two selections are both minor key straight-ahead *salsa* songs. "Contrólate" features a typical call-and-response section between trumpet and *coro* as well as an Armenteros solo over *moña* and *coro* at the end. "Sé tu historia" follows a similar format, with a two-measure minor key *montuno* pattern. "Lo dicen todas" is an Arsenio Rodríguez composition, played Eddie Palmieri style, with a piano solo and a *moña*/trumpet solo section. "Apriétala en el Rincón" is a I-IV-V *montuno* from beginning to end; Armenteros plays continuously over the first part of the piece and again in the *moña* section. "Inocencia" is a *bolero* and the final song on the first part of the album. Armenteros plays a beautiful interpretation of the song's melody toward the end of the piece.

"Trumpet en montuno," a minor key *son*-based *descarga*, initially features Armenteros trading *montuno* sections with the initial four-bar *coro*. Later the trumpet/*coro* call and response is shortened to two-measure sections before a final fade-out section that contains only solo trumpet and rhythm section. "La Cayuga" is an unusual instrumental *danzón-montuno*. The first part of the tune is an Orestes Lopez *danzón* with Armenteros performing the vocal melody. One of the earliest of modern Cuban music styles, the *danzón* predates the *son* and is usually associated with flutes and violins and not the *septeto* trumpet. This is probably why the *montuno* section contains the improvised portion of Armenteros' playing on the piece. "Chocolate en ti" is an instrumental jam session over a one-chord medium-slow-tempo *tumbao*. For some reason, the piece is divided into two different selections on the album, although both appear to be part of the same recording. Armenteros performs a lengthy, slowly developed solo during part 1. Part 2 fades in with a piano

solo, which is followed by a *bongó* solo and a bass solo. The piece
ends with rambunctious soloing by Armenteros.

SAR

Starting in 1980, Armenteros joined SAR Records, which was
owned by Roberto Torres (Armenteros' partner on the earlier
Salsoul recording *Juntos*). Torres produced three of Armenteros'
recordings on SAR. Like the previous Salsoul series, these
recordings are firmly in the *conjunto* mode, with a large horn section and full-blown vocals. Armenteros is featured prominently
throughout the three volumes, albeit in a conservative *típico* format. The first two albums, *Prefiero el Son* and *Y Sigo Con Mi
Son*, were re-released on CD as *Lo Mejor de Chocolate*, volumes
1 and 2. *Prefiero el Son* was released in 1980 and featured, among
others, Jose Rodrigues and Leopoldo Pineda on trombone and
pianist Alfredo Valdez, Jr., who later worked with Armenteros on
recordings with Israel "Cachao" Lopez and with the Caiman All
Stars, which was fronted by the pianist. Rodrigues is the only
trombonist on *Y Sigo Con Mi Son* (released in 1981), and the
sonero is Fernando Lavoy. Aside from Tony Divan (lead singer on
Prefiero el Son), all other personnel is the same on both albums.
The third SAR album, *Chocolate Dice*, was released in 1982 and
has a number of personnel changes. Most significant is the trombone section, which in this case contains veteran Lewis Kahn and
a young Jimmy Bosch.

The formal characteristics of the SAR recordings are similar to
those of the Salsoul recordings. In particular, the production values of *Juntos* are present in these Torres-produced recordings. Because of the formal similarities between the Salsoul and SAR
recordings, the SAR recordings will not be discussed in detail. Although a thorough analysis is beyond the established purview of
this document, these recordings should, and hopefully will, be subjected to a more rigorous examination in the future. Suffice it to

say that there are many outstanding *salsa* pieces on these three volumes, as well as some excellent soloing by Armenteros.

Caiman

Switching to an all-instrumental format, Armenteros recorded three albums for the Caiman label. *Chocolate en Sexteto* was released in 1983 followed by *¡Rompiendo de Hielo!* in 1984. *Chocolate y Amigos* was recorded around the same time but was not released until several years later. These three albums contain some of the most extended and exciting solo playing by Armenteros on record. Based on a more freewheeling and improvisational approach than utilized on most of his previous recordings, Armenteros' playing on the Caiman works extends the trumpet soloing concepts that he had developed in the 1970s on the Eddie Palmieri and Grupo Folklórico albums. Besides Armenteros, these three albums feature Mario Rivera on baritone saxophone and flute, and future *salsa romántica*–producing mogul Sergio George on piano.

While the Salsoul and SAR recordings are very similar in terms of formal characteristics, the three Caiman instrumental recordings represent a major change in musical conception and approach. Although the *descarga* performances on the second half of *Chocolate en el Rincón* foreshadow the *descarga* style of the Caiman recordings, the rest of the selections on the Salsoul and SAR albums are in the mainstream vocal-oriented *salsa* realm. All three albums Armenteros recorded on Caiman in the mid-1980s (*Chocolate en Sexteto, Chocolate y Amigos,* and *¡Rompiendo de Hielo!*) are currently available in CD form. Comments here will focus on the first two of these volumes.

There are three basic formal types used on *Chocolate en Sexteto* and *Chocolate y Amigos.* One type is the *descarga,* which predominates on *Chocolate en Sexteto.* A second type of piece is the instrumental interpretation of a standard song from the Afro-Cuban tradition. This practice is most prevalent on *Chocolate y Amigos*. The final song type is the instrumental *bolero*.

Four of the six selections on *Chocolate en Sexteto* are straight-out *descargas* authored by Armenteros. Two of the four *descargas* are remakes of pieces recorded previously on the Grupo Folklórico albums. "Chocolate's guajira" is a very loose interpretation of "Choco's guajira" on volume one of the Grupo Folklórico set. While this recording lacks the vocal *coro* of the original, much of the initial trumpet melody is identical. Another difference between the two *guajira* recordings is the use here of a piano performing the *guajeo* instead of the *tres* on the original. The second version is also faster in tempo than the Grupo Folklórico original.

The other remake is the *guaguancó* "Trompeta en cueros," which was originally included on the second Grupo Folklórico volume. In this case, the similarities are greater than in the two versions of the *guajira*. Armenteros begins both versions of "Trompeta en cueros" with a rubato solo. He plays completely solo on the Grupo Folklórico rendition; on the *Chocolate en Sexteto* version he plays over a series of out-of-tempo percussion figures. In both cases, the initial solo section is followed by a continuation of the trumpet solo over a percussion *rumba* sans bass and chordal instruments. Much of the trumpet solo in this section is a prewritten (albeit with many improvised embellishments) melody that is quite similar on both recordings. At the end of this section, Armenteros plays the *coro* melody and brings in the rest of the ensemble. On the original, the *coro* comes in with the same melody and initiates a call-and-response section with the trumpeter. On the *Chocolate en Sexteto* version both horns perform the initial *coro* figure and Mario Rivera plays the second (and final) *coro* on baritone saxophone before Armenteros goes completely solo. The original recording features a *tres* solo instead of the Sergio George piano solo of the Caiman remake. Instead of trading with the *coro* toward the end of the piece, as on the Grupo Folklórico version, Armenteros trades solo sections with

Rivera on this remake. The other two *descargas* on *Chocolate en Sexteto* are both *son-montunos* written by Armenteros. Both "Montuno caliente" and "Trompeta en montuno" contain extended soloing by members of the band.

A second type of composition featured on the Caiman recordings is the traditional Afro-Cuban standard. This type of piece is represented on *Chocolate en Sexteto* by the *son-pregon* "El manicero (The Peanut Vendor)," which was an internationally popular success in the 1930s. There are three Afro-Cuban standards on *Chocolate y Amigos*. "Son de la loma" is one of the most famous of Cuban songs and was originally recorded in the early 1920s by the seminal *son* group Trio Matamoros. Likewise, "Guantanamera" and "La Macarena" are standard songs that are recognized not just by Latin Americans but throughout the world. Although there are many *descarga* elements present in these renditions of Cuban standards, the lyricism of Armenteros is showcased in his inventive interpretations of these famous melodies.

"Mi sentir" on *Chocolate en Sexteto* is a rhythmic *bolero-beguine*, while the two *boleros* on *Chocolate y Amigos* feature sophisticated synthesizer-based arrangements by Sergio George in a preview of his future career as a star-making producer for RMM and other commercial Latin music labels.

Armenteros' work as a featured sideman on these and other labels during the same time period is equally impressive. In addition to pursuing his own projects, Armenteros spent much of the late 1970s travelling the world with Sonora Mantancera; following this tenure, Armenteros rejoined Machito's band for most of the 1980s. Among the recordings he performed on during the 1970s was *With a Touch of Brass* (1974) by the New York band Tipica Novel. While on tour in Venezuela with Sonora Mantancera in 1979, Armenteros recorded *Se Empató el Sonero* with Sonero Clasico del Caribe, which consisted of a number of veteran Venezuelan musicians who specialized in the Cuban *son/septeto* style. In a departure, Armenteros lent his authentic Caribbean trumpet stylings to a *calypso* record album entitled *Knockdown Calypso '79* by Trinidad veteran Growling Tiger. In the 1980s, Armenteros performed as a sideman on numerous albums. He appeared with Machito on three albums recorded in 1982 and 1983 in conjunction with a historic series of appearances by the band in London during the early 1980s. Departing from his normal *salsa* context, Armenteros appeared with an American jazz group on pianist Cedar Walton's *Eastern Rebellion 4*, which featured, among others, noted jazz trombonist Curtis Fuller. Aside from his work as a leader, Armenteros recorded prolifically on the Caiman label as a sideman during the 1980s. Among the recordings was *Super All-Star '84*, which featured an all-star line up including Tito Puente and Paquito D'Rivera. In a more traditional mode, he recorded on *Pionero del Son* with Alfredo Valdés, Sr. in 1984 and on *Con Tumbao* with Los Guaracheros de Oriente (Clarke 1998).

CHOCOLATE: ELDER STATESMAN

In the late 1980s and early 1990s, legendary Cuban bassist Israel "Cachao" Lopez made an impressive reappearance on the Afro-Cuban musical scene. In addition to recording a two-volume set of Grammy award–winning CDs entitled *Master Sessions, I and II*, in 1995, Lopez and his cast of characters filmed a documentary, *Como Su Ritmo No Hay Dos*, which was produced and directed by actor Andy Garcia. The group included both younger musicians (trombonist Jimmy Bosch and saxophonist Paquito D'Rivera) and veterans (Armenteros and pianist Alfredo Valdez, Jr.). Cachao also revived the traditional *danzón* and the *charanga* with this group. In fact, this ensemble was two bands in one, with instrumental changes made to reflect either the *danzón* or the *son* tradition. When a *danzón* was performed, the ensemble included a string section and the flutist Nestor Torres. A horn section replaced these players when a *descarga* was performed. Like the members of

Grupo Folklórico in the mid-1970s and the Cuban purists of the early *salsa* era, Cachao's goal was to create an Afro-Cuban renaissance. Armenteros' trumpet playing on these Lopez dates was one of the crucial elements in providing authenticity to this *charanga/ conjunto/descarga* recreation. His junior colleague on trombone, Jimmy Bosch, proved his own firm grasp of the "Chocolate" style. Although Armenteros was in his sixties by the time these recordings were made, age obviously had had little deleterious effect on the trumpet master's performing prowess.

As the twenty-first century begins, Armenteros, now in his seventh decade, remains very active. Following up on the major success of Lopez' *Master Sessions* CDs and documentary film in the mid-1990s, Armenteros recorded two CDs with the Caiman label all-star group, the Estrellas Caiman. Both CDs feature top *salsa* stars under the musical direction of pianist Alfredo Valdez, Jr. The first CD, *Descarga in New York,* was released in 1995 and features, among other selections, an Armenteros interpretation of the Kurt Weill standard "Mack the Knife," which the trumpeter had previously recorded on *¡Rompiendo de Hielo!* from his Caiman period. The Estrellas Caiman's *Descarga del Milenio,* released in 1997, is a slicker production, featuring most of the same performers plus a string section. This second volume is less swinging and freewheeling than the initial recording.

Armenteros is featured prominently on trombonist Jimmy Bosch's first recording as a leader, *Soneando Trombón,* released in 1998 on the Rykolatino label. The year 1998 also marked the first release in a number of years of a new Armenteros-led recording; entitled *Chocolate and His Latin Soul,* the Caiman CD is an instrumental compendium featuring a front line of trumpet and a four-man saxophone section.

The latest generation of Cuba-based musicians and groups did not exist when Armenteros left Cuba. Many of the top musicians on the current Cuban scene weren't even born when Armenteros left Cuba four decades ago. "When I left it was all about Arsenio,

René Alvarez, Arcaño y Sus Maravillas, Beny Moré, Melodia del
40, La Orquesta Ideal de Joseito. These other fellows [Jesus Alemañy, Los Van Van, etc.] weren't around yet" (Armenteros 1999).
When asked about his opinion of current Afro-Cuban/salsa–based
trumpet players, he finds many of them lacking. His main com-
plaint is that they are deficient in originality and individual identity. Two exceptions are Luis "Perico" Ortiz and Jesus Alemañy. Armenteros has a high regard for the well-rounded musicianship of
producer/composer/trumpeter Ortiz. As for Alemañy, Armenteros
admires the young trumpet player's respect for tradition and states,
"he's one of the musicians that preserves the style pretty well" (Armenteros 1999). Armenteros enjoys the Cuban genres such as the
songo and *timba* that have been created by newer Cuban musicians and is happy that the younger bands are often using traditional instruments such as the *rumba*-associated *bata* drums.

At the end of the twentieth century, Alfredo "Chocolate" Armenteros actively and proudly maintains his position as, arguably,
the most important of all Afro-Cuban/salsa trumpet players. In addition to numerous other engagements, on the first Monday of
every month Armenteros can be found at Willie's Steak House be-
neath the elevated IRT #6 train on Westchester Avenue in the
Bronx. As regular guest soloist with pianist Willie Rodríguez' house
band, Armenteros continues to be a living tribute to the Afro-
Cuban *septeto* trumpet tradition.

"SI ACASO"

Overview

"Si acaso," from the Armenteros-led recording *Chocolate Aquí*,
is a *son-montuno* in the key of B♭ major. Table 7.1 provides a time
line of the entire recording and will be referred to in the following
analysis. The transcriptions of the seven trumpet solos in section A
also will be referred to in the text of the analysis.

Table 7.1. Time Line of "Si acaso"

Time-(min./sec.)	Section	Description
	Part A	
0:00	1. Prelude	Material independent of the main composition. Brahms lullaby is performed instrumentally by piano, bass, and percussion.
0:16	2. mm. 1–3	Three measure pickup to main part of composition.
0:20	3. mm. 4–63	Call and response between *coro* and trumpet.
	a) mm. 4–7	*Coro* 1.
	b) mm. 8–11	Trumpet solo 1.
	c) mm. 12–15	*Coro* 2.
	d) mm. 16–19	Trumpet solo 2.
	e) mm. 20–23	*Coro* 3.
	f) mm. 24–27	Trumpet solo 3.
	g) mm. 28–31	*Coro* 4.
	h) mm. 32–35	Trumpet solo 4.
	i) mm. 36–39	*Coro* 5.
	j) mm. 40–43	Trumpet solo 5.
	k) mm. 44–47	*Coro* 6.
	l) mm. 48–51	Trumpet solo 6.
	m) mm. 52–55	*Coro* 7.
	n) mm. 56–59	Trumpet solo 7.
	o) mm. 60–63	*Coro* 8.
	Part B	
1:31	1. mm. 64–103	Piano solo.
2:19	2. mm. 104–118	Piano/bass vamp.
	Part C	
2:32	1. mm. 119–149	Four measure call and response between *coro* and trumpet. Only second half of text is utilized.
2:57	2. mm. 150–166	Rhythm switches to regular *montuno* from vamp.
3:16	3. mm. 167–1752+	*Coro* switches to singing-only text from last measure of *coro* lyrics. Engineer electronically fades recording.

The recording opens with a slow version of the Brahms lullaby. Although the introduction is in the same key as the rest of the performance, it is otherwise totally unconnected musically with the main part of the piece. In addition to the piano statement of the lullaby melody with bass and triangle accompaniment, there are verbal comments by Armenteros. The lullaby is followed by a sudden three-measure introduction to the main part of the song (figure 7.1).

Figure 7.1.   "Si acaso": Opening break

This part of the introduction quickly establishes the two-three *son-montuno clave*. The third measure also contains the anacrusis of the four-measure *coro* (figure 7.2).

Figure 7.2.   "Si acaso": Four-measure *coro*

The first major part (A) of the recording is a sixty-measure call and response between the *coro* and Armenteros. Each of the four-measure statements of the *coro* is followed by a four-measure trumpet improvisation. Because the *coro* begins and ends the A section, there are eight *coro*s and seven trumpet solos. Harmonically, the basic four-measure *montuno* pattern of dominant-tonic differs slightly between the *coro* section and the solo section. The trumpet solos are played over the four-bar *montuno* in the form of a two-measure dominant chord resolving to a two-measure tonic harmony. During the *coro*, however, the resolution to the tonic is delayed by one measure. In this case, the basic pattern is three bars of dominant harmony followed by one measure of tonic.

The second main part is a forty-measure piano improvisation (with spoken comments) over the *montuno* followed by a piano/bass vamp, which introduces the final main section (C) of the recorded performance. The vamp is a four-measure figure, which is repeated eight times. The fourth time through the vamp, the C section starts with the *coro* coming in on the second part of the four-measure pattern.

The trumpet enters at the beginning of the next four-measure pattern, followed again two measures later by the *coro* (figure 7.3).

por - que ma - ña - na_hay que tra - ba - jar   si_a - ca - so

Figure 7.3. "Si acaso": Four-measure *coro* with first phrase missing

Omitting the first line of the lyrics and singing the second line every four measures creates a four-bar diminution of the original eight-measure *coro*/trumpet call-and-response pattern. This stretto-like effect provides for more extensive overlapping between the *coro* and Armenteros.

Sixteen measures after the initial entry of the trumpet, the piano and bass switch from the vamp to a straight *montuno* tumbao. After sixteen bars of *montuno*, the *coro* is shortened even further to the phrase from the last measure of the original *coro* (figure 7.4).

si_a - ca - so   si_a - ca - so

Figure 7.4. "Si acaso": Truncated *coro* using last phrase

This phrase is now sung in the second and fourth measures of the *montuno*, which serves to further truncate the call-and-response pattern. By this time, Armenteros is improvising almost continuously. This continues for eight plus measures as the engineer fades the piece electronically.

The *Coro* and the Trumpet Solos in Section A

The series of *coro*/trumpet solo exchanges in section A consists of eight four-bar *coros* (see figure 7.2) alternating with seven four-measure trumpet improvisations. The *coro* begins and ends this section, which explains the extra *coro* part. The *coro* begins with a three-note pickup starting rhythmically on the upbeat of two followed by the upbeat of three and the downbeat of four. The three pitches, D5, B♭4, and G5, lead to a dotted quarter-note F4 starting on the first beat of the *montuno* phrase structure. The first full measure of the *coro* contains an arpeggiation of the dominant harmony using two dotted quarter- and eighth-note rhythmic patterns. Rising from F4 to C5, the measure ends with a return to the third of the chord on the upbeat of beat four. This usage of dotted quarter- and eighth-note patterns is a common way of representing the two-side of *clave*. After ascending linearly to E♭5 on the upbeat of two in the second measure of the phrase, there is a melodic descent ending with F4 on the upbeat of one in the fourth measure followed by A4 on the upbeat of two and a final G4 on the fourth beat. The three-note figure in the second measure of the *montuno* phrase is an identical rhythmic repetition of the *coro*'s pickup measure and follows a similar melodic line. However, instead of an arpeggio movement as in the initial trumpet pickups, the E♭5 proceeds stepwise to C5. Ascending briefly with three repetitions of D5 (a quarter note and two eighth notes), the descent to F4 continues with two C5s and a B♭4 in a syncopated eighth-note/quarter-note/eighth-note pattern on the last two beats of the third measure in the *montuno*.

One reason for the truncation of the *coro* in section C is that the pickup of the *coro* occupies the same rhythmic area of the *montuno* as in the final measure of the *coro*. All seven of the trumpet solos in section A are initiated rhythmically in the fourth measure of the preceding *coro*. Because five of the solos start on the upbeat of two in the pickup bar, the relationship between solo and *coro* is strengthened. This relationship creates both melodic unity and increased complexity because of the overlapping combination in measure four of the *coro* and the trumpet solo pickups and a further overlapping on the final bar of each solo when the *coro* pickups reoccur.

There are three instances of the trumpet solo continuing into the following *coro*. Solo one ends on the first beat of the following phrase. In solo five, Armenteros extends the solo an entire measure into the sixth *coro* section. Finally, solo seven appropriates almost two full measures of the final *coro*. The figure from the final measure of solo five is repeated in the penultimate measure of solo seven. The trumpet solos (in section A) range in pitch from E♭4 in solos five and seven to C6 in solo three.

The first two solos have quick initial ascents and then descend slowly to the lower register. Activity then returns to the middle range before re-descending to the initial register. Solo one, starting with an F4 on the second half of beat two in m. 7, begins with five consecutive upbeats leading to a G5 on the third beat of m. 8 (figure 7.5).

Figure 7.5.   "Si acaso": Solo one

The first three notes are a second inversion arpeggio of the underlying tonic harmony. On the upbeat of beat one in m. 8 (the first measure of the *montuno* pattern), G5 is the ninth of the dominant harmony and the highest pitch in the first solo. A linear descent from G5 to C5 takes place between beat three of m. 8 and the third beat of m. 9, with a brief detour to F5 on beat two. (There is a subtle rhythmic delay in this part of the phrase which cannot be indicated using traditional notation.) The final module of this solo starts slightly behind the beat and subtly increases in momentum to a final, nine-note,

eighth-note figure that ends up on the forward part of the beat rhythmically. This figure starts on F4 and mimics the opening anacrusis,
but the final D5 of m. 10 (repeated in m. 11) is the highest pitch of
the figure, which soon returns to F4 at the conclusion of the extended
eighth-note figure cited previously.

The second solo is almost identical to the first in terms of
melodic linearity (figure 7.6).

Figure 7.6. "Si acaso": Solo two

An initial arpeggio again leads to a G5 that descends to an F4 and,
as in solo one, ascends to D5 in m. 3 of the phrase; it returns to F4
and G4 at the end of this solo. Although the second solo is almost
identical linearly to the first solo, there is an increase in melodic
embellishment and rhythmic density. The initial pickup arpeggio is
a series of eighth-note triplets consisting of the chord tones surrounding lower chromatic neighbor notes. As in the first solo, the
rhythmic thrust stretches behind the pulse during the middle of
the phrase (most noticeably in the second half of m. 17) and snaps
back to the forward part of the beat by the end of the four-bar section. The rhythm also is increased in density at the end of this
phrase by two sixteenth-note embellishments, which are executed
in a manner that reflects the idiosyncrasies of trumpet technique.
The rhythmic subtlety of the performance of these embellishment
figures cannot be described properly using standard sixteenth-note
notation.

The third solo section also has a quick initial ascent, which, in
this case, is to the highest register of section A (C5). Following an
initial descent to F4, the line eventually returns to A♭5 at the end
of the solo (figure 7.7).

Figure 7.7. "Si acaso": Solo three

Solo three is the most rhythmically complex of the trumpet solos in section A. The first three notes in m. 24 are an excellent
demonstration of the manner in which Armenteros (and other
Cuban soloists) stretch rhythm. These three notes can be notated
rhythmically in two different ways, neither of which is an accurate
representation of what is occurring aurally. If the three notes were
indicated and performed as two eighth notes surrounding a quarter, the underlying rhythmic *clave* would be most closely reinforced. By stretching this three-note figure toward quarter-note
triplets, a rhythmic tension is created that is resolved by a return
to standard eighth-note-oriented syncopation during the next measure and an half. This resolution is partially compromised by a
slightly behind-the-beat statement of these more traditional
rhythms. The stretching of an eighth-note syncopation toward a
quarter-note triplet is a common ploy in Cuban brass soloing. In
addition to the melodic similarities between the second measures
in each of the first three solos, there are reiterations of a rhythmic
cell consisting of an upbeat eighth note leading to a downbeat
quarter note. The rhythmic impetus toward the back of the beat is
also a common feature of these three measures. The last three
measures of solo three are linearly similar to the corresponding areas of the first two solos, with the exception of the final notes in the
phrase, which ascend to A♭5 (a nonchord tone and arguably an un-
intended pitch). The trumpet line in these two measures is the
most rhythmically complex and notation-resistant part of section A
and furthers the elaboration (initiated in solo two) of the original
melodic module in solo one (mm. 10–11).

The fourth solo section, with the exception of the final note, consists of twelve consecutive iterations of G5 (figure 7.8).

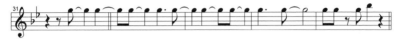

Figure 7.8. "Si acaso": Solo four

These notes are placed to rhythmically reinforce the *clave*. The phrase ends on a B♭5, the only deviation in this solo section from G5. The first eight notes are one and a half beats in duration. Unlike in the first three solos, none of the notes in this solo section stray from the underlying rhythm. Instead of being in front of or behind the beat, each iteration of the G5 lands completely in sync with the rhythm section. For the most part, the *clave* rhythm is reinforced directly during the solo. The pickup notes in m. 31 are placed on the second and third parts of the three-side of the *clave*. The rhythmic placement of the third note on the upbeat of beat one in m. 32 is, in Latin music, a common approach to beat three in the two-side of the *clave*. The fourth note is, indeed, on the third beat and is rhythmically reinforced by the preceding note. The fifth G5 is on the upbeat of the fourth beat of the two-side of the *clave* and leads to the sixth note on beat two of the three-side. Neither of these rhythmic placements coincides directly with the *clave* pattern. However, the upbeat of four on the two-side of *clave* is a commonly reinforced rhythmic area in Cuban music, and the downbeat of two is part of the *timbale cascara* rhythm that sets up the following upbeat figures.

The placement of the seventh G5 is consistent with the upbeat character of the three-side of *clave*. Although the two notes in m. 34 would appear to contradict the *clave*, in Latin music the first beat in a measure is, perhaps, the most innocuous (in contrast to European music), and the upbeat of two is normally played by the bass player in every measure. In m. 35, the notes on the upbeats of one and two reaffirm the *clave*. The final note (B♭5) of the solo lands on the third beat, which is, ironically, a common way to follow the upbeat of beat two on the three-side of the *clave*.

The fifth solo section starts with a three-note pickup phrase on B♭5. The following four measures consist of a descending melodic minor scale from G5 to G4 (figure 7.9).

Figure 7.9. "Si acaso": Solo five

Each note is played three times as two eighth notes and a quarter note. The repeating three-note figure is in direct opposition to the standard practice of Cuban music. Normally, especially in the *conga* and cowbell parts, beats two and four contain stressed eighth-note figures. By placing the eighth notes on beats one and three, a rhythmic dissonance is created. To further reinforce this dissonance, the use of chord extensions dominates the melodic line. Measures 40 and 42 both contain the ninth of the underlying harmony on their first two beats. In m. 41 and m. 43, the three-note groupings are on the seventh of the chord on the first two beats and on the sixth (thirteenth) during beats three and four. Measure 44 breaks the pattern with a jazz-like figure (featuring an ascending triplet arpeggio starting on the lowest note of the recording) that returns the melodic line to the middle part of this solo's range, ending on a C5. This figure is reprised at the end of solo seven.

Linearly, solo six is a recapitulation of solos one and two (figure 7.10).

Figure 7.10. "Si acaso": Solo six

Except for being offset rhythmically, the pickup measure is almost identical to the beginning of solo two. Again descending to F4 in the middle of the phrase (as in solos one and two), the line similarly returns to the middle register at the end of the solo. Solo six (through the ebbing process of its recapitulation) starts the closure of section A.

Armenteros, however, cannot resist heating it up once more in solo seven by playing a highly ornamented series of G5s during the first three measures, similar in many ways to the beginning of solo four (figure 7.11).

Figure 7.11.   "Si acaso": Solo seven

The tension is resolved in the final measures of the solo, which return to the low-middle register using figures that motivically relate to similar episodes in the endings of solos one, two, and six. Armenteros again spills into the first half of the next *coro*. The one-beat displaced reprise of the figure in m. 44 of solo five provides a neat and coherent ending to this series of solos.

NOTES

1. Armenteros 1998. The recorded Armenteros interviews were transcribed into Spanish text and translated into English by Ricardo Luiggi, a professional translator who is knowledgeable about Afro-Cuban/*salsa* music. Much of the biographical material comes from this and other interviews.

2. Some of these Arsenio Rodríguez recordings have been reissued on the *Tumbao* Cuban Classics CDs *Dundunbanza* (TCD-043) and *Montuneado* (TCD-0310).

8

CONCLUSION AND RECOMMENDATIONS

CONCLUSION

Afro-Cuban music has been one of the richest and most important musical traditions to come of age during the past century. This music contains a wide variety of styles, including such genres as *son*, *rumba*, *danzón*, and the religious music of *santería* associated with the *bata* drums. While all of these styles are important, *son* has been the backbone of mainstream Cuban music. From its beginnings at the turn of the last century in the trios of the Oriente province to its golden age in the *conjuntos* of modern Cuba and the *salsa* bands of New York City, *son* has led the way. Ever since trumpet was added to the *son* sextet in the 1920s, this expressive instrument has been a mainstay in most Cuban bands. Between them, Félix Chappottín and his younger colleague Alfredo "Chocolate" Armenteros have been present at almost every major turning point in the development of Afro-Cuban music.

By the late 1920s, when Sexteto Habanero recorded "Coralia" and "Criollo haragan," most of the formal elements that drove *conjunto* and *salsa* groups in later decades were in place. Even though the instrumentation changed in later years, other components such as the two-part *largo/montuno* form already existed. Most importantly, the *clave* and the recurring *montuno* pattern became the fundamental building blocks of the *son* heritage. The call and response between *coros* and either solo singers or instrumental soloists over the *montuno* pattern is another feature of the early *son* groups that has remained essential throughout the history of Afro-Cuban music. It was precisely during these short responses between *coros* that the mainstream Afro-Cuban solo trumpet style developed. Although the solos of the earliest *son* trumpet players—such as Enrique Hernández, José Interián, and the young Chappottín—are relatively simple and unsophisticated, they contain the stylistic elements that fueled the playing of Armenteros, the mature Chappottín, and the other mainstream Cuban trumpet soloists. By the time Sexteto Habanero and Septeto Nacional produced their landmark recordings in the 1920s and 1930s, all of the instruments in the ensemble had realized their particular roles in the *clave*-based musical texture. In particular, the anticipated bass and the *tres*/guitar (later piano) *guajeo* had for the most part achieved their final form by this time.

The *conjunto* of the 1940s as exemplified by Arsenio Rodríguez represents modern Cuban music in one of its most fundamental aspects. With the addition of *congas*, piano, and the trumpet section, the instrumentation of the standard modern *conjunto* was finalized. There are two aspects of the modern *conjunto* that are of concern in the study of trumpet performance. One is the formation of two or more trumpeters into a section. Trumpet arrangements varied from simple harmonizations of melodic lines that were derived from the earlier *son* trumpet solo style to elaborate orchestrations, often with elements borrowed from New York big bands of the time such as the Machito orchestra or Dizzy Gillespie's Afro-Cuban jazz band of the late 1940s. These brass section parts could either be settings behind the vocalists in the *largo* or alternating with the *coro* in call-and-response *montuno* patterns.

Maturity in the trumpet solo style is the second trumpet-related development of the classic *conjunto*. It was in the 1940s that trumpeters like Félix Chappottín and his protege Armenteros became well-known soloists with distinctive improvisational styles. The development of the solo trumpet style from its early *son* roots to its manifestation in the playing of Chappottín and Armenteros has been the main focus of this book and its music analysis component.

When Chappottín as a twenty-year-old joined Septeto Habanero in 1928, he was not the first trumpet player to play with a *son* band, but he was the most important. In the same way that Louis Armstrong took the style developed by older New Orleans trumpeters like Freddie Keppard and King Oliver and developed into the first mature trumpet soloist in jazz, Chappottín innovated a mature Afro-Cuban soloing style from the elemental playing of other early trumpeters such as Hernández, Interián, and Lazaro Herrera. Prior to Chappottín, the trumpet almost exclusively played the melody of the song alternating with the vocalists. On Habanero recordings such as "Coralia" and especially "Lamento esclavo," Chappottín shows that he is not afraid to take off and improvise. By the time he recorded "Lamento esclavo" in 1931, he had almost fully developed the trumpet solo style that brought him fame with Arsenio Rodríguez and during his three-decade-plus leadership of Chappottín y Sus Estrellas. His solos on songs like "Dundunbanza" with Rodríguez and "Camina y prende el fogón" with his own band amply demonstrate why Félix Chappottín is considered by many to be the most important trumpet player in Afro-Cuban music history.

In his early recorded solos with René Alvarez and Arsenio Rodríguez, Alfredo "Chocolate" Armenteros showed that he was ready to grab the baton from Chappottín. On "Para las niñas y para las señoras" with Alvarez and "No puedo comer vistagacha" with Rodríguez, Armenteros demonstrates a power and fluidity of technique that surpasses his older colleagues and a sophisticated rhythmic conception that is surprising for a player in his early twenties.

In a sense, Armenteros played the role of Miles Davis or Clifford Brown to Chappottín's Armstrong and updated the soloing style of the Cuban trumpet.

Because the development of New York *salsa* and the prime years of Armenteros' trumpet playing career coincided, it was important to examine the music of that period in detail. The relationship between Eddie Palmieri and Armenteros is particularly vital in analyzing the trumpeter's approach to extended soloing. Finally, by looking at the recordings Armenteros released as a leader, insight can be gained into his creative approach to music.

"Bilongo" as recorded by Eddie Palmieri on his *Superimposition* album is one of the most important *salsa*-era recordings to feature the soloing of Armenteros. More than twenty years after his first recordings in Havana with René Alvarez and Arsenio Rodríguez, Armenteros is at his peak on "Bilongo" and his other recordings at this time. Most of the formal aspects of "Bilongo" are the same as those of its prototypes in the *son* and *conjunto* ensembles: an extended *largo* section and a typical *montuno* section based on a four-measure pattern. There also are two significant differences between the *salsa* ensemble on the Palmieri recording of "Bilongo" and the classic Cuban *conjunto*: the additions of the *timbales* and the extended trombone *moña*. One of the changes in instrumentation that took place in the development of *salsa* was the completion of the three-drum battery when the *charanga*-associated *timbales* joined the prevailing *congas* and *bongos*. The primary effect of this instrument, with its accenting ability and attached cowbells, was an increase in the rhythmic intensity of the musical fabric. A carryover from Palmieri's earlier band La Perfecta, the continuous trombone *moña* plays a very important and dynamic role in supporting the trumpet solo on "Bilongo." The trumpet solo on "Bilongo" is much longer and more virtuosic than any solos would have been in the *conjunto* days. The increase in solo length partially reflects the *descarga* Cuban jam sessions of, among others, Israel "Cachao" Lopez.

When Armenteros began his career as a leader on the mid-1970s, he returned to the *conjunto* tradition of short solos alternating with *coros*. However, as "Si acaso" from the album *Chocolate Aquí* indicates, he has not abandoned the virtuoso playing style he exhibited on the Palmieri albums. As the music analyses of "Bilongo" and "Si acaso" demonstrate, Armenteros has a complete grasp of the *septeto* style. His playing style combines the time-stretching, syncopated, eighth-note/quarter-note triplet-based, rhythmic sophistication of Chappottín and Florecita with a trumpet performance technique that far surpasses that of his contemporaries. Armenteros' solos are loaded with *septeto*-style influences such as three-against-four rhythmic figures and minor key modal shifting.

As a septuagenarian, Alfredo "Chocolate" Armenteros is still active as one of the pillars of Afro-Cuban trumpet performance. In the past few years, he has not only released a CD—*Chocolate and His Cuban Soul*—as a leader, but he has, among other things, been a featured soloist on a recording and appeared in a movie with the Chico O'Farrill big band. Now the elder statesman of Cuban trumpeters, Armenteros continues to play in the *septeto* style that he learned as a young man from his musical mentors, Chappottín and Florecita.

RECOMMENDATIONS FOR FURTHER STUDY

While this book provides a beginning, there is still much to be learned about the lives and music of Félix Chappottín and Alfredo "Chocolate" Armenteros. More thorough biographical investigations of these two men need to be undertaken. While the emphasis in this book has been on music analysis, it is important that ethnological and biographical research is done in Cuba on both of these men and their social milieu before the passage of time distorts or destroys the pertinent data. This is especially important in the case of Chappottín in that he is the older of the two and has been deceased for two decades. A detailed discography needs to be created of his work in the 1930s and with bands other than Sexteto Habanero, Arsenio Rodríguez, and his own group. Information about his work with these three groups also needs to be clarified and expanded.

Even though Armenteros is still alive there is still much work to be done in creating a proper biography of this important musician. There need to be additional interviews with the trumpeter as well as with others familiar with his background. It would be useful to do field research in the Las Villas province of Cuba, where information about his family and youth is available. His professional roots in Havana also need to be researched in this manner. Additional music transcriptions and analyses from various stages of his career are necessary to gain a fuller understanding of his playing style and its development.

In the area of Afro-Cuban brass playing, there are a number of avenues of inquiry. The work of other trumpet players needs to be analyzed and their lives researched. Although this book has focused on Chappottín and Armenteros, there have been numerous other important trumpet players involved in the history of Afro-Cuban music. Generations of distinguished trumpeters from the earliest *son* players to modern-day Latin jazz star soloists have all contributed to a remarkable body of work. In the earliest days of the *septeto,* these included such brass players as Enrique Hernández, José Interián, Lazaro Herrera, and Enrique "Florecita" Velazco. Mario Bauza, Carmelo Alvarez, El Negro Vivar, Luis Escalante, and Armando Armenteros are just a few of the many Cuban trumpeters to have emerged in the 1940s, 1950s, and 1960s. In New York this same era produced numerous players of various origins. These include Pedro "Puchi" Bouloung, Victor Paz, David Gonzales, Tony Cofresi, and Roy Roman. Many talented trumpeters came of age in the past three decades, including Ray Maldonado, Luis "Perico" Ortiz, Arturo Sandoval, Jesús Alemañy, and Ray Vega. Even this relatively long list represents a small percentage of the many talented trumpet players who have been involved in this great brass tradition.

Another topic that needs to be further analyzed is the brass section. As discussed briefly in chapter 3, brass arranging developed in a different way in the *conjunto* than it did in the jazz-influenced New York City bands of leaders like Machito and Tito Puente. These implications need to be examined in greater detail.

Yet another brass-related subject that needs to be studied is the use of the trombone in Afro-Cuban and *salsa* music. Like its smaller cousin the trumpet, the trombone merits study in terms of its solo style and its role in the Afro-Cuban/*salsa* ensemble. While the mainstream use of trombone in Afro-Cuban music and *salsa* does not have the long history that the trumpet does, many distinguished players have come along since Generoso "Tojo" Jiménez and others originated the solo style in the 1950s. These include Barry Rogers, Jose Rodrigues, Lewis Kahn, Reynaldo Jorge, Papo Vásquez, Jimmy Bosch, and many other excellent trombonists.

Although this particular research project is concerned with trumpet playing, this subject area constitutes only a small corner of the Afro-Cuban music world. Many musicians and groups deserve to have their music subjected to thorough critical and academic examination. Bandleaders like Machito, Arsenio Rodríguez, Arcaño, Cachao, and Tito Puente are obvious choices as analytical subjects. Sexteto Habanero and Ignacio Piñeiro's Septeto Nacional are historically as important to Cuban music as early American bands led by Fletcher Henderson and Louis Armstrong are to jazz. Singers like Beny Moré, Celia Cruz, and Miguelito Cuní, and a number of well-known instrumental performers are all likely candidates for further research in the Afro-Cuban genre. Most of the leaders of the *salsa* movement in the 1960s and 1970s are now world famous figures; artists like Eddie Palmieri, Willie Colón, Larry Harlow, and others will one day be accorded fuller academic inquiry.

In addition to individuals, there needs to be more research work done on general historical issues. One major project that sorely needs to be undertaken is a thorough documentation of the recorded canon. Because the musicians are aging, it is important to establish a Smithsonian-like archive of interviews. Not only would this help in establishing the aforementioned documentation; this archive would be important in its own right by providing an invaluable resource for scholars.

Though the primary focus of this academic work is the *son/conjunto/salsa* tradition, other genres of Cuban music are worthy of attention. An obvious choice is the other mainstream dance band style: the *danzón/charanga* style. Only its irrelevance to brass playing downplayed its role in this study. Another area that is of paramount significance to *son* and other modern Cuban styles is the folklore music associated with the *rumba*, the *comparsa*, and the *santería* religion. A relatively unknown body of Cuban music is the rich theater tradition, as exemplified by composers Ernesto Lecuona and Eliseo Grenet. Although Robin D. Moore's book *Nationalizing Blackness: Afrocubanismo and Artistic Revolution in Havana, 1920–1940*, is an important resource for this music, further study (including modern-day re-creations of these theater works) needs to be undertaken. The final type of Cuban music that calls for further investigation is the Cuban-composed European concert music that incorporates elements from the folklore and mainstream styles of the island. Perhaps the most famous of these composers are Alejandro García Caturla and Amadeo Roldán.

Finally, a comprehensive history of Cuban music (in the Gunther Schuller jazz tradition) is a project that needs to one day come to fruition. However, before that kind of long-term project can take place, the research must be undertaken and the data gathered. This information must be collected before much of it disappears.

APPENDIX A

Glossary of Terms

Botijo—an instrument fashioned from a large ceramic jug into which the performer directed his airstream to create the sound. (Similar techniques were used at the same time in the United States by jug bands associated with the Mississippi delta blues.)

Cascara—a drum-shell tapping rhythm.

Chachachá—a slow rhythmic dance derived from the *danzón*.

Clave—the fundamental rhythmic unit of Cuban music. The two-measure pattern, once established, is repeated throughout the performance. The *clave* pattern consists of a "two-side" and a "three-side." In their simplest representation, the two-side contains two downbeat quarter-note rhythms on the second and third beats and the three-side consists of three notes on the downbeats of one and four and the upbeat of two. The *clave* of a particular piece can be either three-two or two-three.

Comparsa—a folk style of carnival music that features percussion instruments, trumpets, and vocals.

Conjunto—a term most often associated with the type of ensemble led by *tres* player Arsenio Rodríguez in the 1940s. The *conjunto* evolved from the *son* ensemble of the 1920s and 1930s.

The addition of the *conga* drum and the creation of a brass ensemble are two of the main changes between the early *septeto* and the modern *conjunto*.

Coro—The *coro* is a repeating phrase sung by a chorus of two or more singers. The phrase will occupy all or part of a recurring *montuno* pattern. Normally, the *coro* alternates *montunos* with a solo singer or instrumentalist.

Descarga—an Afro-Cuban jam session.

Guaguancó—one of the major forms of the *rumba*. The *guaguancó* is the version of the *rumba* that is most commonly used by the modern *conjunto*.

Guajeo—a repeated rhythmic vamp typically played by the *tres* or the piano.

Guaracha—an uptempo Cuban music genre that is similar to the *son* and contains a *montuno* section.

Guiro—a percussion instrument, traditionally a hollowed-out gourd, that is played with a scraper.

Largo—the initial part of an Afro-Cuban song form. The *largo* is in most cases more complex in structure than the second part or *montuno*.

Mambo—the section of an arrangement featuring horn lines and new musical material.

Maracas—hand-held rattles or shakers made from gourds filled with beans.

Marimbula—an instrument with African roots that is built along the architectural designs of the *mbira* or thumb piano; on the *marimbula*, metal strips are fastened to a large resonating wooden box. The strips are tuned by varying their lengths and the performer sits on the box and plays notes by plucking the metal bars. The *marimbula* is strongly associated with the *coros de son*.

Moña—a short repetitive horn line (either written or improvised).

Montuno—a short repeating two-, four-, or eight-measure phrase, based on a simple chord progression, which contains the call-

and-response portion of a piece. The most common usage of the *montuno* is to support the interchange of *coro* (chorus) and *sonero* (solo singer).   However, in many cases the *coro* may exchange *montuno*s with an instrumental soloist. The *montuno* is also commonly used for extended instrumental soloing.

Rumba—traditional secular music and dance genre, rendered by vocals and percussion, or later, in its commercialized form, by a standard dance band.

Salsa—a term coined in New York City during the late 1960s renaissance of the classical Cuban music style. Primarily instigated by Puerto Rican musicians like Eddie Palmieri and Johnny Pacheco, the term *salsa* often refers to the Cuban style in general.

Septeto—Spanish for *seven*; refers to the Cuban trumpet style that evolved when the *son* ensemble of the 1920s and 1930s added a seventh performer: a trumpet player.

Son—the single most popular dance music genre of twentieth-century Cuba, usually (but not always) performed by a group comprised of six pieces. Considered a perfect balance of African and Spanish musical elements, the *son* is the most common influence on modern Cuban music and *salsa*.

Son pregon—a music form derived from the *son* that is based on the calls of the street vendors in Havana.

Sonero—the solo singer, especially referring to the singing in the *montuno* section of a song.

Son-montuno—a form derived from the *son* genre that features an extended *montuno* section.

Típica—Spanish for the English word *typical*; when referring to Cuban music, *típica* denotes adherence to the *rumba* or *son* tradition.

Tres—a guitar-like instrument that holds three sets of double strings. It is the primary chordal instrument in the *son* ensemble.

Tumbao—a repeated pattern played by the bass and the *congas*.

APPENDIX B

Musical Example: "Bilongo"

"Bilongo" - trumpet introduction and background figures.

"Bilongo" - trumpet solo

APPENDIX C

Interview of Alfredo "Chocolate" Armenteros
(Spanish Transcription)

AUGUST 3, 1998: TAPE 1, SIDE B

Andy González (A): ¿Cuál fue la primera música que tu recuerdas cuando eras niño?

"Chocolate" Armenteros (C): La primera musica que yo recuerdo cuando era niño—en mi casa había un radio d' esos y yo escuchaba "En Mi Campo," el Septeto Habanero, el Septeto Nacional . . .

A: ¿Y ellos estaban transmitiendo en vivo?

C: En la epoca que yo nací no lo pude oir en vivo, pero entonces pasaron a los fonógrafos y en mi casa había fonógrafo tambien y estaban todos esos discos grandes y había que darle manigueta. Después el problema era que no podíamos ir a bailar los mucha-chos—y si yo estoy pegao a la primita o la que sea, me decían "Al-fredito, te toca a ti darle manigueta" y yo decía "¡no, no ——!"

A: (Se rie). ¿Y cuál fue la primera experiencia musical—

C: ¿Que me llevó a mí a la instrucción?

A: *Sí.*

C: Bueno, mi difunto padre fue músico, tocaba trombón cuando joven. Entonces, el padre de Richard Egües, flautista de la Aragon, fue mi primer maestro que vivía en una de las propiedades que teníamos allí los Armenteros puestas. Y estaba yo en la escuela pública y el llega a buscar muchachos que querían tocar música para hacer la banda infantil y yo fuí uno de los primeros que levante la mano. Pues yo empecé con la banda infantil. Y lo primero, en esa epoca, lo que hacían es, te daban el libro del solfeo y la ——. Ahí viene todo—harmonía y todas las áreas. Cuando tú vas por la segunda o tercera parte, te dan el —— del instrumento. Te preguntan después "Que instrumento a usted le gusta"—yo tuve el instrumento que me gustaba—siempre fuí loco con la trompeta. Pero el único que después de la trompeta siempre me gustó fue el saxofón tenor.

A: *¿Y llegaste a tocarlo?*

C: Nó. Entonces me dieron la boquilla de la trompeta para hacer embocadura primero, cómo se soplaba y to', entonces yo, con el (puentecito)—ese era Richard Egües y yo, muchacho, yo iba con Richard a ayudarlo a limpiar la academia en el pueblo y lo que hacíamos era practicar —— y cuando el maestro, el padre de el, me dice "ahora le toca a usted. Ya le voy a enseñar las escalas." Ya yo me sabía las escalas porque estaba to' los días en eso—gracias a eso empecé con la banda infantil. Tú sabes que la banda infantil—cuando tu tocas en banda es como la escuela—lo que tú tocas son operturas—son obras y esas cosas—así que cuando me dicen a mi de sonero que estudió música, de veras—lo primero que tú estás leyendo en la música—lo que tú empiezas—con el primer libro de bajo—tú que eres bajista—ya estás tocando obras—

A: *Sí.*

C: Porque son las primeras que hay que dar—después ya tú vas cogiendo la parte que más te agrada de la música—tú sabes que es la parte que yo escogí—porque después de la banda infantil solo toqué comparsas y eso me encanta, me facilitó. Pero para tener compromisos, ya tuve la oportunidad de entrar a tocar los shows, los cabareses, Tropicana y esas cosas—

A: *Bueno, este, vamos a seguir porque ya con lo que me dijiste me contestaste 6 o 7 preguntas—*

C: (Se rie.)

A: *¿Cuál fue tu primera experiencia tocando con un grupo?*

C: La primera experiencia que yo pasé tocando con un grupo fue con un grupo [en verdadera] fue cuando yo estaba con René Alvarez, que fue cuando ya me nombraron que ya entré a un profesionalismo que yo nunca me sentí así. Yo siempre estaba ——. Ese disco que tú ves aquí en mi cama—18 de marzo del 1949—esa es la primera experiencia que se pasa musical—porque las demás todos estabamos los muchachos juntos.

A: *¿Cuándo tú te viniste aquí para—*

C: Yo me fuí en el año 49.

A: *Así que cuando tú llegaste, ¡lo primero que hiciste fue grabar!*

C: Lo primero que hice fue entrar a [martiberona] a tocar con el Conjunto Habanero, con el Septeto Habanero cuando estaba todavía el director—el que cantaba . . . se me olvida el nombre porque son muchos años—estaba [Bejerín, estaba el Chino bongosero todavía, Chaucho el que cantaba la segunda voz . . . 'toy buscando lel nombre del director . . . Gerardo! Gerardo Martinez era el director. Yo tocaba el martiberona—y de ahí pues, me escucharon y me llamó René Alvarez y ahí es que grabo ya con René—

A: *Los Astros.*

C: Ese, "Los Astros de René Alvarez," el único conjunto que había frente a Arsenio Rodríguez. Pero mi delirio era tocar, que era mi

sueño y siempre lo dire y estoy satisfecho de ir a tocar con Arsenio.
Un día nos toca como a los tres meses tocar una gira en la cerve-
zeria [Polar] frente a frente y cuando termina Arsenio, entramos
nosotros y viene Arsenio con Chappottín y le dice cuando me escucha dice "¡ese es el hombre que yo necesito!" y entonces me
llamó y me habló "¡Muchachito! ¿Quieres empezar conmigo
mañana?" Fíjate tú decirme eso, si yo estoy desesperao—"Yea, yea,
yea!!!" Fíjate que ahí está la foto en el disco cuando yo me junté
con el—que yo no tenía ni el uniforme—me regaló la corbata, la
única que yo tengo igual.

A: ¿Y que pensaba René Alvarez que Arsenio le estaba robando la
trompeta?

C: No, eso es así. Eso es lo mismo que tu tienes hoy en día. Tú tienes
una orquesta, tienes trabajo y tienes músicos. No tienes trabajo, no
tienes músicos. Y yo era loco para tocar con Arsenio—ese era mi an-
helo. Y —— tuve la oportunidad de grabar con René Alvarez, no me
quejo—estoy bien satisfecho. Ahora, cuando llega Arsenio—tú sabes,
cuando tú sales de la escuela que ya quieres llegar—¡coño trabajar
con Arsenio en aquella epoca era ——! Pa mi Amalia en las nubes no
estaba mejor que yo. Sinceramente, que todavía lo digo con mucho
corazón, mucho orgullo—para mi es un orgullo y privilegio es más,
que me regaló un número que se llama ahora "Asi me bote de gueño
(?)"—no es mío, el le puso mi nombre para que yo cobrara ese dinero
y me hiciera el primer uniforme con el—

A: Ajá

C: —— conmigo no era nada de eso. Yo era orgulloso del caminito
que él me llevaba.

A: Quiero hablar sobre Florecita.

C: ¡Aaaa, ese era mi ídolo! Entre Florecita y ——. Enrique Velazco—le pusieron Florecita porque el cogía los números y era flo-
reándolo—por eso le pusieron Florecita.

A: *¿Qué edad tenía Florecita cuando tú lo conociste?*

C: Cuando yo conocí a Florecita yo tenía 21 años y el regresaba de Méjico—ya él era mayor, estaba por los 47 o 48 años... Oye el único privilegio que me queda en el mundo en mi mente y orgulloso—El único que Florecita le aguantaba, con lo relajado que yo soy, yo le decía "Y qué, mi abuelo" y me abrazaba—a mí na'más, a más nadie. Y me tocó la oportunidad que él se fue de la comparsa "La Jardinera" y me llamaron a mí pa' que fuera el sucesor de él y asi que qué mas privilegio podría pedirle a la vida—porque ese fueron, entre Florecita y Chappottín, yo hice asi, yo decía "Bueno si Florecita aquí hace así y Chappottín hace eso, oye por qué yo no puedo hacer algo en el medio?" Y ahí fue que busqué mi estilo. Todos tenemos un seguidor siempre que nos gusta—pero ese fue... y con mucho gusto y mucho cariño... Toda la vida gracias a eso ahí, la experiencia de ayer en la vida de hoy—y bien orgulloso, de ahí salí.

A: *Si porque él no sabía nada de Florecita y yo le toqué unas cosas, tú sabes, Florecita con Miguelito Cuní—*

C: No, eso era... [Él] estaba tocando aquí (señalando) y ve que alguien le va a pasar por aquí y a él no le importa, se quitaba la trompeta y ahí le pasaban pa'que no le rompieran la trompeta—te digo a ti—yo fuí privilegiado. Cuando yo le dije mi abuelo, él me miró así y me abrazó y después [la gente me decía] "coño, qué tú le dijiste? ¡Florecita no le aguanta a nadie que le digan abuelo!" Pero mira yo me safé—pues yo se lo decía con cariño porque lo veo como mayor, no que "mi abuelo" por viejo—coño con el cariño que uno siente—y él se dió cuenta—el único al que se lo admitía...

A: *¿Y tú llegaste a grabar junto a Florecita?*

C: Seguro que sí y tú lo sabes bien—tú me haces esa pregunta y yo se que es pa' la entrevista pero tú sabes que yo te dije a ti cuando nos encontrabamos con René y en cualquier momento no dudes que te encuentras a Joseito Fernandez—

A: *¡Aaaaa, ahora sí!*

C: Y tocaban Chocolate, Alfredo y Florecita tocamos juntos . . . Oye mi china. . . .

A: *¿Y cuales otros músicos en otros instrumentos te influenciaron?*

C: Bueno pues mira ahí estaba en esa epoca, después de Florecita, Chappottín, está Lázaro el pecoso que es mayor que tú has oído, que es un sonero lindo, melódico tocando. Tú sabes, yo lo admiraba, me gustaba escucharlo como al igual escuchaba a todos los otros trompetistas. Yo admiro todo el que toca la trompeta. Porque yo soy yo, el otro es el otro, el otro el otro . . . Ahora, la teoría mía musical, mi línea de mi solo está influenciada por Florecita y Chappottín en el centro . . . Traté de no imitar a ninguno . . .

Rick Davies (RD): What about other instruments?

C: Ahora tú me hablaste y yo te voy a contestar. Entonces, estaba un saxofón alto llamado [Bruno Guijaro?] que era el primer saxofón alto de la orquesta de Julio Cuevas, que era un tiro inspirando en eso, a mi siempre me gustó—porque a mí, lo que me gusta del músico en cualquier instrumento—a mi me gusta todo lo que es música, pero me gusta cuando cantan, me gusta que me canten, que me digan algo, que tengan un mensaje. Tu sabes que todos estudiamos la música—la tenemos todos en las manos—cinco líneas y cuatro espacios. No es ni tuya, ni mía, ni de él, ni de nobody. Cada uno saca su estilo—que es lo que a mi me gusta comunicar. ¿Cómo tú puedes comunicar? Cantas, tienes la suerte que le gustaste a una gente, te salvaste. ¿No le gustaste? Está bien, no dejas de ser músico por eso. Hasta que [edad viene borrando] lo que tú quieres.

A: *¿Y la música de jazz de los EEUU llegaba a Cuba?*

C: Siempre nosotros en Cuba oíamos esa música, fíjate tú cuando yo vine—dentro de la pregunta cabe esto que yo te voy a contar—para decirte si llegaba o no llegaba. Cuando yo vine a los EEUU en el año 57 yo era loco por conocer a Roy Eldridge y a Coleman Hawkins y existía el metropol. Ya yo tenía en mi casa un disco que salieron los trompetistas que mejor interpretaron en esa época el ——. Y yo voy y le digo a Roy Eldridge lo llamé en mi poco inglés—que si me hacía un favor y él le pidió permiso a Coleman Hawkins—porque dijo "Es que Coleman Hawkins fue el que hizo época en EEUU con ——" y entonces Coleman Hawkins le dice "Toca trompeta ——." En Cuba siempre se oyó la música americana—toda la vida. Y yo tuve la suerte de haber tocado toda esa música—pero dentro de la orquesta, como solista nó. Porque yo llego a hacer un solo americano es "con el rabo encendido" y yautía y todas esas cosas. Yo siempre he sido sonero—compasero y sonero. Todo eso me fascina, sé tocartela en una banda. En el septeto completo porque esa es [la dicción]—Pero a la hora que me dicen un solo... arroz con frijoles negros . . .

A: *Hay que ser fiel al ritmo, tú sabes . . .*

C: Yo soy —— me gusta mi música, me cayó bien y con eso he tenido la suerte y la oportunidad de conocer el mundo entero en los festivales de lo que sea mas grandes del mundo he estado—donde van los mas grandes de la música esa, yo he estado—pero yo con lo mío. He tenido la oportunidad de tocar con muchas bandas grandes pero mi estilo lo han querido dentro de ellos, que es diferente, yo no me he salido de esa porque yo no—si no enseñé bien a hablar español te digo que por lo menos me entienden mi trompeta que suena en español—ahora díme tú del inglés. [Se rien.]

A: *Ahora, cuál fue las circunstancias de tú ir de Cuba y venir pa'ca pa vivir?*

C: Bueno, cuando yo tocaba con la Sonora Matancera, fuí a Venezuela a los carnavales y fue la orquesta de Machito y [Buddy Watson] me escuchó Machito y me hicieron una oferta de venir para acá. Eso fue en el año 51. Entonces yo le dije "Bueno a mi me gustaría ir para Nueva York," a mí siempre me ha gustado—yo soy bolandero, yo no tengo sitio, a mí to' los sitios me gustan, pa mí to's son iguales. Entonces yo le dije "el problema es que yo en el 51 no voy," porque yo estaba, ya tenía en mente hacer la banda con mi primo hermano Beny Moré y a mí me gusta hacer lo que yo quiero. Y es un gran orgullo para mí haber hecho la banda que yo hice con él, que tuvo una acogida de ser la primera banda bailable en Cuba—y acompañado de (Beny) la hice. Ahora, después de eso tengo la oportunidad de venir a Nueva York con Fajardo y está la orquesta de Machito y me dice Mario Bauzá y Machito "la oferta que te hicimos en Caracas está directa" y le dije "ahora sí la acepto," porque ya yo logré algo. Yo acepté, entonces viene con un contrato [que tocar directamente para ellos y con la banda de Machito] a ocupar la silla de Mario Bauzá y residente.

A: *Tú dijiste algo que me cayó a mí bien importante y eso es: la orquesta de Beny Moré que era la primera banda para los bailadores del público, no para ningún hotel . . .*

C: No, no, no, no, no eso era un orgullo—Beny Moré es mi primo hermano y mi compadre dos veces. Bartolomé Maximiliano Moré Armenteros—primo hermano mío y después compadre—padrino de la última boda mía en Cuba, padrino de la última hija mía que hice en Cuba. Sinceramente—para mí eso es un orgullo. Cuando usted habla de algo Andy, créemelo—si algo me preguntas y no lo sé te digo—no te contesto por no hacerme de—si no sé, no te digo—mañana busco la forma de encontrarme con alguien. Pero lo que yo te hablo lo dice Alfredo Chocolate Armenteros de verdad porque es lo que yo he vivido, no te hablo lo que he leido en el periódico.

A: *Sí—me dí cuenta que eso fue verdad—la primera banda bailable que era para el público—o sea, todas las otras bandas eran para las sociedades de hoteles, de turistas . . .*

C: Mira, lo de nosotros era el cabaret, este de San Susino [bajo Hermes Matri lo que este abuelo que era jefe ahí] fue a hablar conmigo y con el que quería a Beny para exclusividad a él con la banda. Y le dije "no—que Beny vaya . . . nosotros tocamos para el público porque nosotros—el público es lo verdadero y es lo que nos gusta a nosotros—tocar al público. Créeme, yo no hice la banda porque—empezando que yo no soy músico que me gusta el trabajo esteril—yo entré a Tropicana y cuando pasaban cuatro semanas ya yo mandaba a —— pa coger mi dinero—de eso—a mí no me molesta—la vida mía—lo que yo más he vacilado—doy gracias a Dios de las cosas buenas—he tenido suerte para eso es que vamos a Europa—tenemos un día en Londres, otro en Alemania, otro acá . . . a mi me encanta moverme—así—eso es lo que a mí me gusta. Ahora, trabajo esteril—cuando tu tienes un trabajo esteril, aunque tu ves gente diferente, ya tu ves las mismas caras—

A: *Y no solamente eso, no te dá inspiración—*

C: A mí no me dá inspiración. Se pone uno monótono—se pone uno maquinario—aunque toquemos los mismos números—los tocamos hoy en casa de Chocolate, mañana vamos a tocar los números en tu casa, hay otro ambiente, vamos a la casa de este y es otro ambiente—aunque sea el mismo número, yo nunca he sido músico que me ha gustado trabajo esteril. Me ví obligado en Cuba porque trabajo esteril es y al tener responsabilidad, tener casa, muebles e hijos ya tenía que responsabilidades—pero cuando pude safarme [gracias a Dios que hay buenas cosas. Eso va ilustrado.] (Se rien.)

A: *Tenemos aquí una historia cronológica de tu carrera aquí en los Estados Unidos.*

C: Sinceramente le doy gracias a todas las buenas cosas. Después que tuve el privilegio de llegar aqui, tuve el privilegio de ser el trompetista en aquella época, que los directores me llamaban a mí para que le buscara trompetistas porque tuve la oportunidad de grabar aquí cuando entré con [Anto Mate?] con Poncho Leña grabé tambien. Con Joe Coco, con Joe Coco le grabamos que cantaba más que _____ con Joe Coco le grabamos a un Moncho, el que tocaba caracatikiti—

A: *Eee . . . Mon Rivera.*

C: Mon Rivera—con la banda de Joe Coco le grabamos—

A: *Ese es Dolores—*

C: Óyeme—ese fue el triunfo de él!

A: *Dolores.*

C: Ahi toca—¿Tú sabes quien toca ahí? [El Negro Vival, Mario y Louie] y Chocolate. Somos los que tocamos ahí —lo que nos ponían el nombre—eso lo lograbamos nosotros. [Y maína] to' eso—ahí empezó. Tuve la oportunidad tambien, cuando llegó Raul Marrero de Mejico de grabarle "Sin Sangre en las Venas" que fue el que lo levantó cuando llego de Mexico—

A: *Ajá—*

C: Okei? Entonces tuve la oportunidad de grabar con Arsenio mismo aquí dos o trés números—porque ya en eso tenía que irme de vez y dejé a Nilo Agudin por [gusto]. Entonces tuve la oportunidad de grabar con Septeto La Playa—

A: *Aa, sí sí—*

C: Que [Vitin, Pato Calaomi, y Ivan ——] allí estaban—esos son caminos porque no ponemos nombres. Tuve la oportunidad de grabar al sonero mayor—muy querido mío, Ismael—grabarle "El Nazareno"—donde está "el hombre bueno no le teme a la oscuridad"; grabarle al difunto de Orlando Contreras todos los boleros esos cuando era [la teca] discos. To' eso lo he grabado yo. Tuve la oportunidad tambien que para mí es un gran privilegio que Vincentico Valdés na' más que ponía el nombre de la revista cuando le grababan la única grabación que hice con Vincentico Valdés puso aunque sea Alfredo Armenteros—ahí está, así que figúrate. Después con Larry Harlow los primeros cuatro álbumes de Larry Harlow. Primero "Heavy Smoking"—

A: *Cuando estaba Monguito, ¿nó?*

C: No, primero "Heavy Smoking"—que ahí estaba Felo Grito. Después vino [Guarachita] que es donde entra Monguito. Después viene "Las Luces" y "Bajándote" que es donde está Ismael Miranda. Esos son los primeros cuatro. De ahí, paso a Eddie Palmieri y tú sabes que hicimos cantidad porque tú estabas ahí, que ahí viene "Chocolate Ice Cream" y todas esas boberías —— que me acuerdo que eso fue una cosa que se hizo así y de ahí pues vino Charlie Palmieri tambien ["La Vecina y La Esta"] y "La hija de Lola" y así llegué a tener la oportunidad de grabar con [Cedar Walton] el americano allá en Holanda que él lo que toca es jazz y yo le dije "yo no toco jazz" y dice "el estilo tuyo yo lo quiero dentro de esto que yo toco." El me dió la oportunidad y lo grabé. Ahora acabo de grabar con Marc Ribot, el guitarrista. Grabé con [Joe Azuba] el bajista que tú lo conoces, de allá de Los Angeles, acabo de grabar allá ahora—

A: *Y grabaste con Steve Touré tambien—*

C: Bueno, ——. Y después de ahí, gracias a Dios hasta ahora.

A: *Ahora, tu primera grabación, bajo tu nombre—*

C: Bajo mi nombre fue cuando grabé "Chocolate Aquí" que uso dos cantantes, estás tú, y esta que usé dos partes, te acuerdas, llevé a Nicky y fue Jerry tambien y después no va Nicky sino Julito Collazo con la batería y había una parte con eso y tú sabes [que es Montu].

A: *¿Oye y qué de la vida de Montú?*

C: Bueno tú sabes que el trabajaba aquí y le dieron un tiro en la mano. Yo lo ví en Puerto Rico y ahora lo sacaron—pero esta gente no me dan la dirección exacta—

A: *Tú sabes que yo encontré copias nuevas de—*

C: (Se rie.) Sí, me la llevaron al SOB—el mismo tipo y me dice "no, la dirección es esa" y yo voy allí y no lo veo porque yo tengo que cobrar mi derecho—mira todos los números que yo tengo ahí. El primero es Niko y después Nelson. Y él mismo me llevó a su persona.

A: *Encontré el disco—*

C: Sí, yo lo tengo.

A: *Lo encontré nuevo—*

C: Bueno pues yo lo tengo—pues este fue el primero que yo hice, te acuerdas que te decía, "Es que no sé si grabo instrumental o con dos cantantes pero a mí me gustan grupos pequeños ahora, pa esto, tú sabes, pa moverme." ¿Te acuerdas? Grabé dos estilos por eso— en uno uso Nicky —— y despues en otro uso a Julito Collazo pa escoger ahí fue la primicia pa eso—

A: *Y después—*

C: Viene—entonces viene—

A: *El de Salsoul, ¿nó?*

C: No con la [Kingtronix] y después cambio a la Salsoul—

A: *Sí.*

C: Con [Kingtronix] que fue con Roberto Tones cuando "El Caminante"—

A: *Tú sabes que ellos sacaron—*

C: Sí yo se, yo los tengo. Y ahora me acaban de sacar los—cuando mi orquesta ya Chocolate, que esta "La Taza de Chocolate," . . . Yo tengo que ir ahí a buscarlo. Ellos me lo dijeron. Yo fuí allí y me tiraron una foto.

A: *Sacaron los dos volúmenes de Folklórico.*

C: Tambien yo se lo dije a René: "Aquí hay una grabación pa discos y pa cassettes, y ahora viene este que es otra cosa." Pero tú sabes—Andy, yo me alegro ———. Yo sigo aquí tranquilito. Yo tengo lo que yo le pedí a Dios pa' mi retiro. Mira, cuando yo vine a este pais con la madre mía, 108 y Broadway, 255 West de la 108 y Broadway—piso siete. Ahora me retiré—piso siete. ¡Son los siete mares y los cuatro vientos! A mí que si yo vivo con el corazón limpio. No me interesa na' que sea de nadie. Es tuyo, es tuyo. Si no puedo—si tengo dinero tuyo y de momento me hizo falta, te llamo—"Andy, mira me dieron este dinero 'I'm sorry' yo lo tuve que necesitar, pero dáme un breiquecito, que yo . . . "

A: *Seguro.*

C: Ese ha sido mi camino toda mi vida y es como camino en la calle—dondequiera que voy puedo llegar teniendo dinero vengo y firmo—porque tengo garantía pa eso.

A: *Ahora, una pregunta, cuando tú estás haciendo un solo—¿Qué son las cosas que tú piensas?*

C: Chico, sinceramente te voy a decir una cosa, Andy. Esa pregunta me la han hecho varias gentes. Yo sé que yo hablando—tú sabes que hay muchas formas—ejemplo: te voy a empezar. Estamos en un estudio de grabación que tu lo que ves son las caras del que está aburrido y el que está atras . . . Ahora, cuando yo siento la música y me inspiró lo que se está tocando, ahí hay impulso. Ahora me voy por ahí y me voy endulzando. Eso es un solo. Ahora voy a tocar un concierto, tú sabes que eso es lo mas dificil que hay, está to' el mundo sentao escuchando. Tú ves uno detrás bostezando (lo demuestra y se rien)—to' eso hay que mirarlo. Ahora, cuando ves uno que está así y está gozando, ya me inspiró. Y ahí hay otro solo. Eso es la inspiración del solo. Porque nosotros no somos mecánicos, ahora tú tienes una idea. El solo no es una cosa que yo lo llego así. Es como el tiempo. Está—nos levantamos y está lloviendo. Esta entrevista ahora fue fomentada en día sabrosito. Y yo tengo aire acondicionado. ¿No hay aire acondicionado? Estamos sudando. —— Hay una inspiración para la cosa ahí el momento, esta lo que tú sientes en el momento. El solo es la vibración que tú sientes hacia ti en ese momento. En eso no hay nadie que sepa ni pio. Ahora el mecánico es el que siempre está en lo mismo. Por eso es que yo no puedo ser un doble. Yo —— porque no me acuerdo lo que hice. Puedo repetirte una frase—que me viene la coda y me acordé de una frase y vaya—porque tenemos una firma—una identificación, pero lo demás olvídate.

A: *Mucha gente cuando estoy soplando mucha gente me dice "coño, tú tocaste un tumbao en esta parte, coño eso estaba cabrón . . ."*

C: Y tú ni te acuerdas.

A: *¡No me recuerdo!*

C: El momento que te emocionaste. Eso viene emocionado. Porque si yo estoy haciendo un solo, yo depende de ti, el ritmo—

A: *Ajá.*

C: Depende del ritmo. Y tú me oíste que hice una frase y te gustó y automaticamente tú haces así, Andy, y me cambias un tumbao que me pone a gozar y yo te pongo que estamos los dos—gozando. Eso es lo que hay en solo. El solo no es mecánico, es momentaneo. El solo es una cosa que te sale momentaneamente. Y eso se llama inspiración.

A: *Ahora esta próxima pregunta, no sé, porque todo el mundo tiene su manera de expresar esto—"¿Cómo tú interpretas la clave?"*

C: Bueno la clave, es cuestión de sentirla. La clave, cualquier ritmo que tú tocas na'más tiene dos y trés. Ahora, como que tú eres músico y somos todos y tenemos la música, cada vez que nosotros vamos a tocar [de] un papel no es "one-two-three-four"—¡ta! Lo mismo te empieza la música en el primer tiempo, en el segundo, que en el tercero, que en el cuarto. Entonces, si tú sientes la clave, y en español nosotros le decimos Anacruza, lo que le da la sal— Tarará riri riri (sonando la clave con las manos). La clave es una cosa que es más bien de sentimientos—si no la sientes, no la pones. Porque después te vas a encontrar con la discusión en que yo me encontraba con muchas personas, que yo estoy haciendo un solo y me están haciendo una clave atravesá y yo tengo que parar y después me llaman y me dicen "Chocolate, pero si la clave es dos y tres," Sí, dos y tres pero ¿dónde la pones? ¿Dónde la co-lo-cas? Eso es más bien hay que sentirla. Si no la sientes, no la bajas. Por eso dicen "si no la bailas, no la tocas" (se rien). Eso es lo que yo siento. La clave son na'más que cinco golpes, en la forma que tú la vires, cuéntala pa' que veas. En guaguanco, en rumba: pa-pa-pa pa-pa. Cinco. Pa-pa pa-pa-pa son cinco. Tú le puedes dar el viraje que quieras "Five beats. No mo'." No hay seis. Igualito que cuando me hablan de música moderna y yo digo "para mi la música sera moderna cuando le pongan seis líneas." Ahora nadie es culpable que hoy en día el público nuevo entienda y acepte los alaridos de la [Bonachita] y los de [Kin Kon], y en otra época no aceptaban eso. No hay na' moderno, ya to' eso está escrito—aquí nadie inventa na'. Desde que tú abres el libro de música pa' estudiar—ves la fuga de Bach, ves esto de Beethoven—¿Quién inventó más na'? El mismo libro que yo leí cuando tenía nueve años de —— [Lagos]. Ahora tengo setenta y no ha cambiado, igual, es lo mismo. Si hay siete claves—y siete tonos igual. Moderno no hay na'.

RD: *We can skip that one.*

A: *Bueno aquí hay una pregunta que si tú puedes dar una descripción sobre lo que es el són, la rumba, la guaracha, la guajira . . .*

C: Muy fácil. Viene entendido para todo el público americano y europeo—yo interpreto—si usted escucha de verdad el "blues," estás escuchando una guajira con "different beats" o que son las tonalidades menores todas.

A: *Sí. O tambien se puede decir un lamento, ¿no?*

C: Tambien—ese lamento es el grito del guajiro. Ese es lo que siente el guajiro. La Guajira es el lamento—ese es conclusión. El montuno es lo que se llama el "jazz" vamos a hacer una melodía de cuatro barras o de ocho—y todo es inspiración. Eso es todas las líneas melódicas y harmónicas. Entonces el bolero-són; el bolero es el "fox trot"—en "low" y después viene y cambia al "swing."

A: *¡Imagínate los bailadores!*

C: A bueno, ese es el detalle. ¿Ahora, tú sabes como yo te lo figuro mas rápido que me van a entender to' el mundo? Cuando usted empieza a enamorar la hembra que le gusta, usted no empieza corriendo a cien millas (se rien). Imagínate—la vas llevando poquito a poco—tú sabes.

A: *Una pregunta sobre los bailes en los sitios grandes como "El Polar" sin amplificación—¿Cómo se oye la cosa?*

C: Bueno el problema que te voy a explicar—las sociedades casi todas eran anteriormente de mampostería, llamamos, que son de ladrillos.

A: *Ajá.*

C: Ya eso resuena. Fíjate que toda la— los — de hoy en día que ya tú te puedes acordar es bajo acustico que es natural, siempre la tienen pal ——. Porque cuando tocas allí, hay que ser de loceta. Entonces tú le das a la conga aquí, y la trompeta no es eso. La trompeta suena sola. Entonces los cantantes usaban lo —— pero era mampostería. En cualquier sitio que tú tocas donde mejor suena la música es cuando tú traes, te encaramas en una tarima, con grande que sea el sitio, y la tarima sea de madera—porque si es mampostería, la resonancia de donde cae—se confunden los soneros. Esa es la acústica. Esa es la grabación es que yo le he puesto aquí a dos o trés que me vinieron a entrevistar. Y yo le pongo el cuarteto genuino de una—eso lo que grabamos—un micrófono pa' la banda, el micrófono del cuarteto—nosotros le dabamos directo pero como si—[y es seco] porque ese es grabado en el estudio de radio, como —— tú sabes que la tarima está alta, abajo esta la bóveda y es de madera. Viene el cuadrado del público, entonces cuando tú tocas el eco te lo dá el mismo público. Y la música está ahí porque ahí está el micrófono—pero es la bóveda que tiene . . .

A: *A mi me dijeron que cuando se bailaban són en uno de esos pues en "El Polar" o algo así, que el público bien callado—*

C: No, no allá no se gritaba—

A: *—oyendo la banda.*

C: Allá no se hablaba. Tú vas a bailar, vas a bailar. Eso que tú ves aquí "Andy González y Chocolate" y estamos haciendo un solo y to'el mundo bla-bla-bla. La primera experiencia dura que yo pasé fue cuando llegué al Japón con la banda de Machito, que nos pusimos ahí a tocar a doce mil y pico de japoneses. Eso era un silencio del carajo. Y uno acostumbrado a la bulla de aquí. Pero es la que se aprende. Dicen "la experiencia de ayer es la vida de hoy." —— Tú sientes el afecto que es pero entonces no escuchas y hay cuatro gente que van a escuchar—experiencia vivida cuando el difunto Nat King Cole trabajaba aquí en un bar y tocaba en un bar y ahí lo sacaron y le dijeron "usted no es de aquí." Entonces, igualito que van a buscar prospectos para el beisbol y para el basquetbol por ahí, lo hay para la música. Te recuerdas de que empezamos—yo siempre le decía a usted "dondequiera que vayas a tocar, haya persona o no haya nadie— toque. No sabe quien es que está sentado allí y le puedes hacer así al alma." Eso es lo que yo aprendí. Tú sabes lo que es eso que yo pensar al tocar en el teatro—

SEPTEMBER 9, 1998: TAPE 2, SIDE A

C: La experiencia de ayer fue la que me enseño la vida de hoy. Entonces pa' mi no hay calor. Cuando me dicen aquí "Ay que calor" y "ay que frío" yo digo: "yo quisiera haber sido compositor de los que tuviera dinero," porque aquí que frío y hay que calor. Yo estoy acostumbrado en pleno agosto, en un agosto en Puerto Rico y en Cuba ——, [y ahí llego con ese cuello con corbata]. Pero ya [la costumbre sabe hacer leyes]. A mí me da igual. Ese es el problema. No hay otro—[la costumbre sabe hacer leyes]. Ya después vino to' esto. Fíjate que aquí cuando dejaron entrar a tocar con —— y eso se jodió to esto. E, cará—suerte tuviste porque estudiaste y seguiste estudiando y puedes tener demanda por tí y yo puedo tener demanda por mí —— puede tener demanda por él pero el que no tuvo demanda se jodió y se quedó ahí. Y entonces te dice que esto está malo. ¡Estará malo pa' tí, pa' mí está bueno! Eso es lo que pasa. Analízalo pa'que tú veas.

A: *Es verdad.*

C: Sí, es la verdad. Mira, el son no se puede salvar con un solo [de esos]. Nosotros somos músicos y la gente está acostumbrada—la orquesta más humilde que había en aquella época tenían uniforme. Fíjate él mismo [Eddie], cuando se tiro —— que fue lo que paso. [Eddie sí que estaba. . . .]

A: *Ahora*—

C: Espérate que no me he dado el pase. (Se rie.) Te lo dije 'orita cuando me hablaste y me quedé parao. ¿Que tú te crees, que yo voy a empezarlo con 70 años ahora?

[Esta parte no se entiende.]

A: *Yo le estaba diciendo [a RD] que yo estoy preguntando cosas que no están en la lista . . .*

C: Seguro que sí.

A: *Porque cuando me interesa algo…*

C: A, eso está bien. Y si está a mi alcance, por qué no, si lo mismo que tú me estás haciendo yo lo hacía cuando era muchacho. Gracias a eso que hice caso—que hice caso. Hice caso y por eso estoy aquí donde estoy.

A: *Eso es verdad.*

C: Cuando me dicen algo yo "mira no ha visto un joven nacer a un viejo" (se rien).

A: *Mira los pobrecitos que tienen la enfermedad que se ponen muy viejos a los seis años—*

C: Porque hay quien nació en esta esquina y no sabe esa esquina, Andy. Nosotros somos privilegiados. Nosotros viajamos pa'ca y viajamos pa'lla. Tú sabes con quien tú te sientes bien compartiendo porque yo si no me siento bien compartiendo contigo, pa' que coño voy a hacer hipocresías—

A: *Ahí está.*

C: [Te veo y te hago la política y vuelvo a decir "e, cómo estas Andy." Y no comparto pero ya nosotros nos conocemos. ¿Y así cuanta gente no quisiera compartir con uno? ¿Que jodedor aquí no quiere sentarse al lao de uno que tiene un nombre: "Coño si estaba con Andy González al lao mío ahí, [que lo traje para ver]." Te lo quieren dar to' ——. Los que somos asi nobles porque nosotros al final somos músicos y al final vamos a estar siempre dentro de los músicos porque yo no hago na', mira yo voy a la bodega porque yo no voy al ——. Pero ahí no hay nadie. —— ¿Qué yo voy a hablar con esa gente? Pero yo me siento y le sigo la corriente: "ay no, no—la cervezita." ¿Yo qué puedo hablar con esa gente, Andy? Pero como que —— tengo que compartir tambien porque…

A: *No—sí, sí.*

C: Como es eso. Tú sabes, yo me acuerdo aquí todos los morenos americanos "A, yo lo ví por televisión, que esto, que mire . . . " coño [pues hazme un regalo? Halago? Regalado?] y to' porque yo no le tengo que decir a nadie que yo soy fulano ni hago esto ni hago na, yo no ando con eso. A mí—lo mismo estoy que me encuentras a las cuatro de la mañana tomando cerveza alla atrás . . . y oliendo. Y así era mi difunto primo-hermano Beny Moré. Nosotros fuimos privilegiados—yo sé que cuando me invitas tu pa' Pito Café, voy pa' Pito Café. Ahora cuando tú me ves ya que ya oí to' esa mierda de Pito Café, tú me vez que me voy buscando venirme pa' 'ca pa' los —— la barrita que a mí me gusta—ahí lo que voy es a vacilar—otro a descargar. Si no quiero ir pa' ahí, me voy pa'l —— alla detrás es otro tipo de descarga—pa cambiar el movimiento, porque si no, si te [estancas] te jodiste. Bueno, venga la pregunta ahora que ya me dí el pase.

A: *¿Cuáles son tus grabaciones favoritas?*

C: Coño esa sí es la mas dura. Chico porque a mi nunca me ha gustado [lo que yo hago] (se rie). Sí, no soy hipócrita. La grabación más favorita que yo tengo en mi vida fue ese primer disco que tú ves ahí. Ese que me ha traído hasta ahora. Después de ahí pa'ca no me ha gustado mas na'. Ahora, me siento feliz. Y yo aplaudo al público que me aceptó.

A: *Te digo una cosa. Cuando él me empezó a preguntar cosas de ti, yo le dije a él "el solo que tu cogiste en el ["Para las Niñas y Para las Señoras"]—se puede hacer una transcripción—*

C: Como trató Tito Puente con Meñique—

A: *Sí, sí, sí pero ese solo—se puede poner en un libro—*

C: Yo mismo no lo he hecho mas nunca. [Eric] mismo me dijo a mí —— "Chocolate—¿Qué tú estabas pensando cuando hiciste esa grabación?" Y yo le dije —— qué tú estás —— por mi madre Andy, yo pensaba que Arsenio Rodríguez me escuchara tocar na' más porque ———. Como fue y sucedió. Ahora yo—si te digo otra cosa es mentira. Yo lo hice asi y más na'.

A: *Yo le dije a él (RD) que estudiantes de música, del son, de la clave, de la música de Swing—*

C: Ahí está—

A: *Que hay cosas pasando en ese solo tuyo—tan corto que es, porque eran na'más que ocho barras o algo así—*

C: Ocho barras, si eran trés minutos lo máximo—

A: *Ocho barras hiciste una declaración de quien tú eras—ya tú tenías tu identidad—tan joven—y no solamente eso—si tú lo analizas muzicalmente—*

C: A, y cuando escribes lo que dice ahí no lo toco (se rie).

A: *No, pero lo que yo digo es que cualquier estudiante del son o de la música—*

C: Tiene que agarrarse ahí.

A: *Sí, si ellos estudian ese solo, ellos van a saber lo que es el "swing" del son.*

C: ——— Aquí está, míralo aquí—"Conjunto René Alvarez."

A: *Sí, es una grabación que él (RD) no tiene, porque eso es dificil de encontrar.*

C: Nó, si es 78 y yo lo pude sacar, asi, no se oye muy bien pero se oye.

A: *Yo no sé porque la gente no sacan ese disco en CD . . .*

C: Orita se acuerdan—porque to'el mundo está buscando la forma que se muera alguien, pa' despues llamarlo. No ves que [Fania] creía que yo me había muerto y nunca me llamaron pa' pagarme mi royalty y cuando me le presenté así dicen "coño, un muerto

vivo." Yo supe siempre que era así muerto pero, aquí estoy. Y va
por ahí. Aquí mi amigo me llama—Andy, llevo cuatro días con un
amigo mío querido en Miami—eso es del cara'—va a ir a buscar el
otro, que no se veían desde hace no sé que tiempo y es un grán
amigo mío—somos tres na'más pero somos —— risa y jode de
años— Como nosotros que empezamos con el folklórico.

A mí me hacen la entrevista de folklórico y yo le digo como era
eso. Te acuerdas que te dije cuando llegó Fernandez que empezó
René a hacer arreglos y se jodió—te dije "Andy se jodió esto." Eso
era sin arreglos [y todos aportabamos de to']—te lo dije y ¿no fue
así?

A: *Así fue.*

C: —— una cosa que nosotros hacíamos con cariño y nos gustaba,
que carajo [y Paquito hermano cuando llegas tú] —— se jodió to'.

A: *Sí, mano . . .*

C: Yo le hago la historia, te acuerdas que nosotros teníamos tres
números montaos—fuimos a tocar a [——] y el público se para,
que estaba el saxofonista que era el director músical ahí "Se acabó
lo de Folklórico." Y René vira para mí, tú también, to' el mundo
[porque yo era el más viejo] "¿coño, ahora que hacemos?"

"Olvidate d'eso. Mira, me haces un redoble ahí, sol menor, tú
verás. Y yo haciéndole, con los cueros y la trompeta [y cuando
hize eso—trompeta en cuero. Le dije que él está—no habían
más números.] Yo le hago el cuento ese a mucha gente, a mí no
me importa que me digan que es mentira—mi abuelo me enseño a decir, que más vale que yo haga el cuento a que no lo
haga. Y él sabe que fue así, no había más na' y el público se puso
de pie y René estaba, te acuerdas, temblando porque coño [es-
taba —— tú no viste el sitio ya pero pa' estar al campo con la
Cuba Linda]—Aah—cuidao, atrás con la confianza, coño.
Porque hibamos de corazón. Cuando llega mi negro pa [prefi-
ción de arreglos y eso], se jodió esto pa'l carajo, si nosotros ya

hicimos aquí puro pulmón, sin interés del carajo, tú sabes, lo que saliera . . .

Déjame ver por donde está. . . . (buscando en el cassette) Porque tengo a René Alvarez con el —— cuando estaba con la melodía del 40 . . . yo tengo que adivinar por donde es que está.

(Se escucha "Lindo Yambú.)

APPENDIX D

Interview of Alfredo "Chocolate" Armenteros
(English Translation)

AUGUST 3, 1998: TAPE 1, SIDE B

Andy González (A): What is the first music you remember hearing as a child?

"Chocolate" Armenteros (C): The first music I remember from my childhood—in my house there was one of those radios and I listened to "En Mi Campo," the Septeto Habanero, the Septeto Nacional . . .

A: Were they broadcasting live?

C: In my time I wasn't able to hear it live, but then came the phonographs. In my house there was a phonograph also and we had those big records and you had to turn the crank. Then the problem was that the guys couldn't go dancing [with girls]—and if I'm dancing close with my cousin or whatever, they would say "Alfredito, it's your turn to turn the crank!" and I would say "No, no! _____"

A: (Laughs). And what was the first musical experience—

C: Which led me to take classes?

A: *Yes.*

C: Well my deceased father was a musician, he played the trombone when he was young. So, Richard Egües's father, flute player for Aragon, was my first teacher. He lived in one of those properties that we the Armenteros had. I was in public school and he shows up looking for kids who want to play music so he can make a children's group and I was one of the first to raise his hand. So I started with the children's group. And the first thing in those days, what they did is they gave you the solfège book and the ———. That gives you everything—harmony and all the different areas. When you are on the second or third part, they give you the ——— of the instrument. They ask you "what instrument do you like?" I took the instrument that I liked—I was always crazy about the trumpet. The only instrument after the trumpet, I always liked the tenor saxophone.

A: *Did you ever play it?*

C: No. So they gave me the mouthpiece of the trumpet to [practice on]. First, how to blow and all that, then I went (with "El Puentecito"), that was Richard Egües, and I, man, I went with Richard to help him clean the academy in town and all we did was practice———. And when the teacher, his father, says, "Now it's your turn, I'm going to show you the scales." I already knew the scales, because I was doing them every day. Because of that, I started in the children's band. You know that the children's band, when you play in a band, it's like school. You play pieces and that type of thing. So when they call me a *sonero* that has studied music it's for real. The first thing that you read in music, what you start, with the first book of bass, you being a bass player, you are playing pieces.

A: *Yes.*

C: Because those are the first you have to do. Then you start choosing the part that you like best in music—you know which part I chose. Because after the band, I only played *comparsas*, and I love that. But in order to have compromises, I had the opportunity to play in shows, cabarets—Tropicana and those places.

A: *Well let's continue because already with what you told me you answered six or seven questions.*

C: (*Laughs.*)

A: *What was your first experience playing with a group?*

C: My first experience playing with a real group was when I was with René Alvarez, which was when I was recognized. I had entered a level of professionalism that I had never experienced. I was always ——. That record that you see there on my bed, March 18, 1949, was the first experience which can be considered musical, because all the rest were just the guys getting together.

A: *When did you come here for—*

C: I left in '49.

A: *So when you arrived the first thing you did was record!*

C: The first thing I did was go into [Martiberona] to play with the Conjunto Habanero, with the Septeto Habanero when they still had the director, the one that sang… I forget the name, it's been a long time. There was [Bejerin], el Chino Bongosero, [Chaucho] who sang back-up… I'm trying to remember the name of the director… Gerardo! Gerardo Martínez was the director. I played in [Martiberona] and from there, well, I was heard and René Alvarez called and that's how I recorded with René.

A: *Los Astros.*

C: That's right, "Los Astros de René Alvarez," the only group next to Arsenio Rodríguez. But my dream was to play, I'll always say it, with Arsenio, and I'm content that I did. One day after about three months [with René] we got a gig at the Polar brewery head to head and when Arsenio finishes, we get on. When I come on, Arsenio says to Chappottín, when he hears me, he says, "That's the man I need." So then he calls me and says "Hey kid, you wanna to start with me tomorrow?" Imagine saying that to me, as desperate as I am. "Yea, yea, yea!" You'll notice the photo on that record from when we got together. I didn't even have a uniform. He gave me the tie, the only one like it that I have.

A: *And what did René Alvarez think about Arsenio stealing his trumpet?*

C: Well, that's the way it is. Same as it is today. When you have a band—you have work and you have musicians. You don't have work, you don't have musicians. And I was dying to play with Arsenio. That was my aspiration. —— I had the chance to record with René Alvarez and I can't complain. I'm very satisfied. Now, when Arsenio arrives, you know, when you get out of school you want to make it right away. Damn, working with Arsenio back then was the best. I felt like Amalia up in the seventh heaven didn't have it any better than me. Honestly, I still say it with a lot of heart and a lot of pride. I'm proud and privileged. What's more, he gave me a tune called "——." It isn't mine; he put my name on it so I would get some money to make my first uniform with him.

A: *Right.*

C: —— with me it wasn't any of that. I was proud of my little path he was leading me on.

A: *I want to talk about Florecita.*

C: Aaaah! That's my idol. Florecita and ——. Enrique Velazco. They called him Florecita because he took tunes and "flowered" them.

A: *How old was Florecita when you met him?*

C: When I met Florecita I was twenty-one years old and he was returning from Mexico. He was already older; he must have been around forty-seven or forty-eight. Man, the only privilege that I have left in this world which makes me proud—the only person Florecita allowed—me being so relaxed, I would say, "What's up, grampa," and he would hug me. Only me, no one else. I had the opportunity when he left the comparsa "La Jardinera," and they called me, to be his successor. What bigger privilege could I ask of life? Because between the two of them, Florecita and Chappottín, I did the following: I said, "if Florecita does it like this, and Chappottín like that, why can't I do something in the middle?" And that's how I got my style. We always follow someone who we like and that was him. And with lots of love and care. All my life, thanks to that, yesterday's experience in our life today—and very proud, that's where I came from.

A: *Yea, because he didn't know anything about Florecita and I put on some stuff for him, you know, Florecita and Miguelito Cuní . . .*

C: I'm telling you—he'd be playing here (*pointing*) and sees someone who's going to pass by here, he didn't care, he'd stop playing while the person went by so they wouldn't hit his trumpet. I tell you I was privileged. When I called him "grampa" he looked at me and hugged me, and then people would say, "what did you say to him? Florecita doesn't let anyone call him grampa!" But I pushed it, because I said it to him with love because I saw him as my elder, not *grampa* to mean he was an old man. It's with the love one feels, and he realized. The only one he allowed it.

A: *Did you ever work with him?*

C: Yes I did and you know it well—you ask me that question and I know it's for the interview but you know that I told you that when we got together with René, at any moment, you can bet you would find Joseito Fernandez—

A: *Aaaa! Now you're talking!*

C: And Chocolate, Alfredo, and Florecita, we played together. Man, I tell you . . .

A: *What other musicians in other instruments influenced you?*

C: Well, look, in those days, after Florecita and Chappottín, there was Lazaro el Pecoso, who is older than you've heard, who is a beautiful, melodic player. You know, I admired him and I liked to listen to him, just like I liked to listen to other trumpet players. I admire anyone who plays the trumpet. Because I'm me, the other guy's the other guy, etc. Now my musical theory, my solo line, is influenced by Florecita and Chappottín, in the core. I tried not to imitate anyone . . .

RD: *(In English) What about other instruments?*

C: Now you asked me and I'm going to answer. Then there was this alto saxophone named [Bruno Guijaro?], the first saxophone for the Julio Cuevas orchestra who was great inspiring in that. I always liked him. Because what I like in a musician in whatever instrument—I like everything that's music; but I like it when they sing. I like them to sing, to tell me something, to have a message. You know we all study music; we have it in our hands. Five lines and four spaces. It's not yours, nor mine nor his nor anybody's. Everyone has his own style, which is what I like to communicate. How does one communicate? You sing. If you're lucky enough that some people like you, you're set. If they didn't like you? That's OK, it doesn't take away that you're a musician. Until age [erases what you want?]

A: *Did jazz from the U.S. reach Cuba?*

C: In Cuba we always listened to that music. When I came—this fits into the question you asked—to tell you whether it reached Cuba or not. When I came to the U.S. in '57, I was dying to meet [Roy Eldridge and Coleman Hawkins]. The Metropol already ex-

isted. I had, in my house, a record that featured the best inter-
preters on the trumpet in that period from around the world. So I
go and I say to Roy Eldridge, in the little English I know, I ask him
to do me a favor. And he asked Coleman Hawkins' permission because he said "Coleman Hawkins was the one who made it in the
U.S. with ———" and Coleman Hawkins says, "Play the trumpet, —
—." In Cuba we always heard American music—all my life. And I
was lucky enough to have played all that music, but within an orchestra, not as a soloist. Because if I were to play an American solo,
it would be *con el rabo encendido* [*lit*: "with my tail on fire"] and
yautia and all that stuff. I was always a *sonero—compasero* and
sonero. I love all that stuff [jazz] and I can play it in a band, in a full
septet because that is [diction]. But ask me for a solo and it's rice
with black beans.

A: *We have to be faithful to the rhythm, you know.*

C: I am ———. I liked my music, it fit me well and with it I've had
the luck and the opportunity to see the whole world. I've been in
the biggest festivals in the world, where the best musicians play.
But I go with what's mine. I've had the opportunity to play with a
lot of big bands, but they have wanted my style, which is different.
I haven't left that because—if I didn't learn Spanish well, I tell you
at least they understand my trumpet, which plays in Spanish. Now,
you tell me about English (*they laugh*).

A: *Now what were the circumstances around you leaving Cuba
and coming here to live?*

C: Well, when I played with the Sonora Matancera, I went to
Venezuela to the carnivals, Machito's orchestra was there.
[Buddy Watson] and Machito heard me, and they made me an
offer to come here. That was in '51. So I told them, "well I would
like to go to New York. I'm a drifter, I don't have a place, I love
it everywhere. It's all the same to me. So I said, "the problem is
that in 1951 I can't go," because I had already planned to make

a band with my cousin Beny Moré, and I like to do what I want. And it makes me very proud to have made that band that I made with him. It was known to be the first danceable band in Cuba—and I made it with Beny. Now after that, I have the opportunity to come to New York with (Fajardo) and Machito's orchestra is there. Mario Bauzá and Machito tell me, "the offer we made you in Caracas is still on," and I said, "now I accept," because I had already achieved something. I accepted, then they bring me a contract to play directly for them and occupy Mario Bauzá's place as resident.

A: *You said something that strikes me as important, that Beny More's orchestra was the first group for the dancers in the audience, not for some hotel—*

C: Yes, that has made me very proud. Beny Moré is my cousin and twice a godfather. Bartolomé Maximiliano Moré Armenteros, my cousin and then a godfather, in my last wedding in Cuba, godfather of the first daughter I made in Cuba. Honestly, that makes me proud. When you talk about something, Andy, believe me, if you ask me something and I don't know the answer, I'll tell you. If I don't know, I'll tell you, and tomorrow I'll look for a way to find out through someone else. But what I'm telling you comes from Alfredo "Chocolate" Armenteros, and it's true because it's something I lived, not something I read in the papers.

A: *Yes. I realized that it's true—the first danceable band for the audience. All the other bands were for hotels, tourists . . .*

C: Look, our thing was the cabaret [San Susino, under Hermes Matri]. That old man that was the owner came to speak with me and with him. Because he wanted Beny Moré exclusively for him. And I said, "——. We play for the audience because the audience is the real thing, and that's what I like, playing for them." Believe me, I didn't make that band to—for starters, I'm not a musician that likes sterile work. I went to Tropicana and after four weeks I sent for my money. It doesn't bother me. In my life, I thank God for the good things. I've been lucky to travel: to Europe, one day in London, another in Germany, another over here. I love to move around. Now sterile work, when you have sterile work, even if you see different people, you see the same faces.

A: *Not only that, it doesn't inspire you.*

C: It doesn't inspire me. You get monotonous, you get like a machine. Even if we play the same tunes, today we play them at Chocolate's house, tomorrow we go play some tunes in your house, there's another atmosphere, we go to his house and it's a different atmosphere. Even if it's the same tune, I have never been a musician that liked sterile work. I was forced to in Cuba because sterile work is—having responsibilities, having a house, furniture, and children, I had to be responsible. But when I could get loose, [thank God there are good things. That shows]. (*They laugh.*)

A: *We have here a chronological history of your career here in the United States.*

C: I am sincerely grateful to all the good things. After I had the privilege of arriving here, I had the privilege of being the trumpet player, during that period, that the directors called so I could find them a trumpet player, because I had the opportunity to record here when I came with [Anto Mate?], I also recorded with Poncho Leña. With Joe Coco we recorded, Joe Coco who sang more than ——. We recorded with a Moncho, the one who sang "Caracatiquiti" . . .

A: *Umm . . . Mon Rivera.*

C: Mon Rivera, with Joe Coco's band we recorded—

A: *That's Dolores—*

C: Man, that was his success!

A: *Dolores.*

C: You know who plays in that tune? [El Negro Vival, Mario and Louie], and Chocolate. We're the ones that play in that song. They gave us the name, we achieved that. —— all that, that's where it started. I also had the opportunity, when Raul Marrero arrived from Mexico to record "Sin sangre en las venas" for him, which is what made him when he arrived from Mexico.

A: *Right.*

C: OK? Then I had the opportunity to record two or three tunes here with Arsenio. Because around then I had to leave and I left (Nilo Agudin) with pleasure. Then I had the opportunity to record with the La Playa Septet.

A: *Ah, yes, yes.*

C: [Vitin, Pato Calaomi, and Ivan ——] were there. Those are paths because we don't give names. I had the opportunity to record with the "Sonero Mayor," very dear to me, Ismael (*Rivera*), to record "El Nazareno" for him—where "the good man is not afraid of the dark" is; to record all those ballads for Orlando Contreras when it was [*la teca discos*]. I recorded all that. I had the opportunity to record also, which for me is a great privilege that Vincentico Valdés put Alfredo Armenteros in the booklet when I recorded the only song that I did with him, there it is. Then with Larry Harlow I did his first four records. First "Heavy Smoking"—

A: *When Monguito was playing, right?*

C: No, first "Heavy Smoking," which featured [Felo Grito]. Then came [Guarachita], which is where Monguito comes in. Then come ["Las Luces" and "Bajándote"], which is where Ismael Miranda comes in. From there I go on to Eddie Palmieri, and you know we did a lot because you were there, "Chocolate Ice Cream" and all that silliness come from there. I remember that was something that was done like that and then came Charlie Palmieri also, ["La vecina y la esta" and "La hija de Lola"] and that's how I came to have the chance to record with [Cedar Walton], the American, over in Holland. What he plays is jazz so I told him "I don't play jazz," and he says "I want your style within what I'm doing." He gave me the chance and I recorded. Now I just recorded with [Mark Ribot] the guitarist. I recorded with [Joe Azuba] the bassist, who you know, from Los Angeles, I just recorded over there now—

A: *You also recorded with [Steve Turre]*—

C: Well, ——. And after that, thank God, until today.

A: *Now, your first recording, under your name*—

C: Under my name was when I recorded "Chocolate Aquí" where I use two singers. You're on it. I use two parts, remember, I took Nicky, and Jerry sings also, and then it isn't Nicky but Julito Collazo with the drums, there was a part like that and you know that it's [Montu].

A: *What ever happened to [Montu]?*

C: Well you know he was working here and they shot him in the hand. I saw him in Puerto Rico and now they took him out, but these people don't give me the right address—

A: *You know I found new copies of*—

C: (*Laughs.*) They took it to SOB, the same guy and he tells me "this is the address." So I go and I don't see him, because I have to claim my right. Look at all the numbers I have over there. The first one is Nico's and then Nelson's. And he took me to see him.

A: *I found the record*—

C: Yea I have it.

A: *It's new*—

C: Well I have it. So this is the first one I made. You remember I told you "I just don't know whether to record instrumental or with two singers." But I like small groups now, for this, you know, to move. You remember? I recorded in two styles because of that. In one I use Nicky —— and then in the other I use Julito Collazo, to choose. That was the beginning of that.

A: *And then—*

C: Then comes—

A: *The Salsoul one, right?*

C: No, with [Kingtronix] and then I switch to Salsoul—

A: *Right.*

C: [Kingtronix] was with Robert Tones during "El Caminante"—

A: *You know they came out with—*

C: Yea I know, I have them. And now they came out with the— when my orchestra ["Ya Chocolate"], which has "La Taza de Chocolate…" I have to go look for it. They told me. I went over there and they took a picture of me.

A: *They came out with both volumes of Folklórico—*

C: I also told René, "Here's a recording for records and cassettes," and now there's this one which is something else. But you know, Andy, I'm glad ——. I'm still here, relaxed. I have what I asked of God for my retirement. Look, when I came to this country with my mother, 108 and Broadway, 225 West 108 and Broadway, seventh floor. Now I retired, seventh floor. It's the seven seas and the four winds! I live with a clean heart. I'm not interested in anything that's anybody's. If it's yours, it's yours. If I can't—if I have money of yours and suddenly I need it, I call you, "Andy, look they gave me some money, I'm sorry, I had to need it but give me a break because I . . . "

A: *Of course.*

C: That has been my path all of my life, and it's how I walk on the street. Wherever I go I can arrive with money. I sign my name, because I'm guaranteed for it.

A: *Now, one question, when you are doing a solo, what do you think about?*

C: Man, I'm going to tell you something honestly. Several people have asked me that question. I know that me talking—you know there are a lot of ways—for example—I'm going to start. We're in a recording studio and all you see are the faces of the one that's bored and the one in the back. Now, when I feel the music and I get inspired from what's being played, there's an impulse. Now I go this way and start getting sweet. That's one solo. Now I'm going to play a concert, you know it's the hardest thing to do, everyone is sitting down listening. You see one in the back yawning (*pause, they laugh*)—you have to look at all of that. Now when you see one that is like this and he's having fun, now I'm inspired. There's another solo. That's the inspiration for a solo. Because we are not mechanical, now you have an idea. A solo isn't something that comes to you just like that. It's like the weather. It's—we wake up and it's raining. This interview occurred on a beautiful day, and I have air-conditioning. No air-conditioning? We're sweating. ——. There's an inspiration for that solo—it's what you're feeling in the moment. The solo is the vibration that you feel towards you in that moment. No one knows anything about that. Now the robot is the one that is always doing the same thing. That's why I can't be a double. I — — because I can't remember what I did. I can repeat a phrase— the coda comes to me and I remember a phrase, because we have a signature, and identification, but the rest—forget it.

A: *A lot of people, when I'm playing, a lot of people tell me, "man you played a tumbao in that part, damn, that shit was smoking!"*

C: . . . and you don't even remember.

A: *I don't remember!*

C: You got excited in the moment. That comes when you are excited. Because if I'm doing a solo, I depend on you, the rhythm.

A: *Right.*

C: It depends on the rhythm. And you heard me do a phrase and you liked it and automatically you go like this, Andy, and you switch up the *tumbao* and I'm loving it and I make it so we're both loving it. That's what's in a solo. The solo isn't mechanical, it's in the moment. The solo is something that comes to you in moment, and that's called inspiration.

A: *Now this next question, I don't know because everyone has their own way of saying this. How do you interpret the clave?*

C: Well the *clave* it's a matter of feeling it. The *clave*, any rhythm that you play simply has two and three. Now, since you are a musician, and all of us are, and we have music, any time we're going to play from a paper, it isn't "one-two-three-four" bam! The music might start on the first beat, on the second, on the third or on the fourth. Then, if you feel the *clave*, and in Spanish we call it *Anacruza*, what gives it salt—Tarara riri riri (*while he claps the clave*). The *clave* has to do with feelings; if you don't feel it, you don't get it. Because then you find yourself in the argument that I have found myself in with several people, where I am doing a solo and they're giving me an upside-down *clave* and I have to stop and they say to me, "Chocolate, the *clave* is two and three." Yea, two and three but where do you put it? Where do you place it? You really have to feel it. If you don't feel it you can't get it. That's why they say, "if you don't dance it, you can't play it" (*they laugh*). That's what I feel. The *clave* is nothing but five beats, no matter how you turn it, count it and see. In *guaguancó* and *rumba*: pa-pa-pa pa-pa. Five. Pa-pa pa-pa-pa. It's five. You can turn it any way you want. "Five beats, no mo'." It's not six. Just like when they talk to me about modern music and I say, "to me music will be modern when they make six lines." Now, nobody is guilty of the fact that these days the new audience understands and accepts the shrieks of [la Bonachita] and of [King Kong] and in another time they didn't accept that. There is nothing modern, everything's already written, no one invents anything here. From the moment you open a music book to study, you see Bach's fugue, you see Beethoven's this—who invented anything else? The same book that I read when I was six years old by —— Lagos. Now I'm seventy years old and nothing has changed, it's all the same. Don't you see there are seven *claves* and seven tones. There's nothing modern.

RD: We can skip that [next] one.

A: Well, here's a question, whether you can give a description of son, rumba, guaracha, guajira . . .

C: Very simple. It is understood for all the American and European public—I'll interpret. If you really listen to the blues, you are listening to a *guajira* with different beats, or the minor tones.

A: Yes. Or you can also call it a lament, right?

C: Right. The lament is the cry of the *guajiro*. That's what the *guajiro* feels. The *guajira* is a lament—that's the conclusion. The *montuno* is what is known as jazz: we're going to make a four- or eight-bar melody—and it's all improvisation. That is, all the melodic and harmonic lines. The *bolero-son* is the fox trot on low and then it changes to "swing."

A: Imagine the dancers!

C: Well, that's the trick. Now, you know how I can put it to you in a way that everyone will understand? When you try to win the love of a female that you like, you don't start running a hundred miles an hour (*they laugh*). Imagine that. You go little by little, you know.

A: A question about dances at big places like the Polar, without amplification. How does it sound?

C: Well the problem that I'm going to explain to you—the societies used to be all masonry, we call them, which were made of bricks.

A: *Right.*

C: That resonates. Notice that all of the —— of today that you can remember are under natural acoustics, they always have it for ——. Because when you play there, it has to be tiled. So when you hit the conga here, the trumpet isn't it. The trumpet sounds alone. Then singers used the —— but it [was] masonry. Wherever you play, the music sounds best when you get up on stage, no matter how big the place is, and the stage is made of wood. Because if it's masonry, the resonance falls and the *soneros* get confused. These are the acoustics. That's the recording I've played for two or three people that came here to interview me. I put on the genuine quartet we recorded, with one microphone for the band, the quartet's microphone. We did it directly, but as if—and it's sharp because it's recorded in a radio studio, like ——. You know the stage is high, below you have the wooden vault. Then when you play, the audience gives you the echo. And the music is there because there's the microphone—but it's the vault that has…

A: *I was told that when you danced* son *in one of those, well in El Polar or something like that, that the audience was very quiet—*

C: Yea, no one screamed there.

A: *. . . listening to the band . . .*

C: No one talked there. If you're going to dance, you're going to dance. What you see here, Andy González and Chocolate, we're doing a solo and everyone bla-bla-bla. The first hard experience I had was when I arrived in Japan with Machito's band where we played to twelve thousand and some Japanese people. There wasn't a sound. And you're used to the ruckus from here. But it's something you learn. They say that yesterday's experience is today's

life. You feel the effect but you don't listen and there are four people that go to listen—like when the late Nat King Cole worked
here in a bar and played and they pulled him out and said, "you're
not from around here." Then, just like they look around for re-
cruits for baseball and basketball, it's the same with music. You remember that when we started I always told you, "wherever you're
going to play, whether there are people or there aren't, play. You
don't know who is sitting there and you might go like this to his
soul." That's what I learned. You know what it's like for me to think
as I play in the theater—

SEPTEMBER 9, 1998: TAPE 2, SIDE A

C: Yesterday's experience is what taught me today's life. So for
me there is no heat. When they say to me, "it's so hot!" and "it's
so cold!" I say, "I wish I could have been one of those composers
that have money." Because there's cold and there's hot. I'm used
to, in mid-August, August in Puerto Rico and in Cuba ——and
I arrive there with a tie around my neck. But habit breeds custom. It's all the same to me. That's the problem, there is no
other. Habit breeds custom. Then, afterwards, all this came. You
were lucky to have studied, man, and you kept studying, because
there is demand for you and there's demand for me. There's demand for him, but the one who there isn't demand for is fucked
and he stayed there. Then he tells you things are bad. "It may be
bad for you, for me it's fine." That's what happens. Analyze it
and you'll see.

A: *It's true.*

C: Yea, it's true. Look, you can't fix the *son* with one of those solos. We're musicians and people are accustomed—even the hum-
blest orchestra of the time had uniforms. Even [Eddie], when he
went into —— what happened.

A: *Now—*

C: Wait I haven't done my line yet. (*He laughs.*) I told you I would do it a little while ago and I didn't. What do you expect, for me to stop now that I'm seventy?

[This part is incomprehensible.]

A: *I was telling him [RD] that I am asking things that are not on the list—*

C: Of course.

A: *Because when something interests me…*

C: Yea, that's good. And if it's within my reach, why not? I did the same thing you are doing when I was young. Thanks to that I paid attention. I paid attention and that's why I am where I am.

A: *That's the way it is.*

C: When someone says something to me, I say "no young person has seen an old person be born" (*they laugh*).

A: *Look at the poor souls that have the disease that they get old when they're six years old.*

C: Because there are people that are born in one corner and they don't know the other one, Andy. We're privileged. We travel here and we travel there. You know who you feel comfortable sharing with—because if I don't feel comfortable sharing with you, why the hell am I going to waste my time with hypocrisy? I see you and I get into the politics of "hi, how are you, Andy." And I don't share with you. But we know each other. How many people wouldn't like to hang out with you? What partier wouldn't like to sit next to one that has made name, "man I was with Andy González sitting next to me there, [I brought him to see]… they want to give you everything ——. We're noble because in the end we're musicians and we will always be within musicians. Because I don't do anything.

Look, I go to the deli because I don't go to the ———. But there's no one there. ———. What am I going to talk to those people about? But I sit down and go along with it, "Just a beer, thanks." What can I say to those people, Andy? But ——— I have to share also.

A: *Yes, yes.*

C: Right? You know I remember all the black Americans here: "Oh, I saw you on television, this and that," damn well give me a [present]. Because I don't have to tell anyone that I'm so and so, and I do this— I don't do that. You'll just as well find me at four in the morning drinking beers back there, and sniffing. And that's how my deceased cousin Beny Moré was. We were privileged. I know that when you invite me to [Pito Café], I go to [Pito Café]. Now when you see that I heard all that shit at Pito Café, you see me coming back to ———, the bar that I like. I go there to hang—another one goes to jam. If I don't want to go there, I'll go to the ———, back there which is another type of jam, to change the scene, because if you get stuck, you're fucked. So bring on the question cause I did my line already.

A: *Which are your favorite recordings?*

C: Damn, that's a tough one. Because I never liked what I do (*he laughs*). No, I'm not a hypocrite. My favorite recording of my life is that record you see over there. That has brought me here. From then on I haven't liked anything else. But, I feel happy. And I applaud the public that accepted me.

A: *Let me tell you something—when he [RD] started asking me things about you, I told him that the solo you took in "Para las niñas y para las señoras," you can transcribe it—*

C: Like Tito Puente tried to do with Meñique—

A: *Yea, but that solo can be put in a book—*

C: I've never done it. [Eric] asked me, "Chocolate, what were you thinking when you recorded that?" and I told him ———. On my mother, Andy, I only wanted Arsenio Rodríguez to hear me play because ——. That's how I did it.

A: *I told him that music,* clave, son *and swing students—*

C: There it is.

A: *That there are things going on in that solo of yours, even as short as it is, because it's only around eight bars—*

C: You're right eight bars, it was three minutes tops.

A: *In eight bars you made a declaration of who you were—you already had your identity—so young. And not only that, if you analyze it musically—*

C: Yea and then you write it down and I can't play it! (*he laughs*).

A: *. . . any* son *or music student—*

C: . . . has to grab onto that.

A: *If they study that solo, they will know what the "swing" of* son *is.*

C: Here it is, "Conjunto René Alvarez."

A: *It's a recording that he doesn't have because it's hard to find.*

C: It's on 78. I managed to get it, you can't hear it too well, but you can hear it.

A: *I don't know why it hasn't come out on CD yet.*

C: They'll remember it soon. Everyone's waiting for someone to die to call him afterwards. Don't you see that Fania thought I had died and they never called to pay me my royalties. When I showed up they said "damn, the living dead!" I always knew I was kind of dead, but here I am. My friend calls me here, Andy, I spent four days with my good friend in Miami. He got the other one, who he hadn't seen in I don't know how long, who's a good friend of mine. Like you and I who started with *Folklórico*. They interviewed me about *Folklórico* and I told them what that was like. Remember I told you that when [Fernandez] arrived, René started arranging and it got fucked up. I said, "Andy, this is gonna get fucked." We did it without arrangements and we all brought in all sorts of stuff. I told you, and wasn't I right?

A: *Yes you were.*

C: Something we did with care, that we liked and, ——, you arrived and fucked it all up.

A: *Yea man.*

C: I tell the story, remember we had three tunes set up—we went to play at [—— with Eddie] and the audience stands up—and the saxophone player was there, who was also the musical director, "Folklórico has finished," and René comes to me and says "damn, what do we do now?" "Forget it, play a roll on the drum, give me a G-minor, you'll see." And I was doing, with the trumpets and the skins [and when I did "trompeta en cuero"]. I tell a lot of people that story, I don't care if they tell me it's a lie. My grandfather told me it was better for me to tell the story than not to. He knows that's how it went, there wasn't anything else, and the crowd gets up and René was, remember, trembling because he was —— [you didn't see the place but it was in the country with Cuba Linda]. Aah—be careful—don't get comfortable. Cause we put our hearts into it. When my man arrives to do the arrangements everything was fucked to hell. What we were doing was without other interests, you know, whatever came out.

Let's see where it is because I have René Alvarez with . . . When he was with the Melodia del 40. I need to guess where it is . . .

[*Lindo Yambú comes on.*]

BIBLIOGRAPHY

Armenteros, Alfredo "Chocolate." 1998. Interview by Andy González and Rick Davies. Tape recording. New York, New York, August 3.
————. 1999. Interview by Andy González and Rick Davies. Tape recording. New York, New York, January 19.
Austerlitz, Paul. 1993. "Dominican Merengue in Regional, National, and International Perspectives." Ph.D. diss., Wesleyan University, 1993. Ann Arbor: UMI, 9328133.
Baker, David. 1969. *Jazz Improvisation: A Comprehensive Method of Study for All Players*. Chicago: Maher Publications.
Bauer, Scott Matthew. 1996. "Structural Targets in Modern Jazz Improvisation: An Analytical Perspective (Melodic Line, Fats Navarro, Clifford Brown, Kenny Dorham, Freddie Hubbard)." Ph.D. diss., University of California, San Diego, 1994. Ann Arbor: UMI, 9601746.
Berardinelli, Paula. 1992. "Bill Evans: His Contributions as a Jazz Pianist and an Analysis of His Musical Style." Ph.D. diss., New York University, 1992. Ann Arbor: UMI, 9222946.
Berliner, Paul F. 1994. *Thinking in Jazz: The Infinite Art of Improvisation*. Chicago: University of Chicago Press.
Boggs, Vernon W. 1992. *Salsiology: Afro-Cuban Music and the Evolution of Salsa in New York City*. New York: Excelsior Music.

Carp, David, and Bruce Polin. 1998. "Profile: Eddie Palmieri: Form and Substance." October 10. Accessed December 12, 2002 at Descarga.com.

Clarke, Donald, ed., 1998 *The Penguin Encyclopedia of Popular Music*. 2d Edition, London: Viking Press.

Cogan, Robert, and Pozzi Escot. 1976. *Sonic Design: The Nature of Sound and Music*. Englewood Cliffs, N.J.: Prentice-Hall.

Coker, Jerry. 1986. *Improvising Jazz*. New York: Simon & Schuster.

Coolman, Todd. 1996. "The Miles Davis Quintet of the Mid-1960s: Synthesis of Improvisational and Compositional Elements." Ph.D. diss., New York University.

Davies, Richard. 1998. "The *Conjunto* Trumpet Style: Chappottín, Florecita, and Chocolate." *IAJE Jazz Research Proceedings Yearbook*. IAJE Publications, 15–20. Manhattan, Kansas.

———. 2001. "Alfredo 'Chocolate' Armenteros." *Music from Cuba: Mongo Santamaría, Chocolate Armenteros, and Cuban Musicians in the United States*. Edited by Charley Gerard. Westport, Conn.: Praeger.

Descarga. 1998–1999. Hard copycover Latin music catalog. 1999.

Dietrich, Kurt Robert. 1990. "Joe 'Tricky Sam' Nanton, Juan Tizol and Lawrence Brown: Duke Ellington's Great Trombonists, 1926–1951." Ph.D. diss., University of Wisconsin, Madison, 1989. Ann Arbor: UMI, 9009559.

Dufrasne-González, J. Emmanuel. 1985. "La homogeneidad de la musica caribeña: sobre la musica comercial y popular de Puerto Rico." Ph.D. diss., University of California, Los Angeles, 1985. Ann Arbor: UMI, 8513108.

Fernández, Olga, trans. 1995. "You Have to Move with the Times," by Ester Mosak and Margarite Zimmerman. *Strings and Hide*. Havana: Editorial José Martí..

Ferrara, Lawrence. 1991. *Philosophy and the Analysis of Music*. New York: Greenwood.

Floyd, Samuel A., Jr. 1995. *The Power of Black Music*. New York: Oxford University Press.

Gates, Henry L. 1988. *The Signifying Monkey: A Theory of Afro-American Literary Criticism*. New York: Oxford University Press.

Gerard, Charley, and Marty Sheller. 1989. *Salsa!: The Rhythm of Latin Music*. Crown Point, Ind.: White Cliffs Media Company.

González, Andy. 1997. Interview by Rick Davies. Tape recording. Bronx, New York, July 29.

Hernández, Erena. 1986. "Dos Poetas Del Son." *La Musica en Persona*. Havana: Editorial Letras Cubanas.

Larkin, Colin, ed. 1995. *The Guinness Encyclopedia of Popular Music*. New York: Stockton.

Levine, Mark. 1989. *The Jazz Piano Book*. Petaluma, Calif.: Sher Music.

Lezcano, Jose Manuel. 1991. "Afro-Cuban Rhythmic and Metric Elements in the Published Choral and Solo Vocal Works of Alejandro García Caturla and Amadeo Roldán." Ph.D. diss., Florida State University, 1991. Ann Arbor: UMI, 9132977.

MacGaffey, Wyatt, and Clifford R. Barnett. 1962. *Twentieth Century Cuba, The Background of the Castro Revolution*. New Haven, Conn.: HRAF.

Manuel, Peter. "The Anticipated Bass in Cuban Popular Music." *Latin American Music Review*. (Austin) 6.2: 249-61. 1985.

———. 1995. *Caribbean Currents: Caribbean Music from Rumba to Reggae*. Philadelphia, Pa.: Temple University Press.

Manuel, Peter, ed. 1991. *Essays on Cuban Music: North American and Cuban Perspectives*. Lanham, Md.: University Press of America.

Mauleón, Rebeca. 1993. *Salsa Guidebook for Piano and Ensemble*. Petaluma, Calif.: Sher Music.

McCracken, Grant. 1988. *The Long Interview*. Sage University Paper Series on Qualitative Research Methods, vol. 13. Beverly Hills, Calif.: Sage.

Moore, Robin D. 1995. "The Commercial Rumba: Afrocuban Arts as International Popular Culture." *Latin American Music Review* 16:165–198.

———. 1997. *Nationalizing Blackness: Afrocubanismo and Artistic Revolution in Havana, 1920–1940*. Pittsburgh: University of Pittsburgh Press.

O'Neill, Jack, ed. 1997. *Cuba: I Am Time*. Bethpage, N.Y.: Blue Jackel Entertainment.

Petruzzi, Leon Thomas. 1994. "Lead Trumpet Performances in the Thad Jones/Mel Lewis Jazz Orchestra: An Analysis of Style and Performance Practices." Ph.D. diss., New York University, 1993. Ann Arbor: UMI, 9333931.

Phelps, Roger P., Lawrence Ferrara, and Thomas W. Goolsby. 1993. *A Guide to Research in Music Education*. 4th edition. Metuchen, N.J.: Scarecrow Press.

Porter, Lewis. 1985. *Lester Young*. Boston: Twayne.

Robbins, James. 1990. "The Cuban *Son* as Form, Genre, and Symbol." *Latin American Music Review* 11:182–200.

Roberts, John Storm. 1979. *The Latin Tinge*. Tivoli, N.Y.: Original Music.

———. 1999. *Latin Jazz: The First of the Fusions, 1880s to Today*. New York: Schirmer Books.

Salazar, Max. 1994. "Salsa Hitman." *Latin Beat Magazine*. October: 32 ff.

Schuller, Gunther. 1968. *Early Jazz: Its Roots and Musical Development*. New York: Oxford University Press.

———. 1989. *The Swing Era: The Development of Jazz, 1930–1945*. New York: Oxford University Press.

Sher, Chuck, ed. 1997. *The Latin Real Book*. Petaluma, Calif.: Sher Music.

Vargas, Barbara Kay. 1990. "Salsa Music: Primary Dimensions of Meaning in an Expressive Cultural Form—The Puerto Rican Experience as Chronicled via Salsa Lyric Poetics." Ph.D. diss., University of California, Irvine, 1989. Ann Arbor: UMI, 8915455.

Waxer, Lise. 1994. "Of Mambo Kings and Songs of Love: Dance Music in Havana and New York from the 1930s to the 1950s." *Latin American Music Review* 15:139–176.

DISCOGRAPHY

RECORDINGS FEATURING ALFREDO "CHOCOLATE" ARMENTEROS

Armenteros, Alfredo "Chocolate." *Chocolate and His Cuban Soul.* Caiman CCD-9038, 1998.

Armenteros, Alfredo "Chocolate." *Chocolate Aquí.* Carib Musicana, 1994.

Armenteros, Alfredo "Chocolate." *Chocolate Caliente.* Salsoul 20-7019-2, 1998.

Armenteros, Alfredo "Chocolate." *Chocolate en Sexteto.* Caiman CCD-9001, n.d.

Armenteros, Alfredo "Chocolate." *Chocolate y Amigos.* Caiman CCD-9032, n.d.

Armenteros, Alfredo "Chocolate." *Lo Mejor de Chocolate,* vol. 1. SAR SCD-1009, 1990.

Armenteros, Alfredo "Chocolate." *Lo Mejor de Chocolate,* vol. 2. SAR SCD-1013, 1991.

Chappottín, Félix and Alfredo "Chocolate" Armenteros. *Estrellas de Cuba.* Antilla, n.d.

Estrellas Caiman. *Descarga del Milenio.* Caiman CCD-9037, 1997.

Estrellas Caiman. *Descarga in New York*. Caiman CCD-9035, 1995.

Lopez, Israel "Cachao." *Cachao Master Sessions*, vols. 1 and 2. Crescent Moon/Epic, 1995.

Moré, Beny. *Y Hoy Como Ayer*. BMG/Tropical Series 3203, 1992.

Palmieri, Eddie. *Justicia*. Tico SLP 1188, 1970.

Palmieri, Eddie. *Superimposition*. Tico SLP 1194, 1970.

Palmieri, Eddie. *Vámonos Pa'l Monte*. Tico SLP 1225, 1976.

Rodríguez, Arsenio. *Dundunbanza*. Tumbao Cuban Classics TCD-043, 1994.

Rodríguez, Arsenio. *Montuneado*. Tumbao Cuban Classics TCD-0310. 1994.

OTHER RECORDINGS

Alemañy, Jesús. *Jesús Alemañy's ¡Cubanismo!* Root Jazz/Hannibal, 1996.

Blades, Rubén. *Antecedente*. Elektra/Asylum, 1988.

Chappottín, Félix. *Chappottín y Sus Estrellas*. Antilla, n.d.

Chappottín, Félix. *Perlas del Son*. Areito, n.d.

Chappottín, Félix. *Sabor Tropical*. Ruchito SP107, n.d.

Cuní, Miguelito. *Sones de Ayer*. Rumba Records RLP55508, n.d.

Dorham, Kenny. *Afro-Cuban*. Blue Note, 1955.

D'Rivera, Paquito. *Paquito D'Rivera Presents CubaJazz*. TropiJazz/RMM, 1996.

Gillespie, Dizzy. *Compact Jazz: Dizzy Gillespie*. PolyGram, 1987.

Palmieri, Eddie. *Azucar Pa' Ti (Sugar for You)*. Tico 1122, 1965.

Palmieri, Eddie. *Bamboleate*. Tico 1150, 1967.

Palmieri, Eddie. *Champagne*. Tico SLP 1165, 1968.

Palmieri, Eddie. *Echando Pa'lante (Straight Ahead)*. Tico 1113, 1964.

Palmieri, Eddie. *El Molestoso*. Alegre 8240, 1962.

Palmieri, Eddie. *La Perfecta*. Alegre 8170, 1962.

Palmieri, Eddie. *Lo Que Traigo Es Sabrosa*. Alegre 8320, 1964.

Palmieri, Eddie. *Molasses*. Tico 1148, 1967.

Palmieri, Eddie. *Mozambique*. Tico 1126, 1965.

Sexteto Habanero. *The Roots of Salsa*, vol. 2. Folklyric Records 9054, n.d.

Sexteto y Septeto Habanero. *Grabaciones Completas, 1925–1931*. Tumbao Cuban Classics TCD, 301–304.

INDEX

ABOUT THE AUTHOR

Rick Davies is a professional musician and a music professor at Plattsburgh State University of New York where he directs the jazz program. As a trombonist, he has worked with many jazz, Afro-Caribbean, and pop music performers, including *Jaki Byard, Tito Puente, Skah Shah #1 d'Haiti, Arrow, Blondie, and Wyclef Jean.* Davies has appeared on over one hundred recordings. Since the mid-1980s, he has been associated with *Wayne Gorbea and Salsa Picante*; as music director, he has composed several pieces and recorded numerous solos for their popular CDs. Davies also performs with his own group, *Jazzismo*; their first CD, *Salsa Strut* (released in 2001), features seven of his original compositions.

As a scholar, Davies has written several monographs, chapters, and articles primarily about Afro-Cuban music and *salsa*. He contributed a chapter on Alfredo "Chocolate" Armenteros to *Music from Cuba* (Praeger Press, 2001). Other articles he has written include "Sexteto Habanero, Félix Chappottín, and Early Afro-Cuban Trumpet Playing," "The Conjunto Trumpet Style: Chappottín, Florecita, and Chocolate," and "Americanizing the Eurocentric Music Curriculum."